CASEBOOK SERIES

PUBLISHED

Jane Austen: *Emma* DAVID LODGE
Jane Austen: *'Northanger Abbey'* and *'Persuasion'* B.C. SOUTHAM
Jane Austen: *'Sense and Sensibility'*, *'Pride and Prejudice'* and *'Mansfield Park'* B.C. SOUTHAM
William Blake: *Songs of Innocence and Experience*
Charlotte Brontë: *Jane Eyre*
Emily Brontë: *Wuthering Heights*
Browning: *'Men and Women' and Other Poems*
Bunyan: *The Pilgrim's Progress*
Byron: *'Childe Harold's Pilgrimage' and 'Don Juan'*
Chaucer: *Canterbury Tales*
Coleridge

Congreve
Conrad
Conrad
Dickens
Dickens
Donne
George
George Eliot: *The Mill on the Floss*
T.S. Eliot: *Four Quartets*
T.S. Eliot: *'Prufrock', 'Gerontion', 'Ash Wednesday' and Other Shorter Poems*
T.S. Eliot: *The Waste Land*
Farquhar
Henry Fielding
E.M. Forster
Hardy
Hardy
Gerard Manley Hopkins
Jonson
Jonson
James
John Keats
D.H. Lawrence
D.H. Lawrence
Marlowe
Marlowe
RUSSELL
Marvell
The Metaphysical Poets
Milton
Milton
John Osborne: *Look Back in Anger*
Peacock
Pope: *The Rape of the Lock*
Shakespeare
Shakespeare
Shakespeare

D1346969

Shakespeare

Coriolanus

A CASEBOOK

EDITED BY

B. A. BROCKMAN

M

First edition 1977
Reprinted 1982, 1983

Published by
THE MACMILLAN PRESS LTD
London and Basingstoke
Companies and representatives
throughout the world

ISBN 0 333 19575 2 (paper cover)

Printed in Hong Kong

CONTENTS

ACKNOWLEDGEMENTS

The editor and publishers wish to thank the following who have kindly given permission for the use of copyright material: A. C. Bradley, extract from article *'Coriolanus'* from *Proceedings of the British Academy for 1912,* reprinted by permission of The British Academy. Reuben A. Brower, 'The Deeds of Coriolanus' from *Hero and Saint: Shakespeare and the Graeco-Roman Heroic Tradition* © Oxford University Press 1971, reprinted by permission of the publisher. Kenneth Burke, extracts from *'Coriolanus* – and the Delights of Faction' from *Language as Symbolic Action: Essays On Life, Literature and Method,* © 1966 by The Regents of University of California, reprinted by permission of the University of California Press. Oscar James Campbell, extract from *Shakespeare's Satire,* © 1943 by Oxford University Press Inc., renewed 1971 by Mrs Robert L. Goodale, Mrs George W. Meyer, and Mr Robert F. Campbell, reprinted by permission. Maurice Charney, extract from 'Style' from *Shakespeare's Roman Plays: The Function of Imagery in the Drama,* reprinted by permission of the author and Harvard University Press. T. S. Eliot, extract from 'Hamlet' in *Selected Essays,* reprinted by permission of Faber & Faber Ltd. Una Ellis-Fermor, 'Coriolanus' in *Shakespeare the Dramatist,* edited by Kenneth Muir, reprinted by permission of Methuen & Co. Ltd. Willard Farnham, extracts from *'Coriolanus'* in *Shakespeare's Tragic Frontier,* reprinted by permission of the author and Basil Blackwell & Mott Ltd. G. K. Hunter, extracts from 'The Last Tragic Heroes' in *The Later Shakespeare, Stratford-upon-Avon Studies,* VIII, edited by Brown & Harris, reprinted by permission of Edward Arnold Ltd. L. C. Knights, extracts from 'Shakespeare and Political Wisdom' in *Sewanee Review,* LXI, reprinted by permission of the author. A. P. Rossiter, extract from *'Coriolanus'* in *Angel with Horns, and*

Other Essays: Lectures on Shakespeare, posthumously edited by Graham Storey, reprinted by permission of Longman Group Ltd. George Bernard Shaw, extract from *Man and Superman,* reprinted by permission of The Society of Authors on behalf of the Bernard Shaw Estate. T. J. B. Spencer, extract from 'Shakespeare and the Elizabethan Romans' in *Shakespeare Survey,* X, reprinted by permission of Cambridge University Press. Derek A. Traversi, extracts from *'Coriolanus'* in *An Approach to Shakespeare* published by Hollis and Carter, reprinted by permission of The Bodley Head Ltd.

PUBLISHER'S NOTE

Special titles for this Casebook have been assigned to those studies in Part Two which in their original form bear identical or similar titles. Such special titles are placed within quotemarks to distinguish them from the others.

GENERAL EDITOR'S PREFACE

The Casebook series, launched in 1968, has become a well-regarded library of critical studies. The central concern of the series remains the 'single-author' volume, but suggestions from the academic community have led to an extension of the original plan, to include occasional volumes on such general themes as literary 'schools' and genres.

Each volume in the central category deals either with one well-known and influential work by an individual author, or with closely related works by one writer. The main section consists of critical readings, mostly modern, collected from books and journals. A selection of reviews and comments by the author's contemporaries is also included, and sometimes comment from the author himself. The Editor's introduction charts the reputation of the work or works from the first appearance to the present time.

Volumes in the 'general themes' category are variable in structure but follow the basic purpose of the series in presenting an integrated selection of readings, with an Introduction which explores the theme and discusses the literary and critical issues involved.

A single volume can represent no more than a small selection of critical opinions. Some critics are excluded for reasons of space, and it is hoped that readers will pursue the suggestions for further reading in the Select Bibliography. Other contributions are severed from their original context, to which some readers may wish to turn. Indeed, if they take a hint from the critics represented here, they certainly will.

A. E. DYSON

INTRODUCTION

The last of Shakespeare's tragedies, evidently written and performed in 1608, *Coriolanus* has been long in arriving at a just critical appreciation. Chronologically the companion of *Antony and Cleopatra* and *Cymbeline*, in classical setting the companion of *Julius Caesar, Troilus and Cressida, Timon of Athens* and *Titus Andronicus, Coriolanus* seems spiritually akin more to *Timon, Troilus* and the 'problem comedies' than to the familiar tragedies of Hamlet, Lear, Othello and Macbeth. Indeed, it is only in the last fifty years that *Coriolanus* has emerged from the shadow of the 'great four' to win acclaim for its own 'admirable peculiarities'; one critic has gone so far as to observe that the play is 'one of the supreme tests of a genuine understanding of Shakespeare's achievement'. It has seemed to modern critics a masterful but forbidding play, from which the unsympathetic character of the hero alienates audience and reader alike.

What *Coriolanus* may have seemed to its original audience we can hardly conjecture. As the leading tragedian of the King's men, Richard Burbage must have played the title role; would that we could know how he interpreted it. Certainly the play must have appeared intensely topical, though it seems not to have been a popular success: the unique early text, that of the 1623 Folio, does not reflect the revisions characteristic of plays frequently performed. Recent research has found the play intimately involved with Jacobean political and social conflict. It seems almost certainly to echo current debate over parliamentary versus royal prerogatives, and the enclosure riots in the midlands in 1607 – the most serious civil disturbances for over forty years – must have provided an external application for the play's arguments about class privilege and popular rights. Without doubt, the play is Shakespeare's most immediately political. Modern critics, echoing Coleridge's notes (reprinted below) on *Coriolanus,* have for the most part celebrated 'the wonderful philosophic impartiality in Shakespeare's politics', and have admired the play's equivocal stance toward its protagonist. It has been the singular ill fortune of *Coriolanus,* however, that its earliest recorded productions – and one or two notorious modern ones as well – have taken advantage of its susceptibility to doctrinaire manipulation. The play appears to have been conceived at a time of civil unrest, and it has figured in political and social tempest ever since.

The first recorded production of *Coriolanus* was in the 1682 adaptation of Nahum Tate, who is remembered chiefly for rewriting *King Lear* with a happy ending. His version of *Coriolanus* is slightly less outrageous. Tate frankly addressed his adaptation to 'the busie Faction of our own time', to the combatants in the titanic struggle between Charles II and the Earl of Danby's Tories on the one hand and the Earl of Shaftesbury's Whigs on the other (Dryden's *Absolom and Achitophel* appeared the year before). Tate's philosophic partiality is amply implied in his title – *The Ingratitude of a Common-Wealth: or, The Fall of Caius Martius Coriolanus* – and in the 'Moral' his Dedicatory Epistle recommends: 'Submission and Adherence to Establisht Lawful Power'. Adaptations by John Dennis (*The Invader of His Country,* 1719) and James Thomson (1749) were prompted by the Jacobite rebellions of 1715 and 1745. Shakespeare's own play appeared in the 1720–1 season and in 1754, when it was staged as an anticipation of Thomas Sheridan's production of a hybrid Shakespeare–Thomson *Coriolanus* which held the stage in both England and America until 1820. After 1789, John Philip Kemble became identified with the title role, which he played, according to Leigh Hunt, with lofty austerity. It was a Kemble performance of 1816 which prompted Hazlitt's assessment (reprinted below) of the play's right-wing inclination, though he, like Coleridge, senses an ultimate balance of arguments for and against democracy in the play itself.

Later nineteenth-century productions of *Coriolanus* left

behind the crudities of earlier interpretations. Edmund Kean
presented Shakespeare's play 'with omissions only' in 1820,
and even though the production was unsuccessful (primarily
because Kean did not play Coriolanus in Kemble's accepted
style), Kean evidently realised an important psychological
dimension of the role by alloying the figure of the hero with
that of the boy – an alloy which is prominent in critical interpretations from Swinburne's (reprinted below) onward.
Macready appeared in the role periodically between 1819 and
1838, and by the latter date the production, in the climate of
the Reform Act, Chartism and the depression of 1837,
presented not a foul and fickle mob as antagonist, but (in the
words of a contemporary review) 'the onward and increasing
wave . . . of men who have spied their way to equal franchise,
and are determined to fight their way to the goal'. Although
Phelps and Forrest played celebrated Coriolanuses with the
icy hauteur of Kemble, Macready's production, as Ralph
Berry observes in a recent study of the play's stage history, established a 'fascination with that menacing crowd' which
marked productions of the play down to the 1930s. Two
memorable performances of that decade for obvious socio-
political reasons tended to reassume the ancient aspect of
propaganda. A Comédie Française production in 1933–4 (to
which A. P. Rossiter makes further reference below) was
perceived as an anti-republican assault on the socialist government and led to rioting. Laurence Olivier's 1938 Coriolanus
suggested, according to Laurence Kitchin, an 'embryo Fascist
dictator'. Intrigued by the play's class-conflict aspect, Bertolt
Brecht began an adaptation/translation and, shortly before
his death in 1956, 'toyed' with the possibility of mounting a
Marxist *Coriolanus* 'without additions . . . just by skilful
production'.

    The drastic politicisation of *Coriolanus* in performance un-
derscores the central difficulty in producing it: one has to slant
everything or nothing. Perhaps as a consequence, recent
productions of *Coriolanus* have tried to slant nothing, to
minimise what by now seem well learned political lessons, and
to explore instead the social and psychological dimensions of
the play. In this respect modern productions reflect an interest

in character which, along with thematic examination of the play's politics, marked the earliest, and major elements of the continuing, critical interest in the play. Hazlitt derives the play's politics and action from the character of Coriolanus, and Coleridge observes, in one of the Bristol lectures of 1813, that Shakespeare's technique in presenting Coriolanus proceeds 'not by any one description; but by such opinions, half right half wrong, as the friends, enemies, and the man himself would give – and the reader left to draw the whole . . .'. Awareness of just such a process enabled Una Ellis-Fermor to develop one of the most sensitive assessments of the character of Coriolanus in relation to a theme of the play; in the essay reprinted below, she finds that the play generates tacit impressions about Coriolanus which incite the audience to ask questions which in turn lead to an awareness that Coriolanus's tragedy stems from his betrayal of his own Roman ideal for the simulacrum of his mother.

Though it is also much more, A. C. Bradley's classic essay represents a culmination of the nineteenth-century character studies which valued psychological verisimilitude in dramatic realisation of character. Like his predecessors Taine and Dowden, whose commentaries appear below, Bradley regards Coriolanus as 'the proudest man in Shakespeare', whose pride, at once noble and reprehensible, precipitates his downfall. It is a theme to which recent critics, among them Willard Farnham in this collection, have frequently returned, though with very individual modifications of the precise definition and meaning of this 'tragic flaw'. Swinburne, with his customary strident overstatement, considered the play 'rather a private and domestic than a public or historical tragedy'; its 'final impression is not that of a conflict between patrician and plebeian, but solely that of a match of passions played out for life and death between a mother and a son'. Bradley too considers the play's politics of secondary interest and its tragedy that of 'a huge boy' who cannot resist his mother's chiding. The perception underlying that memorable phrase has figured widely in recent commentaries. Among the essays assembled here, it anticipates Reuben Brower's illuminating study of Coriolanus as a Latinate Achilles, a 'great boy' exposed to the 'complexities and necessary compromises of the Roman–Jacobean political world'.

Although they regarded the play's tragic outcome as a function of character interaction, Bradley, Swinburne, Dowden, and the nineteenth-century critics generally, tended to see character as of compelling interest in itself; they valued Coriolanus and his companions, in Hazlitt's phrase, as 'complete characters'. Consideration of character can hardly be omitted from any dramatic analysis, of course; but later critics have, while remaining alive to the interaction of characters, stressed, like Brower, the wider functions of character: in relation to themes of politics, morality and, of late, ontology; and in relation to the play's dramaturgical construction, its formal design and its generic category.

If Bradley's essay looked backward to the nineteenth century in its assessment of character, it looked ahead to twentieth-century preoccupations in its attempt to understand the singular atmosphere of this play, to define its genre and to comprehend it in relation to the overshadowing 'great tragedies'. In his 'short stricture' on the play, Dr Johnson, whom Bradley quotes, had called *Coriolanus* 'amusing', by which he meant 'engaging the interest', evidently in the manner of the spectacle of a history play. Bradley called attention to the play's lack of imaginative vision, tragic atmosphere and a protagonist whose character explodes like Lear and Hamlet into poetry. He went on to note elements of the play which seem amusing in the modern sense of 'mirthful', and G. B. Shaw declared as perversely as perceptively that the play is 'the greatest of Shakespear's comedies'; these sentiments anticipate one of the most influential efforts to define the genre and peculiar tone of *Coriolanus*, that of O. J. Campbell. In the essay reprinted here, Campbell classifies the play as satire, to which the conventional standards of tragedy are inappropriate. Subsequent critics have felt that Campbell went too far – that there are important elements of authentic tragedy in the play. As William Rosen shows in a fine study too long for inclusion here, the attitude of the audience toward Coriolanus is carefully manipulated – usually to the detriment of Coriolanus. He is derided, his shortcomings are documented relentlessly, and his character is projected with studied antipathy. Nevertheless an audience grants him a begrudging respect, just as even Aufidius concedes him a 'noble memory'. A number of critics have noted aspects of duality in the play: Shakespeare baits his aristocratic no less than his common audience, and he makes Coriolanus something of a *miles gloriosus* even as he makes him a traditional hero. One critic has considered the play not a tragedy at all, but 'an intellectual debate'.

Campbell went a long way toward explaining how the peculiarities of the play could be considered admirable. It remained for his successors to show that the play is admirable in more traditional tragic terms as well. The most influential of these efforts, which employs a historical method frequently applied to the play since then, is that of Willard Farnham (reprinted here). 'Taints and honors', he contends, weigh equally in Coriolanus; his nobility 'seems to issue from ignoble substance'. The play is a tragedy, but a special kind; the world of *Coriolanus* is that of late Renaissance tragedy in which paradox seems constantly on the verge of overwhelming the tragic emotions and 'the essential simplicities of tragic understanding'. Like Hazlitt before him, and almost everyone after him, Farnham shows that Shakespeare made of his Coriolanus something radically different from his model in Plutarch; he goes on to establish what might have been the attitude of Shakespeare's contemporaries toward the 'historical' character: 'It was entirely possible for a man of the European Renaissance to be blind to the faults of Coriolanus and to see in his story an example of the envy and hatred that human mediocrity all too frequently feels toward those who are set apart in the world by greatness of spirit.' This kind of 'historical criticism' has proved especially durable and beneficial in achieving a just assessment of *Coriolanus:* if the play seems inexplicably odd to us, so the reasoning goes, perhaps it seemed less so to its original audience; and perhaps if we can recover part of their understanding we can illuminate our own. So it is that a number of recent studies have documented Jacobean attitudes toward the ideal state (is Menenius's fable of the belly, for example, normative?), toward military in relation to civilian life and especially toward the hero. We are far from agreement about the details of a theoretical political foil to the action of *Coriolanus:* it may be doubted that Shakespeare's contemporaries could agree on an adequate definition of the state any more than we can. Nevertheless it appears that some theoretical norms can be assumed: Renaissance theorists detested the mob, they mistrusted the autocrat and they respected the hero – as warrior and servant, but not leader, of the state. Important studies by Eugene Waith, Richard Marienstras and Matthew Proser (see the Bibliography, p. 225) deal with the hero in terms which anticipate Reuben Brower's extended effort, reproduced below, to comprehend Coriolanus within the heroic tradition. Brower shows that Shakespeare's protagonist does not fit comfortably into either a classical or a Renaissance mould, though both traditions provide antecedent ideals against which he must be measured in order to be understood. In studies from which extracts below are taken, D. A. Traversi and L. C. Knights examine a corollary theme: the attempt, familiar from several of Shakespeare's earlier plays, to encompass a vaguely perceived, but urgently felt, notion of honour in an active life.

While Knights, Brower, Traversi and a host of others have attempted to place Coriolanus in a normative Renaissance framework, one important modern school, represented here by the selections from Traversi, Knights and G. K. Hunter, find inescapable the implications of the play within modern moral frameworks. In the 1930s, a group of critics associated with *Scrutiny,* among them Traversi, condemned the brutal, mechanistic, militaristic world of *Coriolanus* – a world which Traversi finds in the study included here characterised by 'stagnation and mutual distrust, mirroring the ruthlessness of contrary appetites for power'. Perhaps the most influential of such studies of the play is the long chapter, which could not be included here, in G. Wilson Knight's *The Imperial Theme;* he finds its ethos 'hard', 'constricted', and Coriolanus a personification of 'iron, blood, death'. In the tragic climax of the play, this 'blind mechanism' of 'unrelenting iron' is crushed by a mightier power, filial love: war succumbs to love, *virtus* to *pietas*. L. C. Knights reminds us of the power of literature to vivify the truth of two ethical commonplaces: 'that human actuality is more important than *any* political abstraction . . . [and] that politics is vitiated and corrupted to the extent to which . . . we lose our sense of the *person* on the other side . . .'. G. K. Hunter distinguishes the social isolation of Lear and Hamlet from that of the later tragic heroes like Timon and Coriolanus: the later protagonists fail to create a compensatory 'new world of value' inside themselves; they are 'diminished by [their] failure to accept integration into society'. Citing F. N. Lees's influential essay, Hunter examines 'the moral ambiguity of heroes who are both godlike and inhuman'. 'Coriolanus . . . searches for an *absolute* mode of behaviour . . . but the finding it is the destruction of humanity in him.' Subsequent studies have found this a rewarding line of inquiry.

The ethical standpoint from which any critic views the play necessarily colours what he sees in it; it has been difficult for critics to separate questions of artistry from those of ethics (not to mention politics) in the study of this play. This is especially true in two of the most sensitive close readings of the play's imagery and the unique atmosphere which derives from it – the studies of Traversi and Knight mentioned previously. A more dispassionate study, that of Maurice Charney (extracted below), finds the play's imagery a reciprocating function of Coriolanus's character. Charney's analysis stands here for several studies of the play's style which make us aware of the playwright's artistic command and bring us appreciably closer to understanding T. S. Eliot's cryptic declaration that while *Coriolanus* 'may not be as "interesting" as *Hamlet*', it is, along with *Antony and Cleopatra*, 'Shakespeare's most assured artistic success'. T. J. B. Spencer's account of 'Shakespeare and the Elizabethan Romans' represents here a group of studies which illuminate Shakespeare's craftsmanship by examining his imaginative re-creation of classical Rome and his manipulation of Plutarch and other literary sources. Kenneth Burke's formal analysis, included here, considers the play 'grotesque tragedy' and derives its poetics from Coriolanus's suitability as the sacrificial victim of the audience. His account of the play's exploitation of social and political issues for aesthetic ends is especially useful as a corrective to many earlier readings of the play. Like Jan Kott in *Shakespeare our Contemporary,* Burke finds the moral ambiguity of Coriolanus intriguing and deeply meaningful: an attitude as characteristic of the mid-1960s as the distaste Traversi and Knight felt for the play's controlling imagery was of the thirties. A. P. Rossiter takes as his purpose giving the play 'a chance as a tragic play'; he consequently eliminates 'passionate political side-tracks' and considers it an intellectually demanding tragedy 'about the historic process', in which the protagonist is, as in the history plays, the State. These later critics, not unexpectedly, demonstrate more confidence in the play's artistic success than their predecessors. Farnham, for example, writing a decade earlier, could commend the 'delicate beauty' and 'mathematical precision' of the paradoxically repellent but admirable Coriolanus, but when he recalled the play's 'lack of essential warmth' and the extension of cerebral paradox 'beyond the effective reach of merely human pity', he was compelled to term the play 'a magnificent failure'. Needless to say, current critics are inclined to replace Farnham's conclusion with Eliot's. Critics remain disturbed, however, by the aesthetic distance the play erects as a barrier between audience and protagonist, although H. J. Oliver in an important essay defends the attractiveness of Coriolanus and his suitability as a tragic hero. The play may be a tragic masterpiece; but it remains easier to believe in the masterpiece than to celebrate or even define the species of tragedy.

A few studies – among them the one from which Charney's is excerpted – have led to an appreciation of the play's dramaturgy. Harley Granville-Barker's *Prefaces to Shakespeare* detects in it some flagging of Shakespeare's 'imaginative vitality' and 'metaphysical power' and he conjectures that Shakespeare chose 'a subject and characters which he could make the most of by judgement and skill'. These qualities Granville-Barker finds in abundance in the play: it is 'notable for its craftsmanship . . . the work of a man who knows what the effect of each stroke will be, and wastes not one of them'. Particularly interesting are his discussions of the design of cardinal dramatic moments, especially v iii ('Volumnia Comes, and the Conqueror is Conquered'), his discussion of the verse ('the words are often unmusical in themselves, and they may be crushed into the lines like fuel to stoke a furnace') and his observations on 'the dynamic phrase' ('the little said can be made to suggest much left unsaid') and 'the use of silence'. Berry's study of the play's stage history, mentioned earlier, recounts one instance in which brilliant production vivified the dramatic potential of the play, and discovered a moment which could well arouse in an audience those 'tragic emotions' which readers all too frequently fail to experience. Berry considers Olivier's Coriolanus at Stratford in 1959, directed by Peter Hall, 'the most distinguished of our time'. While that production 'exploited the latent comedy of the mother–son domination', its 'overall effect was of terrifying concentration and power. . . . Olivier solved the central problem of the part by disengaging the hero from patrician and plebian, and by presenting him with a degree of sympathy.' The ground is thus prepared for a stunning denouement which entirely befits this strange tragedy. Berry cites the account in Kenneth Tynan's *Curtains:*

Olivier is roused to suicidal frenzy by Aufidius' gibe – 'thou boy of tears'. '*Boy!*' shrieks the overmothered general, in an outburst of strangled fury, and leaps up a flight of precipitous steps to vent his rage. Arrived at the top, he relents and throws his sword away. After letting his voice fly high in the great, swingeing line about how he 'flutter'd your Volscians in *Cor-i-o-li*', he allows a dozen spears to impale him. He is poised, now, on a promontory some twelve feet above the stage, from which he topples forward, to be caught by the ankles so that he dangles, inverted, like the slaughtered Mussolini. A more shocking, less sentimental death I have not seen in the theatre; it is at once proud and ignominious, as befits the titanic fool who dies it.

The most recent critical studies of the play have seen in its tragic spirit specific reflections of themes which have preoccupied our own age. Some critics of the fifties and sixties, for example, read the play as a psycho-analytic account of mother–son conflict. Critics of the sixties and seventies have seen the play, characteristically, as a study of the radical incapacity of language to convey meaning, and as a sceptical study of unresolvable moral ambiguity. This tendency to see the play from a thoroughly modern perspective is no less apparent when we come full circle and consider recent studies of the political theme. In 1945 John Palmer, in *Political Characters of Shakespeare,* could still assert that *Coriolanus* 'is not the dramatisation of a political thesis . . . [nor] a play in which the supreme conflict is one of political principle . . . Shakespeare is intent on persons, not on public affairs.' His successors, while they might grant the point which Palmer is driving at, would be more likely to endorse A. P. Rossiter's formulation of the political nature of the play, reprinted here. In a manner which inverts Hunter and Knights's equally 'contemporary' socio-moral treatments of isolation and personalism in the play, Rossiter considers the play Shakespeare's 'only great political play' which in its tragic conflicts captures the essence of the very process of history. Therein, according to Jan Kott, is the stamp of its modernity: 'History in *Coriolanus* has ceased to be demonic. It is only ironic and tragic.' The play ends, Rossiter concludes, ' "in utter darkness": the darkness of history, from which Shakespeare finally absconded – with *Cymbeline*'.

It is inevitable, and in spite of the example of Nahum Tate perhaps even salutary, that each age should refract Shakespeare through the lens of its own philosophical predispositions. The history of criticism on *Coriolanus* shows Shakespeare's prescience in assessing its critical fortunes: more than most of his 'revised' and 'reinterpreted' plays, its 'virtues lie in th'interpretation of the time' (IV vii 49–50). We may perhaps take a measure of satisfaction in the tendency, manifested in the essays collected here, of current estimates to bring it progressively into esteem.

TEXTUAL NOTE

The twentieth-century studies quote the following editions of *Coriolanus:* O. J. Campbell and M. Charney, *The Complete Works of Shakespeare,* ed. G. L. Kittredge (Boston, Mass., 1936); A. P. Rossiter and G. K. Hunter, *The Complete Works,* ed. Peter Alexander (Glasgow, 1951); R. Brower, the 'Signet

Classic' *Coriolanus,* ed. R. Brower (New York, 1966); and W. Farnham, *Shakespeare: Complete Works,* ed. W. J. Craig (Oxford, 1943), in which quotations in the other recent essays may be conveniently located. The Folio text of the play is a good one, and there is general editorial agreement about the departures from it adopted in modern editions.

PART ONE

Critical Comment
1765–1919

Samuel Johnson (1765)

The tragedy of *Coriolanus* is one of the most amusing of our author's performances.[1] The old man's merriment in Menenius; the lofty lady's dignity in Volumnia; the bridal modesty in Virgilia; the patrician and military haughtiness in Coriolanus; the plebeian malignity, and tribunitian insolence in Brutus and Sicinius, make a very pleasing and interesting variety: and the various revolutions of the hero's fortune fill the mind with anxious curiosity. There is, perhaps, too much bustle in the first act, and too little in the last.

SOURCE: 'Short Stricture' on *Coriolanus* in Johnson's *Shakespeare* (1765).

NOTE

1. As Bradley remarks (see Part Two below), Johnson intends *amusing* to imply 'engaging the interest' (cf. *O.E.D., s.v. amuse*).

William Hazlitt (1817)

Shakespear has in this play shewn himself well versed in history and state-affairs. *Coriolanus* is a store-house of political common-places. Any one who studies it may save himself the trouble of reading Burke's Reflections, or Paine's Rights of Man, or the Debates in both Houses of Parliament since the French Revolution or our own. The arguments for and against aristocracy or democracy, on the privileges of the few and the claims of the many, on liberty and slavery, power and the abuse of it, peace and war, are here very ably handled, with the spirit of a poet and the acuteness of a philosopher. Shakespear himself seems to have had a leaning to the arbitrary side of the question, perhaps from some feeling of contempt for his own origin; and to have spared no occasion of baiting the rabble. What he says of them is very true: what he says of their betters is also very true, though he dwells less upon it. The cause of the people is indeed but little calculated as a subject for poetry: it admits of rhetoric, which goes into argument and explanation, but it presents no immediate or distinct images to the mind, 'no jutting frieze, buttress, or coigne of vantage' for poetry 'to make its pendant bed and procreant cradle in'. The language of poetry naturally falls in with the language of power. The imagination is an exaggerating and exclusive faculty: it takes from one thing to add to another: it accumulates circumstances together to give the greatest possible effect to a favourite object. The understanding is a dividing and measuring faculty: it judges of things not according to their immediate impression on the mind, but according to their relations to one another. The one is a monopolising faculty, which seeks the greatest quantity of present excitement by inequality and disproportion; the other is a distributive faculty, which seeks the greatest quantity of ultimate good, by justice and proportion. The one is an aristocratical, the other a republican faculty. The principle of poetry is a very anti-levelling principle. It aims at effect, it exists by contrast. It admits of no medium. It is every thing by excess. It rises above the ordinary standard of sufferings and crimes. It presents a dazzling appearance. It shows its head turretted, crowned, and crested. Its front is gilt and blood-stained. Before it 'it carries noise, and behind it leaves tears'. It has its altars and its victims, sacrifices, human sacrifices. Kings, priests, nobles, are its train-bearers, tyrants and slaves its executioners. 'Carnage is its daughter.' Poetry is right-royal. It puts the individual for the species, the one above the infinite many, might before right. A lion hunting a flock of sheep or a herd of wild asses is a more poetical object than they; and we even take part with the lordly beast, because our vanity or some other feeling makes us disposed to place ourselves in the situation of the strongest party. So we feel some concern for the poor citizens of Rome when they meet together to compare their wants and grievances, till Coriolanus comes in and with blows and big words drives this set of 'poor rats', this rascal scum, to their homes and beggary before him. There is nothing heroical in a multitude of miserable rogues not wishing to be starved, or complaining that they are like to be so: but when a single man comes forward to brave their cries and to make them submit to the last indignities, from mere pride and self-will, our admiration of his prowess is immediately converted into contempt for their pusillanimity. The insolence of power is stronger than the plea of necessity. The tame submission to usurped authority or even the natural resistance to it has nothing to excite or flatter the imagination: it is the assumption of a right to insult or oppress others that carries an imposing air of superiority with it. We had rather be the oppressor than the oppressed. The love of power in ourselves and the admiration of it in others are both natural to man: the one makes him a tyrant, the other a slave. Wrong dressed out in pride, pomp, and circumstance, has more attraction than abstract right. Coriolanus complains of the fickleness of the people: yet, the instant he cannot gratify his pride and obstinacy at their expense, he turns his arms against his country. If his country was not worth defending, why did he build his pride on its defence? He is a conquerer and a hero; he conquers other countries, and makes this a plea for enslaving his own; and when he is prevented from doing so, he leagues with its enemies to destroy his country. He rates the people 'as if he were a God to punish, and not a man of their infirmity'. He scoffs at one of their tribunes for maintaining their rights and franchises: 'Mark you his absolute *shall*?' not marking his own absolute *will* to take every thing from them, his impatience of the slightest opposition to his own pretensions being in proportion to their arrogance and absurdity. If the great and powerful had the beneficence and wisdom of Gods, then all this would have been well: if with a greater knowledge of what is good for the people, they had as great a care for their interest as they have themselves, if they were seated above the world, sympathising with the welfare, but not feeling the passions of men, receiving neither good nor hurt from them, but bestowing their benefits as free gifts on them, they might then rule over them like another Providence. But this is not the case. Coriolanus is unwilling that the senate should shew their 'cares' for the people, lest their 'cares' should be construed into 'fears', to the subversion of all due authority; and he is no sooner disappointed in his schemes to deprive the people not only of the cares of the state, but of all power to redress themselves, than Volumnia is made madly to exclaim,

> Now the red pestilence strike all trades in Rome,
> And occupations perish.

This is but natural: it is but natural for a mother to have more regard for her son than for a whole city; but then the city should be left to take some care of itself. The care of the state cannot, we here see, be safely entrusted to maternal affection, or to the domestic charities of high life. The great have private feelings of their own, to which the interests of humanity and justice must courtesy. Their interests are so far from being the same as those of the community, that they are in direct and necessary opposition to them; their power is at the expense of *our* weakness; their riches of *our* poverty; their pride of *our* degradation; their splendour of *our* wretchedness; their tyranny of *our* servitude. If they had the superior knowledge ascribed to them (which they have not) it would only render them so much more formidable; and from Gods would convert them into Devils. The whole dramatic moral of *Coriolanus* is that those who have little shall have less, and that those who have much shall take all that others have left. The people are poor; therefore they ought to be starved. They are slaves; therefore they ought to be beaten. They work hard; therefore they ought to be treated like beasts of burden. They are ignorant; therefore they ought not to be allowed to feel that they want food, or clothing, or rest, that they are enslaved, oppressed, and miserable. This is the logic of the imagination and the passions; which seek to aggrandize what excites admiration and to heap contempt on misery, to raise power into tyranny, and to make tyranny absolute; to thrust down that which is low still lower, and to make wretches desperate: to exalt magistrates into kings, kings into gods; to degrade subjects to the rank of slaves, and slaves to the condition of brutes. The history of mankind is a romance, a mask, a tragedy, constructed upon the principles of *poetical justice*; it is a noble or royal hunt, in which what is sport to the few is death to the many, and in which the spectators halloo and encourage the strong to set upon the weak, and cry havoc in the chase though they do not share in the spoil. We may depend upon it that what men delight to read in books, they will put in practice in reality.

One of the most natural traits in this play is the difference of the interest taken in the success of Coriolanus by his wife and mother. The one is only anxious for his honour; the other is fearful for his life.

VOLUMNIA   Methinks I hither hear your husband's
                              drum:
  I see him pluck Aufidius down by th' hair:
  Methinks I see him stamp thus – and call thus –
  Come on, ye cowards; ye were got in fear
  Though you were born in Rome; his bloody brow
  With his mail'd hand then wiping, forth he goes

Like to a harvest man, that's task'd to mow
Or all, or lose his hire.

VIRGILA   His bloody brow! Oh Jupiter, no blood.

VOLUMNIA   Away, you fool; it more becomes a man
Than gilt his trophy. The breast of Hecuba,
When she did suckle Hector, look'd not lovelier
Than Hector's forehead, when it spit forth blood
At Grecian swords contending.

When she hears the trumpets that proclaim her son's
return, she says in the true spirit of a Roman matron,

These are the ushers of Martius: before him
He carries noise, and behind him he leaves tears.
Death, that dark spirit, in's nervy arm doth lie,
Which being advanc'd, declines, and then men die.

Coriolanus himself is a complete character: his love of
reputation, his contempt of popular opinion, his pride and
modesty, are consequences of each other. His pride consists in
the inflexible sternness of his will; his love of glory is a determined desire to bear down all opposition, and to extort the admiration both of friends and foes. His contempt for popular
favour, his unwillingness to hear his own praises, spring from
the same source. He cannot contradict the praises that are
bestowed upon him; therefore he is impatient at hearing them.
He would enforce the good opinion of others by his actions,
but does not want their acknowledgments in words.

Pray now, no more: my mother,
Who has a charter to extol her blood,
When she does praise me, grieves me.

His magnanimity is of the same kind. He admires in an
enemy that courage which he honours in himself; he places
himself on the hearth of Aufidius with the same confidence
that he would have met him in the field, and feels that by putting himself in his power, he takes from him all temptation for
using it against him.

SOURCE: *Characters of Shakespear's Plays* (1817).

S. T. Coleridge (c. 1818)

The wonderful philosophic impartiality in Shakespeare's politics. His own country's history had furnished him with no *matter* but what was too recent, and he [was] devoted to *patriotism*. Besides, the dispassionate instruction of ancient history. This most remarkable in *Julius Caesar*. In all this good-humored laugh at mobs, collate with Sir Thomas Browne.

[I i 179–80.

> Hang ye! Trust ye?
> With every minute you do change a mind.]

I suspect that Shakespeare wrote –

> *Trust* ye? HANG ye.
> With every [minute you do change a mind.]

[I x 12–24.

AUF.   . . . . mine emulation
Hath not that honour in't it had; for where
I thought to crush him in an equal force,
True sword to sword, I'll potch at him some way,
Or wrath or craft may get him. . . .
      . . . . . My valour's poison'd
With only suffering stain by him; for him
Shall fly out of itself: nor sleep nor sanctuary,
Being naked, sick, nor fane nor Capitol,
The prayers of priests nor times of sacrifice,
Embarquements all of fury, shall lift up
Their rotten privilege and custom 'gainst
My hate to Marcius.]

I have such deep faith in Shakespeare's heart-lore (*Herzlehre*) that I take for granted, this is in nature, and not as a mere anomaly, altho' I cannot in myself discover any germ of possible feeling which could wax and unfold itself into such sentiment.

[II i 109–10.

. . . the most sovereign prescription in Galen is but empiricutic.]

An old question: was it without, or in contempt of, historical information that Shakespeare made the contemporaries of Coriolanus quote Cato and Galen? What the blunder of the press[1] after 'empiric' stands for, I cannot recollect. . . .

[IV vii 28–57. The speech of Aufidius.

All places yield to him ere he sits down; etc.]

I have always thought this in itself so beautiful speech the least explicable from the mood and full intention of the speaker of any in the whole works of Shakespeare. I cherish the hope that I am mistaken and, becoming wiser, shall discover some profound excellence in what I now appear to myself to detect an imperfection.

SOURCE: 'Marginalia and Notebooks' in *S. T. Coleridge: Shakespearian Criticism,* ed. T. M. Raysor, 2nd ed. (1960) vol. I, pp. 79–81. Coleridge's *Shakespearian Criticism* was first published 1836–9.

NOTE

1. Coleridge's Stockdale edition reads *empyric qutique;* the first and second Folios read *emperickqutique.* '*Empiricutic*' is coined on the analogy of 'pharmaceutic' and means 'empiric' [Raysor's note].

Edward Dowden (1875)

The subject of Coriolanus is the ruin of a noble life through the sin of pride. If duty be the dominant ideal with Brutus, and pleasure of a magnificent kind be the ideal of Antony and Cleopatra, that which gives tone and colour to Coriolanus is an ideal of self-centred power. The greatness of Brutus is altogether that of the moral conscience; his external figure does not dilate upon the world through a golden haze like that of Antony, nor bulk massively and tower like that of Coriolanus. Brutus venerates his ideals, and venerates himself; but this veneration of self is in a certain sense disinterested. A haughty and passionate personal feeling, a superb egoism are with Coriolanus the sources of weakness and of strength. . . .

Although the play of Coriolanus almost inevitably suggests a digression into the consideration of the politics of Shakspere, it must once again be asserted that the central and vivifying element in the play is not a political problem, but an individual character and life. The tragic struggle of the play is not that of patricians with plebeians, but of Coriolanus with his own self. It is not the Roman people who bring about his destruction; it is the patrician haughtiness and passionate self-will of Coriolanus himself. Were the contest of political parties the chief interest of Shakspere's drama, the figures of the Tribunes must have been drawn upon a larger scale. They would have been endowed with something more than 'foxship'. As representatives of a great principle, or of a power constantly tending in one direction, they might have appeared worthy rivals of the leaders of the patrician party; and the fall of Coriolanus would be signalised by some conquest and advance of the tide of popular power.[1] Shakspere's drama is the drama of individuality, including under this name all those bonds of duty and of affection which attach man to his fellow-man, but not impersonal principles and ideas.[2] The passion of patriotism, high-toned and enthusiastic, stands with Shakspere instead of general political principles and ideas, and the life of the individual is widened and elevated by the national life, to which the individual surrenders himself with gladness and with pride.

The pride of Coriolanus is however not that which comes from self-surrender to and union with some power, or person, or principle higher than oneself. It is two-fold, a passionate self-esteem which is essentially egoistic; and secondly a passionate prejudice of class. His nature is the reverse of cold or selfish; his sympathies are deep, warm and generous; but a line, hard and fast, has been drawn for him by the aristocratic tradition, and it is only within that line that he permits his sympathies to play. To the surprise of the Tribunes, he can accept well-pleased a subordinate command under Cominius. He yields with kindly condescension to accept the devotion and fidelity of Menenius, and cherishes towards the old man a filial regard – the feeling of a son, who has the consciousness that he is greater than his father. He must dismiss Menenius disappointed from the Volscian camp; but he contrives an in-nocent fraud by means of which the old senator will fancy that he has affected more for the peace of Rome than another could. For Virgilia, the gentle woman in whom his heart finds rest, Coriolanus has a manly tenderness, and constant freshness of adhesion:

> O, a kiss
> Long as my exile, sweet as my revenge!
> Now by the jealous queen of heaven, that kiss
> I carried from thee, dear; and my true lip
> Hath virgin'd it e'er since.

In his boy he has a father's joy, and yields to an ambitious hope, and a yearning forward to his son's possible future of heroic action, in which there is something of touching, pater-nal weakness:

> The god of soldiers,
> With the consent of supreme Jove, inform
> Thy thoughts with nobleness; that thou may'st prove
> To shame unvulnerable, and stick i' the wars
> Like a great sea-mark, standing every flaw,
> And saving those that eye thee!

His wife's friend Valeria is the 'moon of Rome',

> Chaste as the icicle
> That's curdied by the frost from purest snow
> And hangs on Dian's temple.[3]

In his mother Volumnia, the awful Roman matron, he rejoices with a noble enthusiasm and pride; and while she is present always feels himself by comparison with this great mother, inferior and unimportant.

But Cominius, Menenius, and Virgilia, Valeria and Volumnia, and his boy belong to the privileged class, they are patrician. Beyond this patrician class neither his sympathies nor his imagination find it possible to range. The plebeians are 'a common cry of curs' whose breath Coriolanus hates. He cannot like Bolingbroke flatter their weakness while he despises them inwardly. He is not even indifferent towards them; he rather rejoices in their malice and displeasure; if the nobility would let him use his sword he would make a quarry 'with thousands of these quarter'd slaves', as high as he could pick his lance. Sicinius the Tribune is 'the Triton of the minnows'. When Coriolanus departs from Rome, as though all the virtue of the city were resident in himself, he reverses the apparent fact and pronounces a sentence of banishment against those whom he leaves behind; '*I banish you.*' Brutus is warranted by the fact when he says

> You speak o' the people
> As if you were a god to punish, not
> A man of their infirmity.

And yet the weakness, the inconstancy, and the incapacity of apprehending facts which are the vices of the people, reflect and repeat themselves in the great patrician; his aristocratic vices counterbalance their plebeian. He is rigid and obstinate; but under the influence of an angry egoism he can renounce his principles, his party and his native city. He will not bear away to his private use the paltry booty of the Volces; but to obtain the consulship he is urged by his proud mother and his patrician friends to stand bareheaded before the mob, to expose his wounds, to sue for their votes, to give his heart the lie, to bend the knee like a beggar asking an alms. The judgment and blood of Coriolanus are ill commingled; he desires the end, but can only half submit to the means which are necessary to attain that end; he has not sufficient self-control to enable him to dispose of those chances of which he is lord. And so he mars his fortune. The pride of Coriolanus, as Mr Hudson has observed, is 'rendered altogether inflammable and uncontrollable by passion, insomuch that if a spark of provocation is struck into the latter, the former instantly flames up beyond measure, and sweeps away all the regards of prudence, of decorum, and even of common sense.' Now such passion as this Shakspere knew to be weakness and not strength; and by this uncontrollable violence of temper Coriolanus draws down upon himself his banishment from Rome, and his subsequent fate.

At the moment when he passes forth through the gates of the city, and only then, his passion instead of breaking violently forth, subdues his nature in a more evil fashion and becomes dark and deadly. He feels that he has been deserted by 'the dastard nobles', and given over as a prey to the mob. He who had been so warm, so generous, so loyal towards his class now feels himself betrayed; and the deadly need of revenge, together with the sense that he is in solitude and must depend upon his own strength and prudence, makes him calm. He endeavours to pacify his mother, and to check the old man's tears; he utters no violent speech. Only one obscure and formidable word escapes his lips:

> I go alone
> Like to a lonely dragon that his fen
> Makes fear'd and talked of more than seen.

And in this spirit he strides forward towards Corioli.

No passage in the play is quick with such bright, spontaneous, almost lyrical feeling as the address of his defeated rival to Coriolanus, when he finds the great leader an unbidden guest within his house at Antium. Enthusiasm about great personalities finds nobler expression perhaps in the writings of Shakspere than in those of any other poet of any country. The reader will recall that wonderful outbreak of admiration and homage from the aged Nestor when he gazes for the first time upon Hector's unhelmeted head: –

I have, thou gallant Trojan, seen thee oft,
Labouring for destiny, make cruel way
Through ranks of Greekish youth, and I have seen thee
As hot as Perseus spur thy Phrygian steed,
Despising many forfeits and subduements,
When thou hast hung thy advanced sword i' the air,
Not letting it decline on the declined,
That I have said to some my standers by,
'*Lo Jupiter is yonder, dealing life!*'
And I have seen thee pause and take thy breath,
When that a ring of Greeks have hemm'd thee in,
Like an Olympian wrestling. [*Troilus and Cressida*, IV v]

And the old man continues in the like strain until almost breath must fail him. The instantaneous and involuntary homage paid by Aufidius to Coriolanus is the same in kind – the overwhelming joy of standing face to face with veritable human greatness and nobility.

But Coriolanus has found in Antium no second home. Honoured and deferred to, tended on, and treated as almost sacred, he is still the 'lonely dragon that his fen makes fear'd'. Cut off from his kindred and his friends, wronged by his own passionate sense of personality, his violent egoism, he resolves to stand

As if a man were author of himself,
And knew no other kin.

But the loves and loyalties to which he has done violence, react against him. The struggle, prodigious and pathetic, begins, between all that is massive, stern, inflexible and all that is tender and winning in his nature; and the strength is subdued by the weakness. It is as if an oak were rent and up-rooted not by the stroke of lightning, but by some miracle of gentle yet irresistible music. And while Coriolanus yields un-der the influence of an instinct not to be controlled, he possesses the distinct consciousness that such yielding is mor-tal to himself. He has come to hate and to conquer, but he must needs perish and love: –

> My wife comes foremost; then the honour'd mould
> Wherein this trunk was framed, and in her hand
> The grandchild to her blood. But, out, affection!
> All bond and privilege of nature, break!
> Let it be virtuous to be obstinate!
> What is that curt'sy worth? Or those doves' eyes,
> Which can make gods forsworn? I melt, and am not
> Of stronger earth than others. My mother bows;
> As if Olympus to a molehill should
> In supplication nod; and my young boy
> Hath an aspect of intercession, which
> Great nature cries 'Deny not.'

The convulsive efforts to maintain his hardness and rigidity are in vain; Coriolanus yields; his obstinacy and pride are broken; he is compelled to learn that a man cannot stand as if he were author of himself. And so the fortunes of Coriolanus fall, but the man rises with that fall.

Delivered from patrician pride, and his long habit of egoism, Coriolanus cannot be. The purely human influences have reached him through the only approaches by which he was accessible – through his own family. To the plebeian class he must still remain the intolerant patrician. Nevertheless, he has undergone a profound experience; he has acknowledged purely human influences in the only way in which it was possi-ble for him to do so. No single experience, Shakspere was aware, can deliver the soul from the long habit of passionate egoism. And, accordingly, at the last it is this which betrays him into the hands of the conspirators. His conduct before Rome is about to be judicially enquired into at Antium. But the word 'boy', ejaculated against him by Aufidius, 'touches Coriolanus into an ecstasy of passionate rage': –

> Boy! O slave!
> Pardon me, lords, 'tis the first time that ever
> I was forced to scold. . . .
> Boy! false hound!
> If you have writ your annals true, 'tis there
> That, like an eagle in a dove-cote, I
> Flutter'd your Volscians in Corioli;
> Alone, I did it. Boy!

And in a moment the swords of the conspirators have pierced him. A Volscian lord, reverent for fallen greatness, protects the body:–

> Tread not upon him. Masters all, be quiet;
> Put up your swords.

So suddenly has he passed from towering passion to the helplessness of death; the victim of his own violent egoism, and uncontrollable self-will. We remain with the sense that a great gap in the world has been made; that a sea-mark 'standing every flaw' has for all time disappeared. We see the lives of smaller men still going on; we repress all violence of lamentation, and bear about with us a memory in which pride and pity are blended.

SOURCE: *Shakspere: A Critical Study of His Mind and Art*
(1875) pp. 317–36.

NOTES

1. I owe this observation to Professor H. Th. Rötscher, *Shakespeare in seinen höchsten Charactergebilden*, (Dresden, 1864) p. 20.
2. 'His [Shakspere's] drama is the drama of *individuality*. . . . Shakspere shows neither the consciousness of a law, nor of humani-

ty; the future is mute in his dramas, and enthusiasm for great principles unknown. His genius comprehends and sums up the past and
the present; it does not initiate the future. He interpreted an epoch;
he announced none.' Joseph Mazzini, *Life and Writings*, vol. II, pp.
133, 134.

3. Observe the extraordinary vital beauty, and illuminating
quality of Shakspere's metaphors and similes. A common-place poet
would have written 'as chaste as snow'; but Shakspere's imagination
discovers degrees of chastity in ice and snow, and chooses the
chastest of all frozen things. . . .

4. H. N. Hudson, *Shakspere: his Life, Art and Characters*, vol II, p.
473.

A. C. Swinburne (1880)

I cannot but think that enough at least of time has been spent if not wasted by able and even by eminent men on examination of *Coriolanus* with regard to its political aspect or bearing upon social questions. It is from first to last, for all its turmoil of battle and clamour of contentious factions, rather a private and domestic than a public or historical tragedy. As in *Julius Caesar* the family had been so wholly subordinated to the state, and all personal interests so utterly dominated by the preponderance of national duties, that even the sweet and sublime figure of Portia passing in her 'awful loveliness' was but as a profile half caught in the background of an episode, so here on the contrary the whole force of the final impression is not that of a conflict between patrician and plebeian, but solely that of a match of passions played out for life and death between a mother and a son. The partisans of oligarchic or democratic systems may wrangle at their will over the supposed evidences of Shakespeare's prejudice against this creed and prepossession in favour of that: a third bystander may rejoice in the proof thus established of his impartial indifference towards either: it is all nothing to the real point in hand. The subject of the whole play is not the exile's revolt, the rebel's repentance, or the traitor's reward, but above all it is the son's tragedy. The inscription on the plinth of this tragic statue is simply to Volumnia Victrix.

A loftier or a more perfect piece of man's work was never done in all the world than this tragedy of *Coriolanus*. . . .

SOURCE: *A Study of Shakespeare* (1880).

H. A. Taine (1883)

... Plutarch's Coriolanus is an austere, coldly haughty patrician, a general of the army. In Shakspeare's hands he becomes a coarse soldier, a man of the people as to his language and manners, an athlete of war, with a voice like a trumpet; whose eyes by contradiction are filled with a rush of blood and anger, proud and terrible in mood, a lion's soul in the body of a bull. The philosopher Plutarch told of him a lofty philosophic action, saying that he had been at pains to save his landlord in the sack of Corioli. Shakspeare's Coriolanus has indeed the same disposition, for he is really a good fellow; but when Lartius asks him the name of this poor Volscian, in order to secure his liberty, he yawns out:

> By Jupiter I forgot.
> I am weary; yea, my memory is tired.
> Have we no wine here? (Iix)

He is hot, he has been fighting, he must drink; he leaves his Volscian in chains, and thinks no more of him. He fights like a porter, with shouts and insults, and the cries from that deep chest are heard above the din of the battle like the sounds from a brazen trumpet. He has scaled the walls of Corioli, he has butchered till he is gorged with slaughter. Instantly he turns to the army of Cominius, and arrives red with blood, 'as he were flay'd', 'Come I too late?' Cominius begins to compliment him. 'Come I too late?' he repeats. The battle is not yet finished: he embraces Cominius:

> O! let me clip ye
> In arms as sound as when I woo'd, in heart
> As merry as when our nuptial day was done. (I vi)

For the battle is a real holiday to him. Such senses, such a strong frame, need the outcry, the din of battle, the excitement of death and wounds. This haughty and indomitable heart needs the joy of victory and destruction. Mark the display of his patrician arrogance and his soldier's bearing, when he is offered the tenth of the spoils:

> I thank you, general;
> But cannot make my heart consent to take
> A bribe to pay my sword. (ɪ ix)

The soldiers cry, Marcius! Marcius! and the trumpets sound. He gets into a passion: rates the brawlers:

> No more, I say! For that I have not wash'd
> My nose that bled, or foil'd some debile wretch, –
> ... You shout me forth
> In acclamations hyberbolical;
> As if I loved my little should be dieted
> In praises sauced with lies.

They are reduced to loading him with honours: Cominius gives him a war-horse; decrees him the cognomen of Coriolanus: the people shout Caius Marcius Coriolanus! He replies:

> I will go wash;
> And when my face is fair, you shall perceive
> Whether I blush or no: howbeit, I thank you.
> I mean to stride your steed.

This loud voice, loud laughter, blunt acknowledgment, of a man who can act and shout better than speak, foretell the mode in which he will treat the plebeians. He loads them with insults; he cannot find abuse enough for the cobblers, tailors, envious cowards, down on their knees for a coin. 'To beg of Hob and Dick!' 'Bid them wash their faces and keep their teeth clean.' But he must beg, if he would be consul; his friends constrain him. It is then that the passionate soul, incapable of self-restraint, such as Shakspeare knew how to paint, breaks forth without hindrance. He is there in his candidate's gown, gnashing his teeth, and getting up his lesson in this style:

> What must I say?
> 'I pray, sir' – Plague upon't! I cannot bring
> My tongue to such a pace: – 'Look, sir, my wounds!
> I got them in my country's service, when
> Some certain of your brethren roar'd and ran
> From the noise of our own drums.' (ii iii)

The tribunes have no difficulty in stopping the election of a candidate who begs in this fashion. They taunt him in full senate, reproach him with his speech about the corn. He repeats it, with aggravations. Once roused, neither danger nor prayer restrains him:

> His heart's his mouth: ...
> And, being angry, does forget that ever
> He heard the name of death. (iii i)

He rails against the people, the tribunes, ediles, flatterers of the plebs. 'Come, enough,' says his friend Menenius. 'Enough, with over-measure,' says Brutus the tribune. He retorts:

> No, take more:
> What may be sworn by, both divine and human,
> Seal what I end withal! ... At once pluck out
> The multitudinous tongue; let them not lick
> The sweet which is their poison.

The tribune cries, Treason! and bids seize him. He cries:

> Hence, old goat! ...
> Hence, rotten thing! or I shall shake thy bones
> Out of thy garments!

He strikes him, drives the mob off: he fancies himself amongst

Volscians. 'On fair ground I could beat forty of them!' And
when his friends hurry him off, he threatens still, and

> Speak(s) o' the people,
> As if you (he) were a god to punish, not
> A man of their infirmity.

Yet he bends before his mother, for he has recognised in her a
soul as lofty and a courage as intractable as his own. He has
submitted from his infancy to the ascendency of this pride
which he admires. Volumnia reminds him: '*My praises made
thee first a soldier.*' Without power over himself, continually
tost on the fire of his too hot blood, he has always been the
arm, she the thought. He obeys from involuntary respect, like
a soldier before his general, but with what effort.

CORIOLANUS   The smiles of knaves
   Tent in my cheeks, and schoolboys' tears take up
   The glances of my sight! a beggar's tongue
   Make motion through my lips, and my arm'd knees
   Who bow'd but in my stirrup, bend like his
   That hath received an alms! – I will not do't . . . .
VOLUMNIA   . . . Do as thou list.
   Thy valiantness was mine, thou suck'dst it from me,
   But owe thy pride thyself.
COR.   Pray, be content:
   Mother, I am going to the market-place;
   Chide me no more. I'll mountebank their loves,
   Cog their hearts from them, and come home beloved
   Of all the trades in Rome. (III ii)

He goes, and his friends speak for him. Except a few bitter
asides, he appears to be submissive. Then the tribunes
pronounce the accusation, and summon him to answer as a
traitor:

COR   How! traitor!
MEN   Nay, temperately: your promise.
COR   The fires i' the lowest hell fold-in the people!

> Call me their traitor! Thou injurious tribune!
> Within thine eyes sat twenty thousand deaths,
> In thy hands clutch'd as many millions, in
> Thy lying tongue both numbers, I would say,
> 'Thou liest,' unto thee with a voice as free
> As I do pray the gods. (III iii)

His friends surround him, entreat him: he will not listen; he foams at the mouth, he is like a wounded lion:

> Let them pronounce the steep Tarpeian death,
> Vagabond exile, flaying, pent to linger.
> But with a grain a day, I would not buy
> Their mercy at the price of one fair word.

The people vote exile, supporting by their shouts the sentence of the tribune:

> COR. You common cry of curs! whose breath I hate
> As reek o' the rotten fens, whose love I prize
> As the dead carcasses of unburied men
> That do corrupt my air, I banish you. . . .
>   Despising,
> For you, the city, thus I turn my back:
> There is a world elsewhere.

Judge of his hatred by these raging words. It goes on increasing whilst waiting for vengeance. We find him next with the Volscian army before Rome. His friends kneel before him, he lets them kneel. Old Menenius, who had loved him as a son, only comes now to be driven away. 'Wife, mother, child, I know not.' (VI ii) He knows not himself. For this strength of hating in a noble heart is the same as the force of loving. He has transports of tenderness as of rage, and can contain himself no more in joy than in grief. He runs, spite of his resolution, to his wife's arms; he bends his knee before his mother. He had summoned the Volscian chiefs to make them witnesses of his refusals; and before them, he grants all, and weeps. On his return to Corioli, an insulting word from

Aufidius maddens him, and drives him upon the daggers of the Volscians. Vices and virtues, glory and misery, greatness and feebleness, the unbridled passion which composes his nature, endowed him with all.

SOURCE: Hippolyte A. Taine, *History of English Literature,* trans. H. Van Laun (1883) pp. 105–11, from the French edition of 1863.

Bernard Shaw (1903)

... Neither [Shakespeare nor Dickens] could do anything
with a serious positive character: they could place a human
figure before you with perfect verisimilitude; but when the
moment came for making it live and move, they found, unless
it made them laugh, that they had a puppet on their hands,
and had to invent some artificial external stimulus to make it
work. This is what is the matter with Hamlet all through: he
has no will except in his bursts of temper. Foolish Bardolaters
make a virtue of this after their fashion: they declare that the
play is the tragedy of irresolution; but all Shakespear's projec-
tions of the deepest humanity he knew have the same defect:
their characters and manners are lifelike; but their actions are
forced on them from without, and the external force is grotes-
quely inappropriate except when it is quite conventional, as in
the case of Henry v. Falstaff is more vivid than any of these
serious reflective characters, because he is self-acting: his
motives are his own appetites and instincts and humors.
Richard III, too, is delightful as the whimsical comedian who
stops a funeral to make love to the corpse's son's widow; but
when, in the next act, he is replaced by a stage villain who
smothers babies and offs with people's heads, we are revolted
at the imposture and repudiate the changeling. Faulconbridge, Coriolanus, Leontes are admirable descriptions of instinctive temperaments: indeed the play of Coriolanus is the
greatest of Shakespear's comedies; but description is not
philosophy; and comedy neither compromises the author nor
reveals him. He must be judged by those characters into
which he puts what he knows of himself, his Hamlets and
Macbeths and Lears and Prosperos. If these characters are
agonizing in a void about factitious melodramatic murders
and revenges and the like, whilst the comic characters walk

with their feet on solid ground, vivid and amusing, you know that the author has much to shew and nothing to teach. . . .

SOURCE: *Man and Superman,* Preface (1903).

T. S. Eliot (1919)

We are surely justified in attributing [*Hamlet*], with that other profoundly interesting play of 'intractable' material and astonishing versification, *Measure for Measure,* to a period of crisis, after which follow the tragic successes which culminate in *Coriolanus. Coriolanus* may be not as 'interesting' as *Hamlet,* but it is, with *Antony and Cleopatra,* Shakespeare's most assured artistic success. . . .

SOURCE: 'Hamlet and His Problems' (1919), reproduced in *Selected Essays, 1917–1932,* 3rd ed. (1973) p. 124.

PART TWO

Twentieth-century Studies

A. C. Bradley

'CHARACTER AND THE IMAGINATIVE APPEAL OF TRAGEDY IN *CORIOLANUS*' (1912)

Coriolanus is beyond doubt among the latest of Shakespeare's tragedies: there is some reason for thinking it the last. Like all those that succeeded *Hamlet*, it is a tragedy of vehement passion; and in none of them are more striking revolutions of fortune displayed. It is full of power, and almost every one feels it to be a noble work. We may say of it, as of its hero, that, if not one of Shakespeare's greatest creations, it is certainly one of his biggest.

Nevertheless, it is scarcely popular. It is seldom acted, and perhaps no reader ever called it his favourite play. Indeed, except for educational purposes, I suppose it is, after *Timon*, the least generally read of the tragedies. Even the critic who feels bound to rank it above *Romeo and Juliet*, and even above *Julius Caesar*, may add that he prefers those dramas all the same; and if he ignores his personal preferences, still we do not find him asking whether it is not the equal of the four great tragedies. He may feel this doubt as to *Antony and Cleopatra*, but not as to *Coriolanus*.

The question why this should be so will at once tell us something about the drama. We cannot say that it shows any decline in Shakespeare's powers, though in parts it may show slackness in their use. It has defects, some of which are due to the historical material; but all the tragedies have defects, and the material of *Antony and Cleopatra* was even more troublesome. There is no love-story; but then there is none in *Macbeth*, and next to none in *King Lear*. Thanks in part to the badness of the Folio text, the reader is impeded by obscurities of language and irritated by the mangling of Shakespeare's metre; yet these annoyances would not much diminish the effect of *Othello*. It may seem a more serious obstacle that the hero's faults are repellent and chill our sympathy; but Macbeth, to say nothing of his murders, is a much less noble being than Coriolanus. All this doubtless goes for something; but there must be some further reason why this drama stands apart from the four great tragedies and *Antony and Cleopatra*. And one main reason seems to be this. Shakespeare could construe the story he found only by conceiving the hero's character in a certain way; and he had to set the whole drama in tune with that conception. In this he was, no doubt, perfectly right; but he closed the door on certain effects, in the absence of which his whole power in tragedy could not be displayed. He had to be content with something less, or rather with something else; and so have we.

Most of the great tragedies leave a certain imaginative impression of the highest value, which I describe in terms intended merely to recall it. What we witness is not the passion and doom of mere individuals. The forces that meet in the tragedy stretch far beyond the little group of figures and the tiny tract of space and time in which they appear. The darkness that covers the scene, and the light that strikes across it, are more than our common night and day. The hero's fate is, in one sense, intelligible, for it follows from his character and the conditions in which he is placed; and yet everything, character, conditions, and issue, is mystery. Now of this effect there is very little in *Coriolanus*. No doubt the story has a universal meaning, since the contending forces are permanent constituents of human nature; but that peculiar *imaginative* effect or atmosphere is hardly felt. And, thinking of the play, we notice that the means by which it is produced elsewhere are almost absent here. One of these means is the use of the supernatural; another a treatment of nature which makes her appear not merely as a background, nor even merely as a conscious witness of human feelings, sufferings, and deeds, but as a vaster fellow-actor and fellow-sufferer. Remove in fancy from *Hamlet, Lear,* and *Macbeth* all that appeals to imagination through these means, and you find them utterly changed, but brought nearer to *Coriolanus*. Here Shakespeare has deliberate-

ly withdrawn his hand from those engines. He found, of
course, in Plutarch allusions to the gods, and some of them he
used; but he does not make us feel that the gods take part in
the story. He found also wonders in the firmament, portents, a
strange vision seen by a slave, a statue that spoke. He found
that the Romans in their extremity sent the priests, augurs,
and soothsayers to plead with Coriolanus; and that the embassy of the women which saved Rome was due to a thought
which came suddenly to Valeria, which she herself regarded
as a divine inspiration, and on the nature of which Plutarch
speculates. But the whole of this Shakespeare ignored. Nor
would he use that other instrument I spoke of. Coriolanus was
not the man to be terrified by twilight, or to feel that the stars
or the wind took part against or with him. If Lear's
thunderstorm had beat upon his head, he would merely have
set his teeth. And not only is the mystery of nature absent; she
is scarcely present even as a background. The hero's grim
description of his abode in exile as 'the city of kites and crows'
is almost all we have. In short, *Coriolanus* has scarcely more atmosphere, either supernatural or natural, than the average
serious prose drama of to-day.

In Shakespeare's greatest tragedies there is a second source
of supreme imaginative appeal – in one or two the chief source
– the exhibition of inward conflict, or of the outburst of one or
another passion, terrible, heart-rending, or glorious to
witness. At these moments the speaker becomes the greatest of
poets; and yet, the dramatic convention admitted, he speaks
in character. Coriolanus is never thus the greatest of poets,
and he could not be so without a breach of more than
dramatic convention. His nature is large, simple, passionate;
but (except in one point, to which I will return, as it is irrelevant here) his nature is not, in any marked degree, imaginative. He feels all the rapture, but not, like Othello, all the
poetry, of war. He covets honour no less than Hotspur, but he
has not Hotspur's vision of honour. He meets with ingratitude
like Timon, but it does not transfigure all mankind for him.
He is very eloquent, but his only free eloquence is that of
vituperation and scorn. It is sometimes more than eloquence,
it is splendid poetry; but it is never such magical poetry as we

hear in the four greatest tragedies. Then, too, it lies in his nature that his deepest and most sacred feeling, that for his mother, is almost dumb. It governs his life and leads him un-complaining towards death, but it cannot speak. And, finally, his inward conflicts are veiled from us. The change that came when he found himself alone and homeless in exile is not ex-hibited. The result is partly seen in the one soliloquy of this drama, but the process is hidden. Of the passion that possesses him when his triumph seems at hand we get a far more vivid idea from the words of Cominius than from any words of his own:

> I tell you he does sit in gold, his eye
> Red as 'twould burn Rome.

In the most famous scene, when his fate is being decided, only one short sentence reveals the gradual loosening of purpose during his mother's speech. The actor's face and hands and bearing must show it, not the hero's voice; and his submission is announced in a few quiet words, deeply moving and im-pressive, but destitute of the effect we know elsewhere of a lightning-flash that rends the darkness and discloses every cranny of the speaker's soul. All this we can see to be perfectly right, but it does set limits to the flight of Shakespeare's im-agination.

I have spoken of something that we miss in *Coriolanus*. Unfor-tunately there is something that a good many readers find, or think they find, and that makes it distasteful to them. A political conflict is never the centre of interest in Shakespeare's plays, but in the historical plays it is an element more or less essential, and in this one it is very prominent. Here, too, since it may be plausibly described as a conflict between people and nobles, or democracy and aristocracy, the issue is felt to be still alive. And Shakespeare, it is thought, shows an animus, and sides against the people. A hundred years ago Hazlitt, dealing with this tragedy, said: 'Shakespeare himself seems to have had a leaning to the arbitrary side of the question, perhaps from some feeling of contempt for his own origin; and to have spared no occasion of baiting the rabble. What he says of them is very true; what he says of their betters is also very true, though he dwells less upon it.' This language is very tentative and mild compared with that of some later writers. According to one, Shakespeare 'loathed the common Englishman'. He was a neuropath who could not endure the greasy aprons and noisome breath of mechanics, and 'a snob of the purest English water'. According to another, he was probably afflicted for some years with an 'enormous self-esteem'. A hero similarly afflicted, and a nauseous mob – behold the play!

I do not propose to join this dance, or even to ask whether any reasonable conjecture as to Shakespeare's political views and feelings could be formed from study of this play and of others. But it may be worth while to mention certain questions which should be weighed by any one who makes the adventure. Are not the chief weaknesses and vices shown by the populace, or attributed to it by speakers, in these plays, those with which it had been habitually charged in antiquity and the Middle Ages; and did not Shakespeare find this common form, if nowhere else, in Plutarch? Again, if these traits and charges are heightened in his dramas, what else do we expect in drama, and especially in that of the Elizabethans? Granted, next, that in Shakespeare the people play a sorry political part, is that played by English nobles and Roman patricians much more glorious or beneficent; and if, in Hazlitt's phrase, Shakespeare says more of the faults of the people than of those of their betters, would we have him give to humble unlettered persons the powers of invective of lordly orators? Further, is abuse of the people ever dramatically inappropriate in Shakespeare; and is it given to Henry the Fifth, or Brutus (who had some cause for it), or, in short, to any of the most attractive characters? Is there not, besides, a great difference between his picture of the people taken as individuals, even when they talk politics, and his picture of them as a crowd or mob? Is not the former, however humorously critical, always kindly; and is a personal bias really needed to account for the latter? And, to end a catalogue easy to prolong, might not that talk, which is scarcely peculiar to Shakespeare, about greasy

caps and offensive odours, have some other origin than his artistic nerves? He had, after all, some little gift of observation,
and, when first he mixed with a class above his own, might he
not resemble a son of the people now who, coming among his
betters, observes with amusement the place held in their
decalogue by the morning bath? I do not for a moment suggest
that, by weighing such questions as these, we should be led to
imagine Shakespeare as any more inclined to champion the
populace than Spenser or Hooker or Bacon; but I think we
should feel it extremely hazardous to ascribe to him any
political feelings at all, and ridiculous to pretend to certainty
on the subject.

Let us turn to the play. The representation of the people,
whatever else it may be, is part of a dramatic design. This
design is based on the main facts of the story, and these imply
a certain character in the people and the hero. Since the issue
is tragic, the conflict between them must be felt to be un-
avoidable and wellnigh hopeless. The necessity for dramatic
sympathy with both sides demands that on both there should
be some right and some wrong, both virtues and failings; and
if the hero's monstrous purpose of destroying his native city is
not to extinguish our sympathy, the provocation he receives
must be great. This being so, the picture of the people is, surely, no darker than it had to be; the desired result would have
been more easily secured by making it darker still. And one
must go further. As regards the political situation the total
effect of the drama, it appears to me, is this. The conflict of
hero and people is hopeless; but it is he alone who makes the
conflict of patricians and plebeians, I do not say hopeless, but
in any high degree dangerous. The people have bad faults, but
no such faults as, in his absence, would prevent a constitutional development in their favour.

I will not try to describe their character, but I will illustrate
this statement by comparing two accusations of their op-
ponents with the facts shown; for these we must accept, but
the accusations we must judge for ourselves. In the first scene
the people are called cowards, both by the hero and by their
friendly critic Menenius. Now there is no sign that they
possess the kind of courage expected of gentlemen, or feel the

corresponding shame if their courage fails. But if they were
cowards, how could Rome be standing where we see it stand?
They are the common soldiers of Rome. And when we see
them in war, what do we find? One division, under Cominius,
meets the Volscians in the field; the other, under Coriolanus,
assaults Corioli. Both are beaten back. This is what Cominius
says to his men:

> Breathe you, my friends: well fought: we are come off
> Like Romans, neither foolish in our stands,
> Nor cowardly in retire.

Nothing hints that the other division has not fought well or
was cowardly in retire; but it was encouraged beforehand with
threats, and, on its failure, with a torrent of curses and abuse.
Nevertheless it advances again and forces the enemy to the
gates, which Coriolanus enters, calling on his men to follow
him.

> FIRST SOL.   Fool-hardiness; not I.
> SECOND SOL.   Nor I.
> FIRST SOL.   See, they have shut him in.
> ALL.   To the pot, I warrant him.

Disgusting, no doubt; but the answer to threats and curses.
They would not have served Cominius so; and indeed, when
Lartius comes up and merely suggests to them to 'fetch off' the
re-appearing hero, they respond at once and take the city.
These men are not cowards; but their conduct depends on
their leaders. The same thing is seen when Coriolanus himself
appeals to the other division for volunteers to serve in the van.
For once he appeals nobly, and the whole division volunteers.
    Another charge he brings against the people is that they can
neither rule nor be ruled. On this his policy of 'thorough' is
based. Now, judging from the drama, one would certainly say
that they could not rule alone – that a pure democracy would
lead to anarchy, and perhaps to foreign subjection. And one
would say also that they probably could not be ruled by the
patricians if all political rights were denied them. But to rule

them, while granting them a place in the constitution, would
seem quite feasible. They are, in fact, only too easy to guide.
No doubt, collected into a mob, led by demagogues, and
maddened by resentment and fear, they become wild and
cruel. It is true, also, that, when their acts bear bitter fruit,
they disclaim responsibility and turn on their leaders: 'that we
did, we did for the best; and though we willingly consented to
his banishment, yet it was against our will'. But they not only
follow their tribunes like sheep; they receive abuse and direction submissively from any one who shows goodwill. They are
fundamentally good-natured, like the Englishmen they are,
and have a humorous consciousness of their own weaknesses.
They are, beyond doubt, mutable, and in that sense untrustworthy; but they are not by nature ungrateful, or slow to
admire their bitterest enemy. False charges and mean im-
putations come from their leaders, not from them. If one of
them blames Coriolanus for being proud, another says he cannot help his pride. They insist on the bare form of their right
to name him consul, but all they want is the form, and not the
whole even of that. When he asks one of them, 'Well then, I
pray, your price of the consulship?' the answer, 'The price is
to ask it kindly', ought to have melted him at once; yet when
he asks it contemptuously it is still granted. Even later, when
the arts of the tribunes have provoked him to such a storm of
defiant and revolutionary speech that both the consulship and
his life are in danger, one feels that another man might save
both with no great trouble. Menenius tells him that the people

> have pardons, being ask'd, as free
> As words to little purpose.

His mother and friends urge him to deceive the people with
false promises. But neither false promises nor apologies are
needed, only a little humanity and some acknowledgement
that the people are part of the state. He is capable of neither,
and so the conflict is hopeless. But it is so not because the people, or even the tribunes, are what they are, but because he is
what we call an impossible person.

The result is that all the force and nobility of Rome's greatest man have to be thrown away and wasted. That is tragic; and it is doubly so because it is not only his faults that make him impossible. There is bound up with them a nobleness of nature in which he surpasses every one around him.

We see this if we consider, what is not always clear to the reader, his political position. It is not shared by any of the other patricians who appear in the drama. Critics have called him a Tory or an ultra-Tory. The tribune who calls him a 'traitorous innovator' is quite as near the mark. The people have been granted tribunes. The tribunate is a part of the constitution, and it is accepted, with whatever reluctance, by the other patricians. But Coriolanus would abolish it, and that not by law but by the sword. Nor would he be content with that. The right of the people to control the election of the consul is no new thing; it is an old traditional right; but it too might well be taken away. The only constitution tolerable in his eyes is one where the patricians are the state, and the people a mere instrument to feed it and fight for it. It is this conviction that makes it so dangerous to appoint him consul, and also makes it impossible for him to give way. Even if he could ask pardon for his abuse of the people, he could not honestly promise to acknowledge their political rights.

Now the nobleness of his nature is at work here. He is not tyrannical; the charge brought against him of aiming at a tyranny is silly. He is an aristocrat. And Shakespeare has put decisively aside the statement of Plutarch that he was 'churlish, uncivil, and altogether unfit for any man's conversation'. Shakespeare's hero, though he feels his superiority to his fellow-patricians, always treats them as equals. He is never rude or over-bearing. He speaks to them with the simple directness or the bluff familiarity of a comrade. He does not resent their advice, criticism, or reproof. He shows no trace of envy or jealousy, or even of satisfaction at having surpassed them. The suggestion of the tribunes that he is willing to serve under Cominius because failure in war will be credited to Cominius, and success in war to himself, shows only the littleness of their own minds. The patricians are his fellows in a community of virtue – of a courage, fidelity, and honour,

which cannot fail them because they are 'true-bred', though
the bright ideal of such virtue become perfect still urges them
on. But the plebeians, in his eyes, are destitute of this virtue,
and therefore have no place in this community. All they care
for is food in peace, looting in war, flattery from their
demagogues; and they will not even clean their teeth. To ask
anything of them is to insult not merely himself but the virtues
that he worships. To give them a real share in citizenship is
treason to Rome; for Rome means these virtues. They are not
Romans, they are the rats of Rome.

He is very unjust to them, and his ideal, though high, is also
narrow. But he is magnificently true to it, and even when he
most repels us we feel this and glory in him. He is never more
true to it than when he tries to be false; and this is the scene
where his superiority in nobleness is most apparent. He, who
had said of his enemy, 'I hate him worse than a promise-
breaker', is urged to save himself and his friends by promises
that he means to break. To his mother's argument that he
ought no more to mind deceiving the people than outwitting
an enemy in war, he cannot give the obvious answer, for he
does not really count the people his fellow-countrymen. But
the proposal that *he* should descend to lying or flattering
astounds him. He feels that if he does so he will never be
himself again; that his mind will have taken on an inherent
baseness and no mere simulated one. And he is sure, as we
are, that he simply cannot do what is required of him. When
at last he consents to try, it is solely because his mother bids
him and he cannot resist her chiding. Often he reminds us of a
huge boy; and here he acts like a boy whose sense of honour is
finer than his mother's, but who is too simple and too noble to
frame the thought.

Unfortunately he is altogether too simple and too ignorant
of himself. Though he is the proudest man in Shakespeare he
seems to be unaware of his pride, and is hurt when his mother
mentions it. It does not prevent him from being genuinely
modest, for he never dreams that he has attained the ideal he
worships; yet the sense of his own greatness is twisted round
every strand of this worship. In almost all his words and deeds
we are conscious of the tangle. I take a single illustration. He

cannot endure to be praised. Even his mother, who has a charter to extol her blood, grieves him when she praises him. As for others,

> I had rather have one scratch my head i' the sun
> When the alarum were struck, than idly sit
> To hear my nothings monster'd.

His answer to the roar of the army hailing him 'Coriolanus' is, 'I will go wash'. His wounds are 'scratches with briars'. In Plutarch he shows them to the people without demur: in Shakespeare he would rather lose the consulship. There is a greatness in all this that makes us exult. But who can assign the proportions of the elements that compose this impatience of praise: the feeling (which we are suprised to hear him express) that he, like hundreds more, has simply done what he could; the sense that it is nothing to what might be done; the want of human sympathy (for has not Shelley truly said that fame is love disguised?); the pride which makes him feel that he needs no recognition, that after all he himself could do ten times as much, and that to praise his achievement implies a limit to his power? If any one could solve this problem, Coriolanus certainly could not. To adapt a phrase in the play, he has no more introspection in him than a tiger. So he thinks that his loathing of the people is all disgust at worthlessness, and his resentment in exile all a just indignation. So too he fancies that he can stand

> As if a man were author of himself
> And knew no other kin,

while in fact public honour and home affections are the breath of his nostrils, and there is not a drop of stoic blood in his veins.

What follows on his exile depends on this self-ignorance. When he bids farewell to his mother and wife and friends he is still excited and exalted by conflict. He comforts them; he will take no companion; he will be loved when he is lacked, or at least he will be feared; while he remains alive, they shall

always hear from him, and never aught but what is like him
formerly. But the days go by, and no one, not even his mother,
hears a word. When we see him next, he is entering Antium to
offer his services against his country. If they are accepted, he
knows what he will do: he will burn Rome.

As I have already remarked, Shakespeare does not exhibit
to us the change of mind which issues in this frightful purpose;
but from what we see and hear later we can tell how he imagined it; and the key lies in that idea of *burning* Rome. As
time passes, and no suggestion of recall reaches Coriolanus,
and he learns what it is to be a solitary homeless exile, his
heart hardens, his pride swells to a mountainous bulk, and the
wound in it becomes a fire. The fellow-patricians from whom
he parted lovingly now appear to him ingrates and dastards,
scarcely better than the loathsome mob. Somehow, he knows
not how, even his mother and wife have deserted him. He has
become nothing to Rome, and Rome shall hear nothing from
him. Here in solitude he can find no relief in a storm of words;
but gradually the blind intolerable chaos of resentment con-
ceives and gives birth to a vision, not merely of battle and in-
discriminate slaughter, but of the whole city one tower of
flame. To see that with his bodily eyes would satisfy his soul;
and the way to the sight is through the Volscians. If he is killed
the moment they recognize him, he cares little: better a dead
nothing than the living nothing Rome thinks him. But if he
lives, she shall know what he is. He bears himself among the
Volscians with something that resembles self-control; but
what controls him is the vision that never leaves him and never
changes, and his eye is red with its glare when he sits in his
state before the doomed city.

This is Shakespeare's idea, not Plutarch's. In Plutarch there
is not a syllable about the burning of Rome. Coriolanus (to
simplify a complicated story) intends to humiliate his country
by forcing on it disgraceful terms of peace. And this, apart
from its moral quality, is a reasonable design. The Romans,
rather than yield to fear, decline to treat unless peace is first
restored; and therefore it will be necessary to assault the city.
In the play we find a single vague allusion to some unnamed
conditions which, Coriolanus knows, cannot now be accepted;

but everywhere, among both Romans and Volscians, we hear of the burning of Rome, and in the city there is no hope of successful resistance. What Shakespeare wanted was a simpler and more appalling situation than he found in Plutarch, and a hero enslaved by his passion and driven blindly forward. How blindly, we may judge if we ask the questions: what will happen to the hero if he disappoints the expectation he has raised among the Volscians, when their leader is preparing to accuse him even if he fulfils it: and, if the hero executes his purpose, what will happen to his mother, wife, and child: and how can it be executed by a man whom we know in his home as the most human of men, a tender husband still the lover of his wife, and a son who regards his mother not merely with devoted affection but with something like religious awe? Very likely the audience in the theatre was not expected to ask these questions, but it *was* expected to see in the hero a man totally ignorant of himself, and stumbling to the destruction either of his life or of his soul.

In speaking of the famous scene where he is confronted with Volumnia and Valeria, Virgilia and her boy, and the issue is decided, I am obliged to repeat what I have said elsewhere in print [*Shakespearean Tragedy*, p. 84]; and I must speak in the first person because I do not know how far others share my view. To me the scene is one in which the tragic feelings of fear and pity have little place. Such anxiety as I feel is not for the fate of the hero or of any one else: it is, to use religious language, for the safety of his soul. And when he yields, though I know, as he divines, that his life is lost, the emotion I feel is not pity: he is above pity and above life. And the anxiety itself is but slight: it bears no resemblance to the hopes and fears that agitate us as we approach the end in *Othello* or *King Lear*. The whole scene affects me, to exaggerate a little, more as a majestic picture of stationary figures than as the fateful climax of an action speeding to its close. And the structure of the drama seems to confirm this view. Almost throughout the first three Acts – that is, up to the banishment – we have incessant motion, excited and resounding speech, a violent oscillation of fortunes. But, after this, the dramatic tension is suddenly relaxed, and, though it increases again, it is never

allowed to approach its previous height. If Shakespeare had
wished it to do so in this scene, he had only to make us wait in
dread of some interposition from Aufidius, at which the hero's
passion might have burst into a fury fatal even to the influence
of Volumnia. But our minds are crossed by no shadow of such
dread. From the moment when he catches sight of the advan-
cing figures, and the voice of nature – what he himself calls
'great nature' – begins to speak in his heart long before it
speaks aloud to his ear, we know the end. And all this is in
harmony with that characteristic of the drama which we
noticed at first, – we feel but faintly, if at all, the presence of
any mysterious or fateful agency. We are witnessing only the
conquest of passion by simple human feelings, and *Coriolanus*
is as much a drama of reconciliation as a tragedy. That is no
defect in it, but it is a reason why it cannot leave the same impression as the supreme tragedies, and should be judged by its
own standard.

A tragedy it is, for the passion is gigantic, and it leads to the
hero's death. But the catastrophe scarcely diminishes the influence of the great scene. Since we know that his nature,
though the good in it has conquered, remains unchanged, and
since his rival's plan is concerted before our eyes, we await
with little suspense, almost indeed with tranquillity, the certain end. As it approaches it is felt to be the more inevitable
because the steps which lead to it are made to repeat as exactly as possible the steps which led to his exile. His task, as then,
is to excuse himself, a task the most repugnant to his pride.
Aufidius, like the tribunes then, knows how to render its fulfilment impossible. He bears a word of insult, the same that he
heard then, – 'traitor'. It is followed by a sneer at the most
sacred tears he ever shed, and a lying description of their effect
on the bystanders; and his pride, and his loathing of falsehood
and meanness, explode, as before, in furious speech. For a moment he tries to check himself and appeals to the senators; but
the effort seems only to treble his rage. Though no man, since
Aufidius spoke, has said a word against him, he defies the
whole nation, recalling the day of its shame and his own
triumph, when alone, like an eagle, he fluttered the dovecotes
in Corioli. The people, who accompanied him to the

market-place, splitting the air with the noise of their
enthusiasm, remember their kinsfolk whom he slaughtered,
change sides, and clamour for his death. As he turns on
Aufidius, the conspirators rush upon him, and in a moment,
before the vision of his glory has faded from his brain, he lies
dead. The instantaneous cessation of enormous energy (which
is like nothing else in Shakespeare) strikes us with awe, but
not with pity. As I said, the effect of the preceding scene,
where he conquered something stronger than all the Volscians
and escaped something worse than death, is not reversed; it is
only heightened by a renewed joy in his greatness. Roman and
Volscian will have peace now, and in his native city patrician
and plebeian will move along the way he barred. And they are
in life, and he is not. But life has suddenly shrunk and dwindl-
ed, and become a home for pygmies and not for him.[1]

Dr. Johnson observes that 'the tragedy of *Coriolanus* is one of
the most amusing of our author's performances'. By 'amusing'
he did not mean 'mirth-provoking'; he meant that in *Coriolanus*
a lively interest is excited and sustained by the variety of the
events and characters; and this is true. But we may add that
the play contains a good deal that is amusing in the current
sense of the word. When the people appear as individuals they
are frequently more or less comical. Shakespeare always en-
joyed the inconsequence of the uneducated mind, and its
tendency to express a sound meaning in an absurd form.
Again, the talk of the servants with one another and with the
muffled hero, and the conversation of the sentinels with
Menenius, are amusing. There is a touch of comedy in the
contrast between Volumnia and Virgilia when we see them on
occasions not too serious. And then, not only at the beginning,
as in Plutarch, but throughout the story we meet with that
pleasant and wise old gentleman Menenius, whose humour
tells him how to keep the peace while he gains his point, and
to say without offence what the hero cannot say without rais-
ing a storm. Perhaps no one else in the play is regarded from
beginning to end with such unmingled approval, and this is
not lessened when the failure of his embassy to Coriolanus
makes him the subject as well as the author of mirth. If we

regard the drama from this point of view we find that it differs
from almost all the tragedies, though it has a certain likeness
to *Antony and Cleopatra*. What is amusing in it is, for the most
part, simply amusing, and has no tragic tinge. It is not like the
gibes of Hamlet at Polonius, or the jokes of the clown who, we
remember, is digging Ophelia's grave, or that humour of Iago
which for us is full of menace; and who could dream of comparing it with the jesting of Lear's fool? Even that
Shakespearean audacity, the interruption of Volumnia's
speech by the hero's little son, makes one laugh almost
without reserve. And all this helps to produce the
characteristic tone of this tragedy.

The drawing of the character of Aufidius seems to me by far
the weakest spot in the drama. At one place, where he
moralizes on the banishment of the hero, Shakespeare, it
appears to some critics, is himself delivering a speech which
tells the audience nothing essential and ends in desperate
obscurity.[2] Two other speeches have been criticized. In the
first, Aufidius, after his defeat in the field, declares that, since
he cannot overcome his rival in fair fight, he will do it in any
way open to him, however dishonourable. The other is his
lyrical cry of rapture when Coriolanus discloses himself in the
house at Antium. The intention in both cases is clear. Aufidius
is contrasted with the hero as a man of much slighter and less
noble nature, whose lively impulses, good and bad, quickly
give way before a new influence, and whose action is in the
end determined by the permanent pressure of ambition and
rivalry. But he is a man of straw. He was wanted merely for
the plot, and in reading some passages in his talk we seem to
see Shakespeare yawning as he wrote. Besides, the un-
speakable baseness of his sneer at the hero's tears is an injury
to the final effect. Such an emotion as mere disgust is out of
place in a tragic close; but I confess I feel nothing but disgust
as Aufidius speaks the last words, except some indignation
with the poet who allowed him to speak them, and an un-
regenerate desire to see the head and body of the speaker lying
on opposite sides of the stage.

Though this play is by no means a drama of destiny we
might almost say that Volumnia is responsible for the hero's

life and death. She trained him from the first to aim at honour in arms, to despise pain, and to

> forget that ever
> He heard the name of death;

to strive constantly to surpass himself, and to regard the populace with inhuman disdain as

> things created
> To buy and sell with groats.

Thus she led him to glory and to banishment. And it was she who, in the hour of trial, brought him to sacrifice his pride and his life.

Her sense of personal honour, we saw, was less keen than his; but she was much more patriotic. We feel this superiority even in the scene that reveals the defect; in her last scene we feel it alone. She has idolized her son; but, whatever motive she may appeal to in her effort to move him, it is not of him she thinks; her eyes look past him and are set on Rome. When, in yielding, he tells her that she has won a happy victory for her country, but a victory most dangerous, if not most mortal, to her son, she answers nothing. And her silence is sublime.

These last words would be true of Plutarch's Volumnia. But in Plutarch, though we hear of the son's devotion, and how he did great deeds to delight his mother, neither his early passion for war nor his attitude to the people is attributed to her influence, and she has no place in the action until she goes to plead with him. Hence she appears only in majesty, while Shakespeare's Volumnia has a more varied part to play. She cannot be majestic when we see her hurrying through the streets in wild exultation at the news of his triumph; and where, angrily conquering her tears, she rails at the authors of his banishment, she can hardly be called even dignified. What Shakespeare gains by her animation and vehemence in these scenes is not confined to them. He prepares for the final scene a sense of contrast which makes it doubly moving and im-

In Volumnia's great speech he is much indebted to Plutarch, and it is, on the whole, in the majestic parts that he keeps most close to his authority. The open appeal to affection is his own; and so are the touches of familiar language. It is his Volumnia who exclaims, 'here he lets me prate like one i' the stocks', and who compares herself, as she once was, to a hen that clucks her chicken home. But then the conclusion, too, is pure Shakespeare; and if it has not majesty it has something dramatically even more potent. Volumnia, abandoning or feigning to abandon hope, turns to her companions with the words:

> Come, let us go:
> This fellow had a Volscian to his mother;
> His wife is in Corioli, and his child
> Like him by chance. Yet give us our dispatch:
> I am hush'd until our city be a-fire,
> And then I'll speak a little.[3]

Her son's resolution has long been tottering, but now it falls at once. Throughout, it is not the substance of her appeals that moves him, but the bare fact that she appeals. And the culmination is that she ceases to appeal, and defies him. This has been observed by more than one critic. I do not know if it has been noticed[4] that on a lower level exactly the same thing happens where she tries to persuade him to go and deceive the people. The moment she stops, and says, in effect, 'Well, then, follow your own will', his will gives way. Deliberately to set it against hers is beyond his power.

Ruskin, whose terms of praise and blame were never over-cautious, wrote of Virgilia as 'perhaps the loveliest of Shakespeare's female characters'. Others have described her as a shrinking submissive being, afraid of the very name of a wound, and much given to tears. This description is true; and, I may remark in passing, it is pleasant to remember that the hero's letter to his mother contained a full account of his wounds, while his letter to his wife did not mention them at all. But the description of these critics can hardly be the whole truth about a woman who inflexibly rejects the repeated in-

vitations of her formidable mother-in-law and her charming
friend to leave her house; who later does what she can to rival
Volumnia in rating the tribunes; and who at last quietly
seconds her assurance that Coriolanus shall only enter Rome
over her body. Still these added traits do not account for the
indefinable impression which Ruskin received (if he did not
rightly interpret it), and which thousands of readers share. It
comes in part from that kind of muteness in which Virgilia
resembles Cordelia, and which is made to suggest a world of
feeling in reserve. And in part it comes from the words of her
husband. His greeting when he returns from the war and she
stands speechless before him:

> My gracious silence, hail!
> Wouldst thou have laugh'd had I come coffin'd home,
> That weep'st to see me triumph? Ah, my dear,.
> Such eyes the widows in Corioli wear,
> And mothers that lack sons:

his exclamation when he sees her approaching at their last
meeting and speaks first of her and not of Volumnia:

> What is that curtsy worth, or those doves' eyes
> Which can make gods forsworn? I melt, and am not
> Of stronger earth than others;

these words envelop Virgilia in a radiance which is reflected
back upon himself. And this is true also of the lines about
Valeria, probably the lines most often quoted from this
drama:

> The noble sister of Publicola,
> The moon of Rome, chaste as the icicle
> That's curdied by the frost from purest snow,
> And hangs on Dian's temple: dear Valeria!

I said that at one point the hero's nature *was* in a high degree
imaginative; and it is here. In his huge violent heart there was
a store, not only of tender affection, but of delicate and

chivalrous poetry. And though Virgilia and Valeria evoke its expression we cannot limit its range. It extends to the widows and mothers in Corioli; and we feel that, however he might loathe and execrate the people, he was no more capable of injury or insult to a daughter of the people than Othello, or Chaucer's Knight, or Don Quixote himself.

SOURCE: *'Coriolanus'*. Second Annual Shakespeare Lecture, *Proceedings of the British Academy* (1912).

NOTES

1. I have tried to indicate the effect at which Shakespeare's imagination seems to have aimed. I do not say that the execution is altogether adequate. And some readers, I know, would like Coriolanus to die fighting. Shakespeare's idea is probably to be gathered from the hero's appeal to the senators to judge between Aufidius and him, and from the word 'lawful' in the last speech:

> O that I had him,
> With six Aufidiuses, or more, his tribe,
> To use my lawful sword!

He is not before the people only, but the senators, his fellow-- patricians, though of another city. Besides – if I may so put it – if Coriolanus were allowed to fight at all, he would have to annihilate the whole assembly.

2. But Prof. MacCallum's defence of this passage is perhaps successful (Appendix F in *Shakespeare's Roman Plays and Their Background,* London, 1910).

3. What she will utter, I imagine, is a mother's dying curse.

4. The point is noticed by Prof. MacCallum (p. 554).

O. J. Campbell

'EXPERIMENT IN TRAGICAL SATIRE' (1943)

I

In *Coriolanus* we have Shakespeare's second and more successful experiment in tragical satire. The structure which in *Timon of Athens* was bare and almost crude has here become a suitable form in which to cast the Roman aristocrat's story. Yet the construction of this last of Shakespeare's tragedies has been almost universally deplored. Critics, realizing that its pattern is very different from the one which the poet employed in his great tragedies, have agreed to brand it as inept. A. C. Bradley, for example, believes that the author's unintentional departure from his usual practice accounts for the failure of the play to produce a sound tragic effect.[1] This usually acute critic did not allow for the fact that Shakespeare, at this time a thoroughly experienced dramatist, might have deliberately experimented with new dramatic structures.

It is natural enough to judge *Coriolanus* by the standards of conventional tragedy; in the first Folio it is entitled *The Tragedy of Coriolanus*. Bernard Shaw was one of the first to see that the play was not a tragedy at all. He solves the problem of *Coriolanus* by propounding a witty paradox. 'It is,' he asserts, 'the greatest of Shakespeare's comedies.' This perverse statement suggests the proper approach to the play. Shakespeare did not attempt to give *Coriolanus* the structure of a conventional tragedy. Neither in his presentation of the central figure nor in his construction of the plot does he follow orthodox tragic principles. Instead of enlisting our sympathy for

Coriolanus, he deliberately alienates it. Indeed he makes the figure partly an object of scorn. Instead of ennobling Coriolanus through his fall and death, he mocks and ridicules him to the end. In brief, he fills the tragedy so full of the spirit of derision that the play can be understood only if it be recognized as perhaps the most successful of Shakespare's satiric plays.

II

Shakespeare found the materials for his play in Plutarch's *Life of Coriolanus,* but he gave the historical events a meaning entirely his own. For Plutarch they yielded a lesson in political restraint and patriotism. As he tells the story continual war has reduced the plebs to dire poverty. Indeed their misery is so great that they demand a change in their constitution – the creation of new officers to be called tribunes, who are to redress the wrongs of the people. This agitation contains a threat of revolution. But the peril is averted because the senate is wise enough to send to the plebs 'certain of their pleasantest old men' to discuss the grievances of the commoners. These ambassadors agree to the creation of the new officers and induce the plebs to join with the patricians in the defense of Rome against a foreign enemy.

Shakespeare completely changes the significance of these events. His play opens 'in the midst of a riot staged by the mutinous masses', who are starving because of a shortage of wheat. For their misery they blame not the drought, which is the real cause of the famine, but their governing class, the patricians, and, in particular, Coriolanus, the leader and mouthpiece of the aristocrats. They hate him for the contempt he has always shown them. Coriolanus in his very first speech proves that their charge is just, for he addresses them as:

> dissentious rogues
> That, rubbing the poor itch of your opinions,
> Make yourself scabs. (I i 168–70)

This unsavory figurative language is characteristic of most of the utterances of the haughty patrician. On the occasion in

question the vituperative torrent is interrupted by a messenger
who brings Coriolanus an order to lead the Roman army
against the Volscians and Aufidius their leader. Since carnage
is his natural element, he responds to this call with
enthusiasm. But even the heroism he summons for the battle
cannot temper his fundamental brutality. When at the first
onslaught of the enemy his soldiers flee in disorder, he berates
them with characteristically foul speech. By insults rather
than encouragement he drives his men back into the fray,
where he does deeds of superhuman valor, defeats Aufidius in
single combat, and brings complete victory to his army.

On his return to the capital, the populace greets him with
wild acclaim and the senators at once nominate him for consul. He craves the office, but his whole nature flares into revolt
against the convention which demands that he stand in the
market place and beg the plebeians for their votes. However,
at the insistence of his dominating mother he submits to the
humiliation of this electioneering. Though his appeal is filled
with disdain, it seems to succeed. But after he has come
through his ordeal and gone home, the tribunes persuade the
crowd that he has mocked them. If they possess any self-
respect, they will at once revoke their 'ignorant election.' This
they do and drive Coriolanus into the rage which the tribunes
anticipate and exploit.

When they inform him of the people's change of heart, he
insults them with mounting violence, until they call in a 'rabble of plebeians' and precipitate a brawl. In the course of this
uproar the people and their officers are driven off. Later they
return to find that Coriolanus has been persuaded by his
mother to allay their anger with fair speech. But his amenity
does not divert them from their intention to drive him into one
of his fits of uncontrollable rage. They call him traitor, and to
the word he reacts as they had planned. He looses upon them
a torrent of abuse. This stimulates the rabble to shout for his
banishment, and in the words of Coriolanus they 'whoop' him
out of Rome. Through his uncontrollable rage he has been
manipulated into a course of action which is to lead to his
self-destruction.

Then he goes straight over to the enemy, and although he

treats all the Volscians with overbearing arrogance, his
military genius enables him to lead their conquering army to
the very gates of Rome. There various representative citizens
meet him with desperate pleas to spare his native city. They
find him adamant. As a last resort his mother, Volumnia, accompanied by his wife Virgilia and his small son, is sent out to
confront him. She feels sure that she can force him to abandon
his dire purpose, for she well knows her irresistible influence
upon the man who in many respects is still her little boy. She
wisely does not ask him to rejoin the Roman forces, but merely to force Aufidius to make peace. Coriolanus is deaf to his
mother's entreaties but cannot hold out against her anger. He
yields in the flurried terror of a frightened child.

Returning to the Volscian army, Coriolanus induces
Aufidius to 'frame convenient peace'. By thus snatching the
fruits of complete victory from the Volscians, he wins the un-
dying resentment of their leader, who lays a clever trap to
catch and destroy the haughty Olympian schoolboy. He
knows how to stimulate Coriolanus to one of his characteristic
fits of wild anger. He uses the same method which the tribunes
had found effective, and insults him publicly. In the presence
of a crowd of confederates he brands him as a traitor to his
adopted country. The accusation has the desired effect.
Coriolanus throws into the teeth of the Volscians his former
triumphs over them and raises their resentment to the killing
point. Then, though the Lords of Corioli protest, the Volscian
plebeians fall upon Coriolanus and kill him.

III

From this brief resumé of the action it should be clear that
Coriolanus, like all Shakespeare's other history plays, embodies
some of the author's political ideas. Some critics, to be sure,
hesitate to attribute any definite political views to him. The
idolators of the early nineteenth century and their modern
representatives are responsible for this transcendental attitude
toward their hero. Shakespeare, they proudly assert, was not
of an age, but of all time. Of all movements in a given era,
political squabbles are the most ephemeral. Therefore to the

idolators an assertion that Shakespeare expressed positive political opinions even in his chronicle history plays was the rankest heresy. A. C. Bradley expressed their view when he wrote, 'I think it extremely hazardous to ascribe to him [Shakespeare] any political feeling at all and ridiculous to pretend to any certainty on the subject.'[2] This betrays a strange view of the dramatist's art. He, less than any other man of letters, dares to retire to an ivory tower, remote from the social interests of his contemporaries, in order to allow the trade winds from eternity to blow through his philosphic mind. Shakespeare based his profound studies of human motive and human passion upon a realistic appraisal of the various milieux in which his characters came to life; and of all the environments in which human beings must live, the political organization most interested Shakespeare and his contemporaries. The problems of Tudor politics obsessed them.

The usual view is that in *Coriolanus* Shakespeare expresses his contempt for the common man and his conviction that political power in the hands of the mob always brings disaster to the state.[3] More recently critics have looked at the other side of the picture and discerned in Coriolanus's conduct an exposure of the brutal methods that dictators in every age must employ to retain their absolute power.[4] Each of these apparently contradictory views is partly correct. Though Shakespeare is not in this play showing his contempt for the common man, he is nevertheless expressing his vigorous disapproval of democracy. In common with all political theorists of his age, he regarded it as the absence of all government – a form of organized disorder.[5]

But he does not lay all the blame for the social chaos on the plebs and its leaders. To his mind Coriolanus is equally guilty. He is a bad ruler. In the many volumes that the fifteenth and sixteenth centuries devoted to the education of a prince, the supreme magistrate – usually the king – is admonished to regard his subjects as his children and to be a father to them. He must sympathize with their trials and dangers and feel keenly his responsibility for their welfare. He must follow the example set by Henry v toward his soldiers in Shakespeare's play of that name. But Coriolanus acts in a manner diametrically opposed. He hates the people. On almost every occasion in which he meets them face to face he berates them and curses them vilely. Inevitably he finds them hostile and recalcitrant to his leadership – brave and efficient though it be in battle. Instead of correcting their faults, he goads them to anarchy by his hostility and violence. Coriolanus is thus as much responsible as the plebs for the political débâcle.

As a political *exemplum* the play presents a case of violent political disorder and reveals its causes. The trouble lies in the fact that no civil group performs its prescribed duties properly. As a result the divinely revealed pattern for the state is disrupted and society reels toward primal chaos. This lesson could not be clearly taught in the terms of tragedy. With its interest concentrated upon the tragic career of Coriolanus the man, an audience might easily ignore the political significance of the play. But the satiric form gave Shakespeare an opportunity to treat derisively both the crowd and Coriolanus, between whose 'endless jars' the commonweal was sorely wounded. A careful analysis of the play will show how skillfully the political teaching, the central theme of every Elizabethan history play, has been fitted to the satiric form of the drama.

IV

The play opens with a picture of a mutinous mob, in this way establishing immediately the atmosphere of social turmoil which is to exercise its destructive power throughout the action and to form a natural milieu for the subversive forces in the little world of Coriolanus's passions. In the midst of the uproar Menenius appears. He is the chief of the many commentators and expositors in this play who serve as Shakespeare's mouthpiece. He performs this service with a fussy garrulity that is intended to rouse our laughter. Later in the play he explains that he is 'a humorous [i.e. crotchety] patrician and one that loves a cup of hot wine with not a drop of allaying Tiber in 't . . . One that converses more with the buttock of the night than with the forehead of the morning. What I think, I utter, and spend my malice in my breath' (II i

51–8 *passim*). The character of this speech, particularly its unsavory metaphors, stamps Menenius as Shakespeare's variant
of the now familiar buffoonish commentator. Like Carlo Buf-
fone he says right things in the wrong way, thus giving to his
comments a kind of outrageous pertinence.

His first speech to the crowd only partly reveals these
characteristics. In order to persuade it to cease its
revolutionary uproar, he tells the fable of the rebellion which
the other members of the body once raised against the belly,

> That only like a gulf it did remain
> I' the midst o' the body, idle and unactive,
> Still cupboarding the viand, never bearing
> Like labor with the rest. (ɪ i 101–4)

But the belly replies that by sending rivers of blood to all parts
of the body it serves as the source of the health and the very life
of the whole organism. The belly, it appears, stands in this
parable for the senators, and for Coriolanus in particular,
because in Rome he and his fellow patricians exercised the
functions of the king. The mutinous members of the body
represent the plebeians.

The audience would have regarded this figure of the belly
and its functions as a speech designed to characterize
Menenius – to stamp him as a garrulous old man. But they
would also recognize it as a conventional way of stating a
familiar principle of current political philosophy. [6] It would
seem like a page torn from almost any political primer.
Because both the plebs and Coriolanus disregard the principles illustrated in Menenius's parable they bring disaster to
Rome and to themselves. The people, in seeking to exercise
the functions of a ruler, were permitting 'the foot to partake in
point of preëminence with the head'. They were instituting a
form of democracy which was universally regarded as a
monstrous body of many heads. [7] Coriolanus himself employs
this figure to describe the proletariat. As he stands outside the
gate of Rome, whence he has been driven by the mob, he exclaims

The beast
With many heads butts me away. (IV i 2–3)

Elsewhere in the play he calls the plebs Hydra. Through the
repeated use of such familiar figurative language the author
impressed his historical lesson upon his audience. No member
of it could fail to recognize the drama as an exhibition of the
forces of democracy at their destructive work. The most obvious lesson that the drama is designed to teach is, then, as
follows: The people should never be allowed to exercise any of
the functions proper to a ruler. That way lies anarchy. But the
career of Coriolanus is to constitute an equally impressive
warning: No ruler must act as cruelly and brutally toward his
subjects as does this man. He is more of a slave driver than a
kind father. Such a magistrate is always an architect of social
confusion.

V

A character cast to play such an admonitory role cannot be
treated like an ordinary tragic hero. And Shakespeare deals
with Coriolanus from the moment of his first appearance
through the whole course of the play to the catastrophe in a
manner directly opposite to the one he invariably adopted for
his real tragic protagonists. In the first place he endows all his
true tragic heroes with many noble traits which appear and
reappear through the play. In particular he puts into the
mouths of other characters words of praise for the hero as they
knew him before he became a slave to one of the subversive
passions. Shakespeare also puts into his hero's mouth reflective soliloquies which reveal his struggles between good and
evil, and win our sympathetic understanding even while he is
losing his battle with destiny. Then, as his protagonist stands
at the very brink of the catastrophe, the poet allows him to
utter a poignant speech which recalls to the minds of the spectators the loftiness of his nature before he had been caught in
the net of his tragic fate. Finally, after the hero's death some
character who has survived the holocaust is likely to utter a
brief encomium or a benediction upon the soul of the dead
man.

These dramatic characteristics are all clearly illustrated in the tragedy of *Hamlet*. In this play Shakespeare finds numerous opportunities to describe his hero's nature before it was overwhelmed with grief and melancholy. Ophelia's lament is the most famous of these portraits of the uncorrupted Hamlet:

O, what a noble mind is here o'erthrown!
The courtier's, scholar's, soldier's eye, tongue, sword,
The expectancy and rose of the fair state,
The glass of fashion and the mould of form,
The observ'd of all observers – quite, quite down.

(III i 158–62)

The same innate gentleness shines through Hamlet's colloquies with the friends of his youth. It comes out clearly in his talks with Horatio, and only a little less appealingly in his conversations with his renegade friends Rosencrantz and Guildenstern.

But it is on the eve of his death that Shakespeare allows the best in Hamlet's nature to reveal itself in a final burst of splendor. He generously forgives Laertes. And he appeals to Horatio's loyalty in terms of idealistic friendship. Shakespeare enriches these speeches by marrying lofty thought to some of his most inspiring verbal music. Moreover Hamlet's death is followed by Horatio's benediction, in which he invokes the deepest religious emotions to add poignancy and elevation to the feelings aroused by the passing of his friend:

Good night, sweet prince,
And flights of angels sing thee to thy rest. (v ii 370–1)

Coriolanus is treated in a completely different fashion. The very first comments made upon him are derogatory. The two citizens who discuss him in the opening scene are detractors. The first of them asserts that Coriolanus has served his country not from patriotic motives but only to please his mother and to flatter his own pride. The second feebly defends Coriolanus by saying, 'What he cannot help in his nature, you account a vice in him.' The first citizen, unimpressed by the notion that innate faults are not vices, replies, 'He hath faults (with surplus) to tire in repetition.' This very first expository scene presents Coriolanus's passion nakedly, stripped of all nobility. It is what Mark Van Doren calls 'an animal pride – graceless, sodden, and hateful'. This initial exposition is but the first of many conversations about Coriolanus, all contributing features to a disagreeable portrait.

The accumulation of derogatory comment does much to set the satiric tone of the play. 'Groups of people,' says Mark Van Doren, 'tribunes, citizens, servants, officers laying cushions in the Capitol, travellers on the highway, the ladies of his household – are forever exchanging opinions on the subject of Coriolanus. And the individuals who share with him the bulk of our attention are here for no other purpose than to make leading remarks about him.'[8] In other words the play is crowded with satiric commentators.

When two or three characters gather together, the subject of their conversation is always Coriolanus. And even his wife's friend Valeria and his mother Volumnia, in contriving what they think is praise of Coriolanus, reveal the savage results of his pride. Valeria's description of the little boy at play becomes a revelation of his father's heady violence. She says, 'I saw him [the boy] run after a gilded butterfly; and when he caught it, he let it go again and after it again, and over and over he comes and up again; catch'd it again; or whether his fall enrag'd him or how 'twas, he did so set his teeth and tear it! O, I warrant, how he mamock't it [tore it to shreds]' (I iii 66–71). Volumnia's comment on this incident – made with complete satisfaction – is 'One on's father's moods'. And she is right. Irascibility and anger are the emotions which Coriolanus most often displays – and properly, for they are the inevitable results of thwarted pride.

Of all the commentators Menenius is the least obvious in his hostility. That is because, being a buffoon, he inevitably draws the fire of some of the derision. Yet in his characterization of the tribunes, his unsavory metaphors arouse laughter, even while they furiously mock. Witness his vulgar description of the tribunes's attempt to act as judges: 'When you are hearing a matter between party and party, if you chance to be pinch'd with the colic, you make faces like mummers, set up the bloody flag against all patience, and, in roaring for a chamber pot, dismiss, the controversy bleeding, the more entangled by your hearing ... When you speak best unto the purpose, it is not worth the wagging of your beards; and your beards deserve not so honorable a grave as to stuff a botcher's cushion or to be entombed in an ass's packsadle' (ii i 81–7, 95–9). This is the buffoon at his expert best.

When this 'perfect giber for the table' (and 'giber' is an almost exact equivalent for our slang 'wise-cracker') turns his wit upon Coriolanus, he realizes that it must combine exposition of the man's nature with his ridicule. Once while attempting to excuse his friend's violence, he says:

His nature is too noble for the world.
He would not flatter Neptune for his trident
Or Jove for's power to thunder. His heart's his mouth;
What his breast forges, that his tongue must vent,
And being angry does forget that ever
He heard the name of death. (iii i 255–9)

The first line of his speech, torn from its context, has been used by many critics to prove that Coriolanus's pride is the tragic flaw in an otherwise noble nature.[9] But Menenius is speaking not of pride, but of headlong anger. Even if the old patrician had meant to say that the pride of Coriolanus was the infirmity of his noble mind, no one in an Elizabethan audience would have mistaken his opinion for Shakespeare's. By the third act even the slowest-minded spectator would have recognized Menenius as a sort of buffoon and his comments as food for laughter.

After this attempt to palliate his hero's anger, Menenius returns to his more characteristic vein of comment. Such is the tone of his description of his friend's appearance when rejecting the old man's appeal to save Rome: 'He no more remembers his mother now than an eight-year-old horse. The tartness of his face sours ripe grapes. When he walks, he moves like an engine, and the ground shrinks before his treading. He is able to pierce a corslet with his eye, talks like a knell and his hum is a battery . . . He wants nothing of a god but eternity and a heaven to throne in' (v iv 14–26 *passim*). This is bitterly derisive comment, utterly inappropriate for a tragic hero on the verge of his catastrophe, but just the sort of talk best calculated to keep alert to the end of the play the satiric attitude of an unsympathetic audience.

VI

This purpose is accomplished throughout the drama in still more direct ways. Instead of revealing a rich inner nature in profound poetic soliloquies, Coriolanus exhibits over and over again his one ruling passion – the choler which Renaissance philosphers regarded as the inevitable result of wounded pride. At every one of his encounters with the people his rage boils at their impertinence. His contempt he displays through the insults which a 'lonely dragon' or Caliban might pour upon 'rank-scented' men. When his soldiers retreat before the attack of the Volscians, he shouts:

> All the contagion of the South light on you,
> You shames of Rome! you herd of – Biles and plagues
> Plaster you o'er, that you may be abhorr'd
> Farther than seen, and one infect another
> Against the wind a mile! You souls of geese
> That bear the shapes of men, how have you run
> From slaves that apes would beat! (I iv 30–6)

For this voice we can feel only aversion. Yet its vigor and its lean thrust form an almost perfect expression of the spirit of Juvenalian satire. Indeed the bare poetic style of this play, lamented by most critics, is exquisitely adapted to the author's derisive intentions.

Understanding the easy inflammability of Coriolanus, the tribunes are able to teach the plebs just how to induce his paroxysms of anger. When thus beside himself, he becomes their easy victim: 'Put him to choler straight,' they advise,

> ... Being once chaf'd, he cannot
> Be rein'd again to temperance; then he speaks
> What's in his heart; and that is there which looks
> With us to break his neck. (III iii 25–30)

By following these instructions the mob produces a rhythmical recurrence of Coriolanus's grotesque rage; and this stimulated repetition of a vice or a folly is of the very essence of satire of every sort. It turns Coriolanus into a jack-in-the-box. Every time his self-esteem is depressed, it springs back with the same choler-distorted face. This emotional automatism deprives his pride and his anger of all dignity. It makes him a natural object of derision.

Coriolanus is also his mother's puppet. Volumnia transforms him into a terrified little boy every time the two confront each other. Shakespeare may have intended her to represent an austere patrician woman of early Rome, a worthy mother of grim warriors. Yet she wins from her son not the respect of a man, but the frightened obedience of a whimpering urchin. His attitude toward her remains completely infantile.

It is Volumnia who has forced her son to become a soldier and to exult in the blood and sweat of war. Plutarch describes Coriolanus as driven to battle by an irresistible impulse of his own nature. But Shakespeare tells us that it was Volumnia, 'poor hen, who clucked him to the wars and home'. This barnyard figure incidentally deprives the martial impulses of Coriolanus of every shred of dignity. As a soldier he was and remains his mother's creature. Her proud boast is the truth:

> Thy valiantness was mine, thou suck'st it from me.
>
> (III ii 129)

When he is at the front, she relieves her anxiety by imagining him wading in triumph through seas of carnage and blood.

Though Volumnia has also bred into her son his contempt for the people, she knows that he must placate them. She realizes that if he is ever to become consul, he must stand in the market place and humbly beg for their votes. So at first she entreats him to go through the distasteful ceremony merely to please her:

> I prithee now, sweet son, as thou hast said
> My praises made thee first a soldier, so,
> To have my praise for this, perform a part
> Thou hast not done before. (III ii 107–10)

But even for his mother's sake Coriolanus refuses to let his disposition be possessed by 'some harlot's spirit', to turn his voice 'into a pipe small as an eunuch', or to allow a 'beggar's tongue make motion through his lips'. His answer to her courteous pleading is a flat, 'I will not do't'.

Then Volumnia loses her temper and soundly scolds her son. Her burst of scorn and anger immediately brings him around, reducing him to the stature of a frightened child, ridiculously eager to pacify an irate parent:

> Pray be content [he almost whimpers];
> Mother, I am going to the market place.
> Chide me no more.
> . . . Look I am going. (III ii 130–2; 134)

The contrast between his arrogant attitude toward all other persons in the drama and his infantile cowering before his mother's severity is ridiculous, and is intended to be so.

His last scene with Volumnia, in which she finally dissuades him from leading the victorious Volscians into Rome, is a kind of incremental repetition of the interview just described. When neither her pathetic appeals, made as she kneels before him, nor his wife's tears divert him from his purpose, his mother again loses her temper. She rises from her knees, crying

> Come, let us go.
> This fellow had a Volscian to his mother;
> His wife is in Corioles, and his child
> Like him by chance. Yet give us our dispatch.
> I am hushed until our city be afire.
> And then I'll speak a little. (v iii 177–82)

The old woman's fierce indignation again cows her son.
Terrified by her anger, he cries out, like a helpless little boy:

> O mother, mother!
> What have you done? . . .
>
> O my mother, mother! O!
> You have won a happy victory to Rome,
> But for your son – believe it, O, believe it! –
> Most dangerously you have with him prevail'd.
>
> (v iii 182–3; 185–8)

This repeated quailing before his mother deprives Coriolanus
of the dignity every tragic hero must possess. He never submits to her will through conviction or a sense of duty. His surrender is never evidence of filial respect. It is always a boy's
frightened submission to a domineering woman. His un-
deviating arrogance toward the rest of humanity thus seems to
be not exaggerated self-esteem, but compensation for the fear
of his mother. He never attains the mean between these two
unnatural extremes of emotion, but careers wildly between
them. This instability renders him at once absurd and
doomed. The forebodings which seize him after his final
yielding to his mother are fulfilled. They set him in the path
which leads straight to his downfall.

When Coriolanus returns to the Volscian army, he finds
Aufidius hostile. He has all along been jealous of the renegade
Roman and now sees a chance to destroy him. Knowing how
easy it is to drive Coriolanus into a fit of blind rage, he sets the
stage for the undoing of his enemy in a scene which constitutes
the finale of the drama. And a masterful scene it is – an admirable catastrophe for a satirically conceived tragedy. It is an
almost exact replica of those in which Coriolanus has collided
again and again with the Roman mob. For Aufidius knows as
well as the Roman tribunes how to manipulate his foe for his
sinister purpose. He stirs the commoners against his enemy by
haranguing them on the subject of Coriolanus's perfidy:

> He has betrayed your business, and given up

> For certain drops of salt your city – Rome,
> (I say 'your city') to his wife and mother;
> Breaking his oath and resolution like
> A twist of rotten silk; never admitting
> Counsel o' the war; but at his nurse's tears
> He whin'd and roar'd away your victory. (v v 91–7)

In the course of this diatribe he taunts Coriolanus with epithets like 'traitor' and 'boy of tears', words which drive the warrior to an almost pathological seizure of rage. Then Coriolanus, shouting insults to the crowd, stirs the Volscian populace to fury. Once aroused, they rush upon him with cries of 'Tear him to pieces – Do it presently – He killed my son! – My daughter – He killed my cousin Marcus! He killed my father.' The lords of Corioli, aghast at the blood-thirstiness of the mob, try in vain to calm it. But Aufidius and his conspirators have aroused the masses to the killing point. With cries of 'Kill, kill, kill, kill, kill him' they fall upon Coriolanus and murder him.

This catastrophe gives final emphasis to the satiric view of Coriolanus. His automatic response to the artfully arranged provocation has at last entrapped him to his death. His end is the direct result of an over-stimulated reflex mechanism. The catastrophe of such an automaton is not tragic. It is so completely devoid of grandeur and dignity that it awakens amusement seasoned with contempt.

VII

This derision is much less absorbing than the pity and terror provoked by a genuinely tragic denouement. For that very reason a satiric play is better suited than a tragedy to present forcefully a political exemplum. In *Coriolanus* our interest is not held by the fall of a great man destroyed by forces beyond his control. It is rather caught by the picture of social and political chaos produced both by subversive forces of democracy and by a man who is temperamentally unable to be a successful ruler. The drama, then, is a satiric representation of a slave of passion designed to teach an important political lesson.

If this is true, why has *Coriolanus* never been a popular play? The principal reason is that critics and producers have invariably regarded it as a tragedy of an orthodox but greatly inferior sort. As a tragedy it lacks, as Stoll suggests, 'constructive mechanism'. Neither Fate nor a villain spins the plot. Coriolanus is destroyed by what is false within his nature. Yet we do not behold the inner emotional conflict that ends in disaster. We never see the dramatic struggle taking place within his mind and spirit. Therefore his nature inevitably seems poor and shallow. More than that, all the positive qualities which he displays are offensive. The remnants of a noble pride appear darkly through a cloud of childish impatience and uncontrolled rage. Finally, his catastrophe fixes ineradicably in the minds of all who expect a tragedy an impression of Shakespeare's artistic ineptitude. Coriolanus is manipulated into a fatal crisis and he meets his end in a riot which his mad fury has precipitated. No proper tragic hero moves thus toward his end in automatic response to artfully arranged stimuli. Nor can a death which comes to a man in a wild brawl signalize any triumph of the spirit.

These are defects only if Shakespeare intended *Coriolanus* to be a tragedy of the usual sort. If he meant the play to be more satire than tragedy, most of these qualities are virtues. Shakespeare naturally avoids arousing sympathy for a man whom he wishes to deride. For this reason he fills the early scenes with trenchant speech of hostile commentators, whose business is to draw a well-rounded satiric portrait of Coriolanus. Then the author traps his victim again and again so that we may see repeatedly the writhings of his anger. Finally he artfully designs a final scene which will make his satiric intention unmistakable. The murder of Coriolanus is not the moving death of a great hero; it is the deserved result of a supreme exhibition of his folly.

The bareness of the plot of *Coriolanus* also contributes to the satiric emphasis of the drama. True to the genius of satire it keeps the minds of the spectators riveted upon the ridicule of human faults. Derision, unless associated with moral indignation, does not easily awaken aesthetic pleasure. But in *Coriolanus* ridicule has been made to serve the teaching of sound political theory and only by a few can the descriptive forces in a healthy state be strongly enough felt to moderate the discomfort which most men feel at the persistent satire of a strong man.

Whatever the success of Shakespeare's two attempts to combine satire and tragedy, a satiric spirit continued to permeate English tragedy even to the year 1642. It first invaded historical tragedies like *Sejanus*, *Coriolanus*, and *Timon of Athens*. Then it spread to every sort of serious play, and is at least partly responsible for the reputation of decadence which clings to all English drama written between Shakespeare's death and the closing of the theatres in 1642. When this development has been fully described, it will become clear that the last two tragedies of Shakespeare did much to determine the character and direction of the movement.

[Shakespeare's contribution to the satiric writing of his own time was substantial.] Though not an innovator in the designing of satiric patterns, he richly filled the forms invented by his contemporaries, vivifying them with his own genial sense for the absurd and later with a deepening scorn of vice and folly. As the spirit of ridicule came more and more to dominate him, he found it increasingly natural to cast his plays in familiar satiric forms. Because this fact has not been recognized, *Troilus and Cressida*, *Measure for Measure*, *Timon of Athens*, and *Coriolanus* have all confused the critics. Only when they recognize that those dramas have been formed on satiric models will they be able to understand them. Only then will they grasp Shakespeare's plan of composition and appreciate the aesthetic effects he wished to produce. The plays will then stand forth as the culmination of the poet's earlier satiric impulses. Their power will, as it were, be released for the first time, and to Shakespeare's achievements as the greatest English writer of comedy and tragedy will be added triumphs in satire for the stage.

SOURCE: 'Coriolanus', in *Shakespeare's Satire* (1943) pp. 198–217.

NOTES

1. A. C. Bradley, 'Coriolanus. Second Annual Shakespeare Lecture', Proceedings of the British Academy 1911–12 (1 July, 1912) 457–73 [reprinted above]. Hazelton Spencer in The Art and Life of William Shakespeare (1940) pp. 346–50, takes a similar view. 'In Coriolanus', says the critic, 'he [Shakespeare] frankly takes the line of least resistance.' The idea is that he simply followed mechanically the facts laid down in his source – 'that is all'.

2. Bradley, op. cit.

3. George Brandes for example, in a chapter in William Shakespeare, a critical Study (New York, 1902) emphasizes the absence in Coriolanus of 'any humane consideration for the oppressed condition of the poor' and his 'physical aversion for the atmosphere of the people'. M. W. MacCallum expresses the more measured view by admitting that 'Shakespeare invariably treats crowds of citizens, whether in the ancient or modern world ... as stupid, disunited, fickle' (Shakespeare's Roman Plays and Their Background, London, 1910, p. 470).

4. Serge Dinamov, Works of Shakespeare, 4 vols, I xix.

5. These ideas have been thoroughly presented in James E. Phillips Jr's The State in Shakespeare's Greek and Roman Plays (New York, 1940) passim.

6. Ibid.

7. William Fulbecke in his Pandectes of the Law of Nations (1602) cites the history of Coriolanus to confirm his contention that the people is the 'beast with many heads'. This example he offers as part of his evidence drawn from history to prove that democracy is contrary to natural law.

8. Mark Van Doren, Shakespeare (New York, 1939) p. 10.

9. John W. Draper in an article caled 'Shakespeare's Coriolanus: A Study in Renaissance Psychology', West Virginia Bulletin (Philological Studies, III) (Sep 1939) 22–36 develops these ideas. He believes that Coriolanus is a perfect illustration of the notions on this subject developed in Plutarch's Morals, La Primaudaye's The French Academie, and Thomas Adams's Diseases of the Soul (1616) first introduced into Shakespeare studies by Lily B. Campbell in her Shakespeare's Tragic Heroes (Cambridge, 1930).

Willard Farnham

'TRAGIC PRIDE' (1950)

Within the larger world of Shakespearean tragedy, *Timon of Athens, Macbeth, Antony and Cleopatra,* and *Coriolanus* make up a world of their own. I take them to be Shakespeare's final tragedies. Their world is well defined and is set off against a world equally well defined which appears in *Julius Caesar, Hamlet, Othello,* and *King Lear,* the other tragedies of Shakespeare's maturity.

When the death of Antony is announced to Octavius in *Antony and Cleopatra,* Maecenas and Agrippa become a chorus and comment upon the hero of the tragedy. Maecenas says:

> His taints and honours
> Wag'd equal with him.

Agrippa caps the comment:

> A rarer spirit never
> Did steer humanity; but you, gods, will give us
> Some faults to make us men. (v i 30–3)

It is rare spirits deeply tainted that Shakespeare places at the center of his last tragic world. The faults given them to make them men are not only great enough to 'wage equal' with their virtues but are also pervasive, and yet these spirits are noble. Their nobility, as we shall find, is one of life's mysteries, for it seems to issue from ignoble substance. In his presentation of this mystery Shakespeare is greatly daring, not merely in risking loss of sympathy for his tragic heroes but in other ways as well. He takes up an advanced position in a realm of late Renaissance tragedy where new refinements of tragic truth are to be discovered in paradox but where the tragic emotions and the essential simplicities of tragic understanding are in constant danger of being overwhelmed by paradox. Here he occupies a country of the mind that may be called his tragic frontier. Here he finds marches of tragedy beyond which he cannot go without deserting tragedy. . . .

In *Coriolanus*, Shakespeare finds within deeply flawed yet noble human character the only tragic mystery that really matters, just as he does in *Antony and Cleopatra*. He also focuses attention narrowly upon a single example, as he does not in *Antony and Cleopatra*. The tragic flaw of the hero reveals itself at the very beginning of the action, and once we have seen it we never wonder whether we have seen it aright. It is constantly in evidence, first as Coriolanus rises to an eminence from which he can reach for the Roman consulship, then as he mars his fortune and enters upon a downward course, and finally as he goes to his destruction.

The hero does not merely stand at the center of the tragedy; he *is* the tragedy. He brings no one down with him in his fall, and his character is entirely sufficient to explain his fall. No supernatural forces are shown to be at work against him. The tribunes and Aufidius work underhandedly to entrap and undo him, but it seems that by taking advantage of the imperfections of his nature they only hurry him into making tragic errors which eventually he would have made of his own accord. The tragic flaw of Coriolanus is pride, as we are told by other characters in the play again and again. The paradox of Coriolanus is that in his pride, or closely connected with it, there is not only everything bad but also everything good by which he comes to be a subject for Shakespearean tragedy.

Shakespeare took from the moral Plutarch the conception of Coriolanus as a notable combination of good and bad qualities, but he changed radically the nature of the combination. He intensified the drama involved in the opposition between the two sets of qualities by binding them much more closely together than Plutarch had bound them. It was Shakespeare himself who created the paradox in Coriolanus, and he did so by making the good and the bad in his character into elements seemingly inseparable and even seemingly interdependent. . . .

As Plutarch sees it, there was nothing paradoxical about the nobility of spirit shown by Coriolanus. His good qualities were thoroughly good and his bad thoroughly bad, and the two sets of qualities were quite separate. His honesty, temperance, and valor had sufficient power in themselves and drew no strength from his insolent haughtiness, which was purely a failing. Plutarch very obviously thinks that these virtues could have existed in Coriolanus, and could have shown to better advantage, if the haughtiness had been absent, for the haughtiness was merely unpolished roughness and had a train of anger that was merely impatience. It was not this haughtiness but his 'great harte' that stirred up the courage of Coriolanus and made him do notable deeds.[1] The separation between his good and bad qualities was all the more distinct because they had separate origins: the good existed because of his heredity and the bad because of the environment of his youth. Certainly Plutarch wants his readers to see the faults of Coriolanus plainly and to draw a moral lesson from them, but he gives the impression that the good characteristics of Coriolanus are the natural man – the true man – and that the bad ones are accidentally acquired. The faults of Shakespeare's Coriolanus are much more deeply rooted than those of Plutarch's Coriolanus. . . .

[In the next section Farnham shows that contemporary French and English theorists could readily see Coriolanus in a favourable light as a member of a ruling aristocracy who quite properly had no love for the hydra-headed multitude. Still, Farnham observes, from the standpoint of contemporary Christian morality he was regarded as contemptible, consumed by the vices of wrath and pride.]

Shakespeare is so far from being blind to the faults of Coriolanus that he makes them as pernicious as any moralist of his age makes them. He gives them, with regard to their effects in this world, the destructive powers of deadly sins, and he allows them to wear the aspects of deadly sins. Outwardly

the Coriolanus of Shakespeare is much like the haughty and
angrily impatient Coriolanus of Plutarch, but inwardly he is a
very different man; for as Coriolanus passes through the
hands of Shakespeare, the overlying haughtiness, the 'hawtie
obstinate minde', given him by Plutarch becomes an underlying pride, a spiritual flaw reaching to the depth of his being,
and this deep-going pride has deep-going wrath in its train instead of mere angry impatience. Moreover, the wrath of
Shakespeare's Coriolanus is much more clearly subsidiary to
pride than the angry impatience of Plutarch's Coriolanus is
subsidiary to haughtiness. Shakespeare's Coriolanus is often a
wrathful man, but always and before all else he is a proud
man. Whenever we see his wrath, we know that it is fed by
pride.

The tragedy made by Shakespeare out of Plutarch's story of
Coriolanus is not that of a noble spirit ruined by lack of education, which is the tragedy that Plutarch outlines. It is the
tragedy of a noble spirit ruined by something in itself which
education cannot touch, or at least does not touch. We do not
hear anything in Shakespeare's play about the hero's lacking
instruction because of his father's death and thus acquiring a
faulty character. On the contrary, we learn that Volumnia,
the strong-willed mother of the hero, has been both father and
mother to him, has devoted herself, according to her lights, to
the education of his character, and has certainly not failed to
teach him how to be manly. By her precepts and her praises
she has stimulated his valor. We have her own word for it that
she does not approve of his unbending pride, and presumably
she has done what she could to check it when she saw it standing in the way of his advancement. She is not the best of
teachers to show him how to overcome his pride, but at least
she can condemn it as something not drawn from her:

> Thy valiantness was mine, thou suck'dst it from me,
> But owe thy pride thyself. (III ii 129–30)

The pride she condemns is what she says it is, a thing of his
own, fixed in his nature. It is in the original substance of his

character and is not an untutored churlishness acquired
through the accident of his father's death.

But there is that about the pride of her son which Volumnia
is quite incapable of understanding. Though she sees clearly
that it can keep him from gaining the highest honors in Rome,
she does not see that it can also keep him from base timeser-
ving. It is more worthy of condemnation than she knows, but
at the same time it is worthy of praise in a way that she does
not even suspect. Her pupil shows reaches of nobility for
which she is not responsible, and he shows them even in his
valor, which is not a virtue of her creation, as she seems to
think, but a virtue grounded in his natural pride. This valor
has been developed but not called into being by her instruction.

The pride of Coriolanus has two very contradictory
faculties. It is the tragic flaw in his character and therefore has
the well-known power of pride the preëminent deadly sin to
produce other faults and destroy good in the spirit of its
possessor; but it is at the same time the basis of self-respect in
his character and thus has power to produce good in his spirit.
Whether destructive of good or productive of good, it is a fierce
pride, accompanied by a wrath that makes it work at white
heat. The wrath is like the pride it accompanies in not always
having the qualities of a deadly sin; it can at times be
righteous wrath, directed against human baseness. Hence
both the pride and the wrath of Coriolanus can be admirable
as well as detestable. Just as taints and honors 'wage equal'
with the sensualistic Antony, so do they with the proud
Coriolanus. . . . [Farnham discusses I i 173–4, 191–4.]

We understand from these lines which Coriolanus speaks
thus early in the play, in justification of all he stands for, that
for him the virtue of all virtues is trustworthiness. The good
man is the trustworthy man, and the trustworthy man is the
complete aristocrat, who not only is born with blue blood but
also lives in accordance with inherited principles and thus by
rules of conduct well established. Such a man, thinks
Coriolanus, runs true to form. You know what he will admire
and what he will detest, and you know that he will not change
his mind except for solid cause. Naturally, a part of the

trustworthiness acquired from aristocratic warrior ancestors is his courage. He can be counted upon in battle to do credit to his noble blood. Since he is not a coward, he does not tell lies, for the liar is a coward afraid to tell the truth; and since he does not tell lies, he flatters no man. Flattery is the weakling's way of gaining favor and advantage in the world, and the trustworthy man will not stoop to it. Especially will the noble trustworthy man, the aristocrat, not stoop to flattery when he deals with the base, untrustworthy man, the commoner. Commoners are

> no surer, no,
> Than is the coal of fire upon the ice,
> Or hailstone in the sun. (I i 178–80)

To say good words to them is to 'flatter beneath abhorring', and to give them tribunes who will 'defend their vulgar wisdoms', as has just been done, is to 'break the heart of generosity'. By this condemnation of the citizens for their lack of trustworthiness and by the attendant revelation of his faith in an aristocratic ideal of trustworthiness Coriolanus asks to be judged according to the measure of his own trustworthiness. That measure, as we shall see, is in one direction admirably large and in another pitifully small.

Thus the drama begins in a way that makes us ask at once whether its author puts himself on the commoners' or the patricians' side. A part of the answer, I think, is that Shakespeare shows a singular detachment in his ability to find human faults on both sides and a singular breadth of sympathy in his ability to find human virtues on both sides. Another part of the answer is that he does not have such superhuman detachment that he never favors one side. The plain fact is that he is on the side of the patricians whenever they are to be taken as representing a theory of government, and that he gives them an advantage even in the first scene of the play. . . .

It seems that as Shakespeare wrote *Coriolanus* he proceeded upon an assumption, made often enough in his day, that the common people were unfit to have ruling power in a state, not only because they were many-minded and had no stability, but also because they were shortsighted and had no power to see the interests of any other group than their own. A democratic government, then, was an evil government, and it might upon very good authority be called no true government at all but only a perversion of government. Of course, the governments that upon good authority could be called true governments were by no means always perfect. The aristocratic government presented in *Coriolanus* is obviously an imperfect one, and the common people who rebel against it are shown to have grievances. But it is significant that although, as the drama develops, we are often invited to sympathize with individual ordinary citizens, we are rarely if ever invited to sympathize with the tribunes, who are the means by which the citizens as a body are becoming a political power and challenging the authority of the patricians – the means, in other words, by which Rome is bringing democracy into being.[2]

The deeply flawed Coriolanus, as Shakespeare sees him, is one of the chief reasons why the government headed by the patricians is imperfect, and yet he is also one of the chief reasons why that government has virtue in it. His pride is patrician pride grown to a self-contradictory greatness that makes it at times a monstrous liability and at other times a magnificent asset to the state. It forces him to set himself off from other men, as better than they – so far off, indeed, that he lacks an understanding of humanity and cannot make any truly unselfish contribution to the public weal; but though it keeps him at all times from knowing what true self-sacrifice for the state can be like, it paradoxically drives him to give himself to the state completely, and heroically, in time of war. In battle Coriolanus is an eminent possessor of the virtue of trustworthiness. . . .

[Farnham goes on to argue that Coriolanus is not a schemer; contrary to the Tribunes' portrait of him, he covets neither power nor dominion, only deferential recognition. He is at once modest and proud, magnanimous and thoughtless.

Paradoxically, his virtues stem from vicious pride. He is devoted not to the ideal, but to securing the recognition which comes from devotion to the ideal. Yet he values integrity above all –

> Know, good mother,
> I had rather be their servant in my way
> Than sway with them in theirs. (II i 220–2)

– and he insults the plebeians in order to ensure that he not deceive them through flattery.

When the people, with the Tribunes' prompting, deceive themselves and turn against him, his mother tempts him into betraying his instinctive, absolute honour for a policy of expedient dissembling. While such a policy has as its ostensible purpose the preservation of aristocratic government, Coriolanus's motive in adopting it is loyalty to his mother – to which he sacrifices every other loyalty. Yet when the Tribunes raise the cry of traitor against him, his outrage produces an honest excoriation of the people reminiscent of celebrated non-flatterers in the classical tradition. Farnham concludes:]

Members of Shakespeare's audience might at first be led to condemn Coriolanus, in the light of contemporary ideas about the viciousness of the man guilty of pride, and then be led to reconsider their condemnation, in the light of contemporary ideas about the virtuousness of the man incapable of flattery. The virtue of the nonflatterer could only too easily, in a corrupt world, be mistaken for envy or pride, as they might remember having been told in some such words as these: 'The world is growne to that corruption that he that cannot flatter is either accompted enuious or reputed proud and arrogant.' [3] So one might have second thoughts, or even third and fourth thoughts, about the degree to which Coriolanus should be condemned for that pride which leads to his banishment.

As Coriolanus says farewell to his family and friends and goes into exile, he makes this promise:

> While I remain above the ground you shall
> Hear from me still; and never of me aught
> But what is like me formerly. (IV i 51–3)

There is unconscious irony in his words, for it fortunes that he lives up to them in a way he does not think of when he utters them. He does not continue to make his mark in the world by continuing to be the honorable man he has been formerly, which is what he means to say he will do. He continues to make his mark in the world only by becoming a traitor. And yet when he follows the course of treason there is nothing in him which is essentially not like him formerly, because with his inordinate love of self and his total lack of any loyalty except that to his mother he has always been potentially a traitor.

Only after a severe soul struggle has Coriolanus undertaken to be a dissembling politician and flatter the people. He undergoes no soul struggle at all as he prepares to become a traitor to his country. His pride gives him a conscience to support in him the virtue of plainspoken honesty, but it does not even intimate to him that for the kind of patrician he has taken himself to be, namely, a trustworthy man born to rule and defend his country, treason is an unforgivable sin. Suddenly, quite without warning, we find him saying in a soliloquy that he hates Rome and will turn to Corioli to do it what service he can. He has the idea that his change of allegiance is entirely natural in a world of 'slippery turns', where fast friends can in a moment become bitter enemies. Later he shows no sign of compunction as he tells Aufidius that he is offering his sword to the Volscians 'in mere spite', to be revenged upon his banishers. He implies by what he says to Aufidius that he owes no more consideration to his own class, the 'dastard nobles' who have not been able to keep him from being banished, than to the Roman plebeians, the 'slaves' who have decreed his banishment.

Once Coriolanus has perpetrated treason, there is really nothing new to be learned about him, since the remainder of his tragedy is a second perpetration of treason brought about by the same deficiency in his nature that is responsible for the first. Everything that happens when he betrays the Volscians has a completely familiar quality. It is true that he does not betray them as he has betrayed the Romans, to get revenge for an insult to his ego; but he betrays them for a purpose sufficiently characteristic – to please his mother. When Coriolanus appears before Rome with his army of Volscians, he seems so fiercely bent upon taking the city and reducing it to fire-blackened ruins that he cannot possibly be turned from his destructive course, and yet his mother, pleading successfully after he has proved deaf to other Roman suppliants, saves the city. She does so by making him feel once more the full power of that authority which to him is her matriarchal sacredness.

At the beginning of her plea Volumnia shocks him by kneeling to him. 'What is this?' he asks:

Your knees to me! to your corrected son!
Then let the pebbles on the hungry beach
Fillip the stars. (v iii 57–9)

The deep respect he shows her promises well for her efforts, but as she proceeds with her plea she finds it useless to search for patriotism in him or to confront him with his wife and child and appeal to his love for them. She also finds it useless to argue deviously, in a manner of which she has once before shown herself a master, that he is too inflexible in his conception of honor. Her argument is extremely plausible. He should realize, she says, that though it would be 'poisonous' to his honor to save the Romans by destroying the Volscians, it would greatly increase his honor to make a peace in which the Volscians and the Romans could enjoy reconciliation and in which the Volscians could acquire merit by showing mercy to the Romans. The truth is that, no matter how good it might be for all concerned if the Volscians could show mercy, Coriolanus has got himself into a position where the decision to grant mercy or withhold it is simply not his to make. Indeed, where there is any question of foregoing a part of the Volscian victory over the Romans, he needs, if he is to be honorable, to lean backward. Coriolanus himself is quite aware that this is the way things stand. He has told Menenius that his affairs are now 'servanted to others' and that any 'remission' for the Romans must come from 'Volscian breasts'. Again we see that Coriolanus has a sense of honesty far more surely grounded than his mother's.

Volumnia finally has success by bringing against Coriolanus the accusation that he is not being honorable so far as *she* is concerned, since he is restraining from her 'the duty which/To a mother's part belongs' (v iii 167–8). There is no man 'more bound to's mother' than he, she would have him know. It is not of any bond of love between her son and herself that she speaks, but only of a bond of duty. Once more she kneels before him, together with the ladies who accompany her. 'Let us shame him with our knees,' she cries. As he remains obdurate, she rises to lead her fellow petitioners back to Rome, but turning to leave she lets him understand that when the city is afire he must be put to further shame by his dishonored mother, for at that time she will yet again 'speak a little'. It is only after this parting shot is delivered that Coriolanus at last gives way.

Thus Volumnia demands that Coriolanus spare Rome at the cost of dishonoring himself, just as she has demanded that he win the Roman consulship at the cost of dishonoring himself. Both times, she gets him to dishonor himself by asking him to honor her. It is true, of course, that in bringing upon him the dishonor of betraying the Volscians she saves him from the dishonor of destroying his native city and keeps him from proceeding to the ultimate violation of the allegiance to which he was born. But the good she does for her son comes far short of balancing the ill, because, though she brings him to the point of saving his native Rome, she cannot bring him to the point of saving his soul as a Roman. She cannot make him reaccept the old allegiance after she has made him turn false to the new, and she cannot even make him feel repentance – not the smallest – for having betrayed Rome in the first place. Hence the result for Coriolanus spiritually is that he is left unmitigatedly guilty of compound treason.

This time, Coriolanus yields to his mother without any sense of losing his integrity. Breaking faith with the Volscians is to him a very different matter from flattering the Roman plebeians, for it leaves his inner being quite untouched. He knows that such faith-breaking is wrong, but his knowledge of its wrongness is so superficial and so unimportant that it is not what keeps him so long from granting his mother's petition. The struggle within him is between his desire for revenge against Rome and his respect for Volumnia as the 'honour'd mould' wherein he has been formed. Once he has decided to put his respect for his mother ahead of his desire for revenge, his spirit is at rest. As for the wrongness of his breaking faith with the Volscians, he feels that he must acknowledge it but not brood over it; and acknowledge it he does, to Aufidius:

> Aufidius, though I cannot make true wars,
> I'll frame convenient peace. (v iii 190–1)

His mother, as we have seen, has tried to make him think that by neglecting to press home the Volscian victory he would be working not against the Volscians, but for them, since he would be allowing them to show mercy and thus act nobly. This specious reasoning makes no impression on him. Bluntly he lays his sparing of Rome to his inability to 'make true wars' for the Volscians, and calls the peace he is about to procure nothing more than 'convenient'. To the very end of his career the pride of Coriolanus gives him brave hatred for all paltering, and this virtue his mother is never able to corrupt, however hard she tries. But to do Volumnia justice, she is by no means villainous when she works to corrupt her son. She is a person of strong character who has succeeded in bending truth to her will and has succeeded so well that she has deceived herself about the nature of truth.

When Coriolanus says to his mother that she has won a happy victory for Rome, but that for him her success is most dangerous, 'if not most mortal', he is looking at the oncoming shadow of his catastrophe. The Volscians are to exact his life in payment for his offense against them, after Aufidius has played out his role of villain. Aufidius is not without generous instincts. Though he can hate Coriolanus as an enemy, he can respect him as a glorious opponent and, when Coriolanus

joins the Volscians, can embrace him as a 'noble thing' that he
can truly love. Even when Aufidius begins to grow jealous of
his too successful associate, he can say, after talking about the
pride of Coriolanus and his defects in general, 'But he has a
merit/To choke it in the utterance' (IV vii 48–9). Yet when
Aufidius is confirmed in his jealousy and feels that the time
has come to ruin Coriolanus, he stops at nothing, either to
justify his aim or accomplish it. To justify his aim he goes so
far as to make the accusation that Coriolanus has worked
against him underhandedly among the Volscians by the
seductive use of flattery. This, of course, is simply not to be
believed. No such use of flattery is shown in the play, and
everything we see of Coriolanus early or late in his career
makes him seem incapable of it. Moreover, there is the admission by Aufidius that he is putting 'a good construction' on his
'pretext to strike' at Coriolanus. To accomplish his aim
Aufidius forms a conspiracy and traps Coriolanus to his
destruction. The scheme of entrapment is exactly the same as
that used by the Roman tribunes, namely, to call Coriolanus
traitor and thereby make him so angry that he must throw all
caution to the winds and expose nakedly whatever is most
offensive in his pride.

Upon his return to Corioli from his victory against Rome,
Coriolanus appears before the Volscians with the declaration
that he is still their soldier and that he is 'no more infected'
with love of his country than when he set forth to fight against
it. This is quite true, and to him it seems to be all that really
matters, but it is also true that (to use the words of Aufidius)
he has sold the blood and labor of the Volscians and has
denied them the full measure of victory which was rightfully
theirs. By admitting his inability to 'make true wars' for the
Volscians, Coriolanus has acknowledged the wrong he has
done them, and yet he has never seen the true quality of that
wrong. He has never been infected with patriotism and has
betrayed his own country without compunction; one would
not expect him to acquire among the Volscians a sure understanding of treason. He knows that he has not kept faith
with the Volscians, but, because of his pride and his consciousness that he is still ready to serve them heroically in any

way short of delivering Rome into their hands, he cannot
abase himself to the point of thinking himself their traitor.
Traitors are scorned as ignoble. How can he, the noble
Coriolanus, be scorned as ignoble by the Volscians, upon
whom he once proved his nobility with his sword? Moreover,
he has done the Volscians a great favor by fighting for them,
even if he has done them wrong by not giving them Rome to
loot and burn. What he has done for them and is still willing
to do for them weighs much more, he thinks, than anything he
has promised to do and not done.

Thus, when Aufidius brings out the word 'traitor' in accusing him before the assembled Volscians, Coriolanus is like
a man struck in the face by an unexpected blow. He is
ludicrously unprepared to meet the attack and is ludicrously
thrown off balance. He can only bluster: 'Traitor! How now!'
When Aufidius presses the attack and loads him with
calculated insults, Coriolanus is toppled into the pit dug for
him. Raging against the Volscians and boasting of his
singlehanded conquest of their city of Corioli, he turns the
Volscian common people against him and falls under the conspirators' swords.

But even as the Volscian people call for his blood a Volscian
lord tries to save him from 'outrage' and pays tribute to his
nobility in these exalted words:

> The man is noble and his fame folds in
> This orb o' the earth. (v v 126–7)

There is another Volscian lord who calls the dead hero the
'most noble corse' that herald ever followed to his urn. And
Aufidius himself ends the play with a speech declaring that
Coriolanus, despite the injuries he has done to the Volscians,
'shall have a noble memory'.

Coriolanus, then, can be thought of as greatly noble, and a
chorus of Volscians urges us at the end of the tragedy to
remember him thus. He is probably the last of the paradoxically noble heroes of Shakespeare's last tragic world. It is likely that few of us would call him the best of those 'rare spirits'

and that many would call him the worst. He is monstrously
deficient as a human being, and his deficiency is the more un-
fortunate because it tends not to foster pity for him but to
destroy any that we might give him. As a tragic hero he
therefore has a marked disadvantage which is not shared by
Timon, Macbeth, or Antony. Each of these others asks for our
pity in a manner not to be denied – even Macbeth, who
himself is pitiless but comes to know pitifully that by being
pitiless he has lost 'honour, love, obedience, troops of friends'.
Coriolanus, the fanatical lover of himself who never knows dis-
illusionment, whose pride is so great that his spiritual self-
sufficiency is never shaken, repels pity at any time, and when
he does not inspire admiration, he is apt to inspire such
detestation as to leave no room for pity.

As Shakespeare gives form to his last tragic world, he is
always daring in his efforts to make the paradox of the deeply
flawed noble hero yield subtle truth. In *Coriolanus* he pushes
this paradox to its limit of tragic validity, and sometimes even
beyond, with the result that he makes it more acceptable to
the mind than to the heart. The deeply flawed Coriolanus who
repels pity is too deeply flawed for Shakespeare's tragic purposes. Most of us who perceive nobility of spirit in him would
doubtless rather praise it than associate with it.

In *Coriolanus* the problem of evil, once terribly urgent for
Shakespeare, is almost completely absorbed within the
dramatic hypothesis of a man who is supremely guilty of pride
the vice and at the same time supremely noble in pride the virtue. Shakespeare constructs the hypothesis with mathematical
precision. He uses the very greatest care to strike a balance
between the repellent Coriolanus and the admirable
Coriolanus, and he keeps the balance in a spirit both ironically superior and dispassionately just. The achievement, though
delicately beautiful, has a quality that can only be called forbidding. About the play as a whole there is a lack of essential
warmth amounting even to bleakness, and it is not for nothing
that the verse is often eloquent but seldom deeply moving,
often impressive but seldom sublime. *Coriolanus* is a magnificent failure in which Shakespeare seems to have brought his
tragic inspiration to an end by taking tragedy into an area of

paradox beyond the effective reach of merely human pity.

SOURCE: extracts from '*Coriolanus*' in *Shakespeare's Tragic Frontier* (1950) pp. 1–2, 207–8, 211–12, 217–19, 226–7, 234–6, 254–64.

NOTES

1. See North's 1579 translation of Plutarch's *Lives*: the 'Life of Caius Martius Coriolanus' and the 'Comparison of Alcibiades with Martius Coriolanus'; *Shakespeare's Plutarch*, ed. T. J. B. Spencer (Harmondsworth, 1968). [Editor's note.]

2. For comment upon *Julius Caesar* and *Coriolanus* as plays representing steps in a development of democracy, see F. T. Wood, 'Shakespeare and the Plebs', *Essays and Studies by Members of the English Assn*, XVIII (1933) 68 ff. A general consideration of Renaissance ideas concerning monarchy, aristocracy, and democracy is to be found in J. E. Phillips, Jr, *The State in Shakespeare's Greek and Roman Plays* (New York, 1940).

3. *Memorable Conceits of Divers Noble and Famous Personages of Christendome* (a translation by 'I. S.' of Gilles Corrozet, *Les Propos memorables des nobles et illustres hommes de la chrestienté*, 1602) p. 273.

L. C. Knights

SHAKESPEARE AND POLITICAL WISDOM: THE PERSONALISM OF *JULIUS CAESAR* AND *CORIOLANUS* (1953)

The land is mark'd for desolation & unless we plant
The seeds of Cities & of Villages in the Human bosom
Albion must be a rock of blood.

Blake, Jerusalem, I V

It is no use pretending that poets can give direct answers to political problems ('We have no gift to set a statesman right,' said Yeats, truly). Nor is a knowledge of literature, however extensive, a substitute for a knowledge of the complex circumstances that make up a particular political problem. Yet if we believe that great literature has something to say about the human situation, that it is great precisely because of its grasp of what man is or may be, then we are surely committed to believing that our knowledge of literature, what we know *from* literature, has some bearing, however indirect, on our thinking about politics. In this essay I shall try to show how Shakespeare, without solving any 'problems' for us, can nourish our thinking about the perennial issues of politics. The plays I want to look at, *Julius Caesar* and *Coriolanus,* have, it is true, an overt political content, but in the manner of their working they are, I think, representative of a wide range of literature. . . .

In [both] *Coriolanus* [and *Julius Caesar*] we are concerned with the public world. But whereas in *Julius Caesar* the 'Roman' background served mainly to throw into relief the chief performers, [in *Coriolanus*] the background (misleading word) is part of the living texture of the play. This Rome, for all its handful of 'citizens', is densely populated, and men press upon each other in the same thick clusters as the buildings:

> stalls, bulks, windows,
> Are smother'd up, leads fill'd, and ridges hors'd
> With variable complexions. . . .

It is a world where men play their public parts as soldiers, officers of state, justices and tradesmen, and the 'multiplying' people swarm in the market-place or yawn in congregations. And corresponding to the felt solidity of the city, itself an effect of poetic evocation, of imagery and allusion, is a moral density and vibrancy. *Coriolanus* is a great tragedy, and a simple schematization of the issues would be as inappropriate to it as to *Macbeth*.

It is, however, only one aspect of the play that I wish to touch on here – the connection that is established between the public and the personal and the manner of its demonstration. Once again, honour – both the public regard that men seek and the social sanction of their actions – is a main subject of the story, and as in *Henry IV, Julius Caesar,* and *Troilus and Cressida* it is subjected to a radical scrutiny. The process starts in the domestic scene (I iii) that follows hard on the splendid 'public' opening. Here Volumnia states explicitly the articles of the faith in which – we are told often enough – she has molded her son.

If my son were my husband, I should freelier rejoice in that absence wherein he won honour than in the embracements of his bed where he would show most love. When yet he was but tender-bodied and the only son of my womb, when youth with comeliness plucked all gaze his way, when for a day of kings' entreaties a mother should not sell him an hour from her beholding, I, considering how honour would become such a person, that it was no better than picture-like to hang by the wall, if renown made it not stir, was pleased to let him seek danger where he was like to find fame. To a cruel war I sent him; from whence he returned, his brows bound with oak. I tell thee, daughter, I sprang not more in joy at first hearing he was a man-child than now in first seeing he had proved himself a man.

This honour, fame, or renown, is associated exclusively with
'masculine' warrior qualities; and although there is no hint in
the play of any under-valuing of physical bravery, we are left
in no doubt of the rigidity and narrowness of the code. In
Volumnia's affirmation the 'honourable' qualities are
repeatedly set over against the values of spontaneous life:

> the breasts of Hecuba,
> When she did suckle Hector, look'd not lovelier
> Than Hector's forehead when it spit forth blood.

If ironic commentary is needed, it is supplied by her grim ap-
probation of her grandson's mammocking of the butterfly. [1]

In the magnificent third act, in the mounting tension in
which the cleft and opposition in Rome is made palpable,
there is a lull in the action whilst the patricians take counsel.
In this scene the theme of 'honour' is taken up again.

VOL   .... I have heard you say,
    Honour and policy, like unsever'd friends,
    I' the war do grow together: grant that, and tell me
    In peace what each of them by the other lose,
    That they combine not there.
COR.   Tush, tush!
MEN.   A good demand.
VOL. If it be honour in your wars to seem
    The same you are not, which, for your best ends,
    You adopt your policy, how is it less or worse,
    That it shall hold companionship in peace
    With honour, as in war, since that to both
    It stands in like request?
COR.   Why force you this?
VOL. Because that now it lies you on to speak
    To the people; not by your own instruction
    Nor by the matter which your heart prompts you,
    But with such words that are but roted in
    Your tongue, though but bastards and syllables
    Of no allowance to your bosom's truth.
    Now, this is no more dishonours you at all
    Than to take in a town with gentle words,
    Which else would put you to your fortune and

> The hazard of much blood.
> I would dissemble with my nature where
> My fortunes and my friends at stake requir'd
> I should do so in honour ...

I think this is one of the few places where without irrelevance we can describe what Shakespeare is doing in the political terminology of a later age: he is revealing the class basis ('my fortunes and my friends') of patrician 'honour'. But he is doing much more than that. For what Volumnia advocates – the passing of counterfeit coin, the use of words that are but roted in the tongue – is nothing less than an abrogation of those qualities of mutuality and trust on which *any* society must be founded. There is a corroding cynicism (and the tone suggests he is half-conscious of it) in the words with which Coriolanus accepts his mother's prompting.

> Pray be content:
> Mother, I am going to the market-place;
> Chide me no more. *I'll mountebank their loves,*
> *Cog their hearts from them,* and come home belov'd
> Of all the trades in Rome. ...
> I'll return consul,
> Or never trust to what my tongue can do
> I' the way of flattery further.

That Coriolanus does not in fact cog the plebeians' hearts, but loses his temper and defies them, is nothing to the point – which is that the structure of his habitual attitudes offers no resistance to the corruption (there is no other word) of Volumnia's persuading. Coriolanus's mind, as the play reveals it to us, is accustomed to move in terms of a rigid but false antithesis. Just as, for him, the only alternative to steel is the parasite's silk (I ix 45), and to the warrior the eunuch (III ii 112–14), so the only alternative to aggressive self-assertion that he can think of is 'flattery'. Now the use that the word 'flattery' has for him has already been made clear; it is a way of holding people at a distance, of refusing to admit relationship.[2] The condition of health for 'Rome' was of course that there should be some degree of mutuality between the different members and classes, as in the fable of the belly, placed – with some effect of irony – at the opening of the play. It is because for Coriolanus large classes of people are reduced to the category of 'it' that, without consciousness of the evil in the words, he can speak of 'mountebanking' the people's loves, of using deceit where deceit is monstrous.

In a sense Coriolanus's tragedy is that he cannot grow up, that, as Wyndham Lewis says, he remains a boy to the end. For although he 'obeys instinct' and submits to his mother's pleading (and there is nobility in his submission) he does not change. It is as an angry boy that he retorts to the taunt of 'boy'. That is his private tragedy; but his own failure to achieve integration is certainly not something that can be dismissed as irrelevant to public considerations. The play is an experiment in *concrete* political thinking, and one of the things that it demonstrates so superbly is that disruption in the state – the body politic – is related to individual disharmony by something more palpable than an Elizabethan trick of metaphor, that the public crisis is rooted in the personal and habitual.[3]

The simple conclusions that I wish to draw are probably by now sufficiently obvious, but when one is in earnest one may as well be explicit. Neither *Julius Caesar* nor *Coriolanus* can be summed up in a moral formula. But, taken together, they point to two related truths of the greatest importance. The first is that human actuality is more important than *any* political abstraction, though more difficult to bear. The second is that politics is vitiated and corrupted to the extent to which, as politicians, we lose our sense of the *person* on the other side of the dividing line of class or party or nation. Both plays – and especially *Coriolanus* – refresh our sense of the actual where today it is most urgently needed.

The point is worth insisting on. There has probably never been a time when social and political thinking has moved so glibly, with so little check, in the realm of the abstract. In England we think in terms of productivity curves, of 'targets' achieved or missed, of the rationalization of industry, of the educational ladder, and so on. Such abstractions are necessary in certain contexts and for certain purposes. The trouble arises when, by constant bandying about, they simply stand opaquely between us and the specific human content, the kind and quality of individual lives, that they are intended to cover. When the cliché phrases become invested with emotion and we cling to them as banners (or savage them as red rags), then whatever we may be doing when we air our views we are certainly not contributing to the health of the state. ('General good,' said Blake with some exaggeration, 'is the cry of the hypocrite and the scoundrel'; adding, with no exaggeration at all, 'he who would do good to another must do it in minute particulars.')

In party and international politics the dangers of abstraction, or – to speak more correctly – of impure quasi-abstraction, are even more plain to see, since it is here that passions from unacknowledged sources are most readily enlisted. 'This was the time,' says Wordsworth, speaking of his period of Godwinian speculation, in . . . *The Prelude* . . .

> This was the time, when, all things tending fast
> To depravation, speculative schemes –
> That promised to abstract the hopes of Man
> Out of his feelings, to be fixed thenceforth
> For ever in a purer element –
> Found ready welcome. Tempting region *that*
> For Zeal to enter and refresh herself,
> Where passions had the privilege to work,
> And never hear the sound of their own names.

And of course there are grosser forms than Godwinian enthusiasms and revolutionary ardors. There is no need, however, to instance the simpler forms of psychological 'projection' which explain so much in the daily press (the ogres always the same, and always in the same stock attitudes). The point is that whenever thought moves in terms of the massive abstractions of 'progressive parties', of 'anti-Fascism', of 'the American way of life', of 'people's democracies', of Socialist virtue and Tory viciousness (or vice versa), it needs to be brought back to the discipline of the actual. It is not our political shibboleths but the decency and integrity of our human responsiveness that in the not so long run decides the fate of nations.

These of course are commonplaces, but they belong to the class of commonplaces that Coleridge described – 'Truths, of all others the most awful and interesting ... too often considered as *so* true, that they lose all the power of truth, and lie bed-ridden in the dormitory of the soul, side by side with the the most despised and exploded errors.' 'Literature can help experience to re-vivify them.

SOURCE: extracts from 'Shakespeare and Political Wisdom: A Note on the Personalism of *Julius Caesar* and *Coriolanus*', *Sewanee Review*, LXI (1953) 43, 48–55.

NOTES

1. The *reductio ad absurdum* of Volumnia's attitude is given us in the 'comic' talk of the Volscian serving men at the end of IV v:

SECOND SERV.   This peace is nothing but to rust iron, increase sailors, and breed ballad-makers.

FIRST SERV.   Let me have war, say I: it exceeds peace as far as day does night; it's spritely, waking, audible, and full of vent. Peace is a very apoplexy, lethargy; mulled, deaf, sleepy, insensible; a getter of more bastard children than war's a destroyer of men.

SECOND SERV.   'Tis so: and as war, in some sort, may be said to be a ravisher, so it cannot be denied but peace is a great maker of cuckolds.

FIRST SERV.   Ay, and it makes men hate one another.

THIRD SERV.   Reason: because they then less need one another. The wars for my money.

2. In the battle scenes he dismisses just praise as flattery, for to accept it would be to admit that other people's opinion counted for him. And the same word serves him to describe an observance of constitutional forms, tempered with a little civility, which is all that is demanded in his relations with the plebeians.

3. On the wider implications of this theme, see D. S. Harding's *The Impulse to Dominate* (London, 1941).

4. *The Friend,* Essay xv, 'Aids to Reflection', p. 1.

T. J. B. Spencer

SHAKESPEARE AND THE ELIZABETHAN ROMANS (1957)

... In writing *Julius Caesar* and *Antony and Cleopatra*
Shakespeare was keeping within a safe body of story. Those
persons had been dignified by tragedies in many countries of
Europe and many times before Shakespeare arose and drove
all competitors from the field. But with *Coriolanus* it was
different. There was apparently no previous play on the subject. It was more of a deliberate literary and artistic choice
than either of the other two Roman plays. He must have discovered Coriolanus in Plutarch. As for Caesar and Cleopatra,
he presumably went to Plutarch knowing that they were good
subjects for plays. But no one had directed him to *Coriolanus*.
The story was hardly well known and not particularly attractive. The story of the ingratitude he suffered, the revenge he
purposed and renounced, was told by Livy, and, along with
one or two other stories of Roman womenfolk (Lucretia,
Virginia), it was turned into a *novella* in Painter's *Pallace of
Pleasure;* there is a mention in *Titus Andronicus*. More than
Julius Caesar or than *Antony and Cleopatra*, *Coriolanus* (perhaps
by the rivalry or stimulation of Ben Jonson) shows a great deal
of care to get things right, to preserve Roman manners and
customs and allusions. We have, of course, the usual Roman
officials, and political and religious customs familiarly
referred to; and we have the Roman mythology and pantheon.
But we are also given a good deal of Roman history worked
into the background. Even the eighteenth-century editors who
took a tooth-comb through the play for mistaken references to
English customs could find very little; and it requires con-

siderable pedantry to check these. Moreover, in *Coriolanus*
there is some effort to make literary allusions appropriate. The
ladies know their Homer and the Tale of Troy. The personal
names used are all authentically derived from somewhere in
Plutarch; Shakespeare has turned the pages to find something
suitable. He is taking great care. He is on his mettle. Dozens of
poetasters could write plays on Julius Caesar or on Cleopatra.
Dozens did. But to write *Coriolanus* was one of the great feats of
the historical imagination in Renaissance Europe.

Setting aside poetical and theatrical considerations, and
merely referring to the artist's ability to 'create a world' (as
the saying is), we may ask if there was anything in prose or
verse, in Elizabethan or Jacobean literature, which bears the
same marks of careful and thoughtful consideration of the ancient world, a deliberate effort of a critical intelligence to give
a consistent picture of it, as there is in Shakespeare's plays. Of
course, Ben Jonson's *Catiline* and *Sejanus* at once suggest
themselves. The comparison between Shakespeare's and Ben
Jonson's Roman plays is a chronic one, an inevitable one, and
it is nearly always, I suppose, made to Jonson's disadvantage. . . . There is a certain naïvety about Ben Jonson's understanding of Roman history. Of course, in a way, there is
more obvious learning about *Catiline* and *Sejanus* than about
Shakespeare's Roman plays. There must have been a great
deal of note-book work, a great deal of mosaic work. It is
possible to sit in the British Museum with the texts of the
classical writers which Jonson used around you and watch
him making his play as you follow up his references (not all, I
think, at first hand). But the defect of Jonson's *Sejanus* is lack
of homogeneity of style and material. Jonson mixes the gossip
of Suetonius with the gloomily penetrating and disillusioned
comments on men and their motives by Tacitus. It is the old
story; 'who reads incessantly and to his reading brings not a
spirit and judgment equal or superior' is liable to lose the ad-
vantages of his reading. After all, it doesn't require very much
effort to *seem* learned. What is so difficult to acquire is the
judgment in dealing with the material in which one is learned.
This is not something that can in any way be tested by collec-
ting misspellings of classical proper names in an author whose

works have been unfairly printed from his foul papers and prompt-book copies. Shakespeare brought a judgment equal or superior to whatever ancient authors he read however he read them. Ben Jonson did not; his dogged and determined scholarship was not ripe enough; he had the books but not always the spirit with which to read them. . . .

SOURCE: extract from 'Shakespeare and the Elizabethan Romans', *Shakespeare Survey,* x (1957) 34–5.

Maurice Charney

STYLE IN THE ROMAN
PLAYS (1961)

. . . The style of *Coriolanus* stands in sharp contrast to both the
other Roman plays, but perhaps most to *Antony and Cleopatra*,
which was probably written only a year or so earlier.[1] We no
longer find the richness and complexity of imagery of *Antony
and Cleopatra*, but a curiously cold, aloof, and objective world.
In this respect the sense of control in *Coriolanus* reminds us
somewhat of *Julius Caesar*, although the two plays cannot be
compared in the relative mastery of their dramatic verse.[2]
Both plays also use a similar two-part form, but *Coriolanus*
rises by a series of mounting climaxes to the high point of
Coriolanus's yielding in v iii, whereas *Julius Caesar* never
builds up to a second climax as strong as the murder of Caesar
in the third act – this creates a certain imbalance in the
development of the action. Despite the poetic and structural
skill of *Coriolanus*, the play appears to be odd and anomalous
and to point ahead to the last plays rather than back to the
period of the great tragedies. It has not only not attracted
critics, but it has seemed to represent an exhaustion of
Shakespeare's powers. One way to answer these judgments is
to examine the play in terms of its dramatic purposes; the
strict application of expression to function makes its style
quite different from that of *Julius Caesar* or *Antony and Cleopatra*.

As a basic premise we need to agree that the style of
Coriolanus is closely linked to the character of the protagonist,
about whom A. C. Bradley has said, 'If Lear's thunderstorm
had beat upon his head, he would merely have set his teeth.'[3]
Coriolanus is an unreflective man of action. His tragedy is

massive and overwhelming, almost like fate, and it does not touch us very personally. We see him setting his teeth against the storm of Fortune when he appears in humble guise at the house of his former enemy, Aufidius. He expresses this great change from Rome's defender to Rome's chief enemy in terms of chance trivialities. Just as fast-sworn friends 'on a dissension of a doit' (IV iv 17) become enemies,

> So fellest foes,
> Whose passions and whose plots have broke their sleep
> To take the one the other, by some chance,
> Some trick not worth an egg, shall grow dear friends
> And interjoin their issues. So with me.
> My birthplace hate I, and my love's upon
> The enemy town. (IV iv 18–24)

Enright finds this soliloquy strange because, 'coming at the turn of the play, at the very hinge of the tragic action, it should refer us to "some trick not worth an egg" '.[4] At a similar juncture Macbeth and Othello react entirely differently.

We have an even stronger example at the end of the play of the inadequacy of Coriolanus as a tragic protagonist. Although he yields to the family group, there is never any real recognition of the tragic folly of his betrayal; his climactic words are simply a realization of his own doom:

> O my mother, mother! O!
> You have won a happy victory to Rome;
> But for your son – believe it, O believe it! –
> Most dangerously you have with him prevail'd,
> If not most mortal to him. But let it come. (v iii 185–9)

There is an awareness of the tragic consequences of mercy here rather than any true self-awareness. The words have none of the quality of Lear's emergence from madness: 'Pray, do not mock me./I am a very foolish fond old man . . . ' (IV vii (59–60). Although the character of Coriolanus is consistent throughout, his next appearance, proud and choleric in Corioles (v, vi), comes as a surprise. Accustomed as we are to

the effects of tragedy, we are not ready to accept the fact that
his yielding seems to have had no influence on his moral being. But neither Coriolanus nor any of the persons in this play
is either inward or meditative or lyric, and there is not much
self-awareness or tragic recognition. Actually, only Menenius
uses figurative language freely and naturally, as in the fable of
belly and members, but his role is limited to that of con-
ciliator. In this atmosphere a rich verbal imagery would defeat
the dramatic purpose, whereas in such a play as *Richard II* it is
just this rich vein of poetic fancy that calls attention to the ineffectual and histrionic nature of the king.

When Coriolanus does use figures of speech, he inclines to
similes rather than metaphors, since they provide a simpler
and more explicit form of expression. Both the vehicle and
tenor of the image are very carefully balanced and limited,
usually by the connectives 'like' or 'as' (I count ninety-three
similes in the play, fifty-seven with 'as' and thirty-six with
'like'). The similes do not suggest new areas of meaning, but
give points already stated an added force and vividness. Their
function is illustrative rather than expressive. In this respect
Coriolanus seems to resemble *Julius Caesar* and Shakespeare's
earlier plays, for the trend of Shakespeare's development is
away from the simile form and toward a dramatically integrated type of metaphor.[5]

Volumnia makes good use of illustrative simile when she in-
structs her son in his role before the people: 'Now humble as
the ripest mulberry/That will not hold the handling . . .' (III
ii 79–80). Coriolanus must be 'humble' before the people, and
the simile emphasizes the exact sort of humility that is expected. Although the mulberry image makes a vivid and
original illustration, it is an embellishment of the basic meaning and not at all indispensable. But the similes in *Antony and
Cleopatra* – for example, Antony's 'indistinct/ As water is in
water' (IV xiv 10–11) – are themselves the meaning of the
passages in which they occur and are not in any way dispen-
sable. This sensitive image of the 'ripest mulberry' has an important dramatic function. Its highly imaginative character
suggests a false tone in what Volumnia is saying. In its context
the image is overwrought, for Volumnia knows her son cannot

feign any sort of humility, no less the supreme humility of the 'ripest mulberry'. It is too self-conscious and lush an image and hints that there is a servile, dishonorable aspect in what Volumnia is proposing. This type of figure raises interesting questions about the function of poetic language in the drama. If the mulberry image appeared isolated from its context in an anthology of lyric poetry, it would certainly seem striking and original, yet in the play its effect is insidious. The poetic quality of the image has been diverted to dramatic ends.

Another example of this principle is in Coriolanus's injunction against flattery in I ix:

> When drums and trumpets shall
> I' th' field prove flatterers, let courts and cities be
> Made all of false-fac'd soothing! When steel grows
> Soft as the parasite's silk, let him be made
> An overture[6] for th' wars! (I ix 42–6)

In the overturning of order that flattery brings, the steel of the soldier (probably his mail coat) will become as soft as the silk of the parasite. It is a vivid contrast of textures, but its imaginative tone is used to suggest the luxury of peace – as if one would expect the silk-clad parasite at court but not the steel-coated man of war to use similes. This pejorative connotation of silk is echoed in the final scene of the play when Coriolanus is accused of 'Breaking his oath and resolution like/ A twist of rotten silk . . .' (v vi 94–5).

The images of peace and civil life put an unexpected music into Coriolanus's verse, although he uses them contemptuously. To prevent flattery, he terms his wounds 'Scratches with briers,/ Scars to move laughter only' (III iii 51–2), which recalls his earlier speech in the Capitol as he escapes from Cominius's oration:

> I had rather have one scratch my head i' th' sun
> When the alarum were struck than idly sit
> To hear my nothings monster'd. (II ii 79–81)

This passage is a graphic illustration of what it means to

'voluptuously surfeit out of action' (I iii 28). War is 'sprightly, waking, audible, and full of vent', while peace is 'a very apoplexy, lethargy; mull'd, deaf, sleepy, insensible . . .' (IV v 237–9). In terms of these values (war is the positive force, peace the negative),[7] we find that the love imagery of the play is curiously transferred to military contexts. In I vi Marcius greets Cominius in the language of the wedding-night:

> O, let me clip ye
> In arms as sound as when I woo'd, in heart
> As merry as when our nuptial day was done
> And tapers burn'd to bedward! (I vi 29–32)

And in IV v Aufidius welcomes his former enemy in these same epithalamial terms:

> But that I see thee here,
> Thou noble thing, more dances my rapt heart
> Than when I first my wedded mistress saw
> Bestride my threshold. (IV v 120–3)

But there is none of this sort of imagery between Coriolanus and his wife Virgilia. In his first dialogue with her, for example, he addresses her as his 'gracious silence' (II i 192) and asks somewhat bluntly: 'Wouldst thou have laugh'd had I come coffin'd home/ That weep'st to see me triumph?' (II i 193–4). The military context evokes a spontaneously vivid imagery that ceases when we move 'From th' casque to th' cushion' (IV vii 43).

Coriolanus's own attitude to words helps to shape the character of the verbal imagery in the play. Suspecting he will have the worst of it, he refuses to parry arguments with the Tribune Brutus, for 'oft,/ When blows have made me stay, I fled from words' (II ii 75–6). Unlike Hamlet or Richard II or even Othello, Coriolanus has a natural antipathy to eloquence that goes beyond the Elizabethan convention that a soldier should be a plain, if not rude, speaker.[8] As Menenius tells the patricians, Coriolanus's aversion to words is part of his hatred of flattery: 'His heart's his mouth;/ What his breast forges, that his tongue must vent . . .' (III i 257–8). He is 'ill-school'd/ In bolted language . . .' and 'meal and bran together/ He throws without distinction' (III i 321–3). There is no subtlety in this man, no use of language as an exploration of consciousness. He says what he thinks and feels and that is the end of it, for words are simply a means to express his bluff honesty. Remember Antony's ironic claim at the height of his oration: 'I am no orator, as Brutus is . . .' (III ii 222). Coriolanus is emphatically 'no orator', and in a play so thoroughly political as this, the inability to make speeches is a claim to integrity.

Coriolanus is also peculiarly oppressed by the reality of words, a weakness the fluent Tribunes and Aufidius know how to turn to their own ends. These antagonists of Coriolanus have, by the way, a striking similarity of function in the two parts of the play. Both display that extempore grasp of circumstance that is the mark of the Machiavel, and the 'plebeian malignity and tribunitian insolence' [9] of Brutus and Sicinius are matched by Aufidius's guiding principle: 'I'll potch at him some way./ Or wrath or craft may get him' (I x 15–16). In III i, for example, Sicinius baits Coriolanus in typical fashion:

> It is a mind
> That shall remain a poison where it is,
> Not poison any further. (III i 86–8)

Coriolanus seizes on this 'shall' as if it were a menacing entity:

> Shall remain?
> Hear you this Triton of the minnows? Mark you
> His absolute 'shall'?
> COM.   'Twas from the canon.
> COR.   'Shall'? (III i 88–90)

And Coriolanus continues to rage against the 'peremptory "shall" (III i 94), the 'popular "shall" (III i 106), which is made to symbolize the whole patrician–plebeian conflict. In terms of the actual situation, Coriolanus's rage is excessive

and strident; he is 'fleeing from words' (II ii 76) rather than
realities.

Aufidius uses the same trick as the Tribunes in V vi, where
he tempts Coriolanus to his doom with three contemptuous
words: 'traitor', 'Marcius', and 'boy'. Coriolanus recoils from
the verbal concussion and repeats the words unbelievingly as
if they had power over him:

> Boy? False hound!
> If you have writ your annals true, 'tis there,
> That, like an eagle in a dovecote, I
> Flutter'd your Volscians in Corioles.
> Alone I did it. Boy? (v vi 112–16)

For the moment, the word and the thing are confounded,
producing a crisis that can only be resolved by violence. The
situation here is the reverse of that in *Antony and Cleopatra,*
where Caesar mocks at Antony's insults: 'He calls me boy,
and chides as he had power/ To beat me out of Egypt' (IV i
1–2). The imperturbability of Caesar cannot be ruffled by
mere words.

Coriolanus's normal speaking voice is often harsh and
vituperative. In his tirades against the people he uses a few
repeated image themes (especially food, disease, and
animals), but our interest is not so much in the images
themselves as in their expletive force. After the Romans are
beaten to their trenches by the Volscians, for example, 'Enter
Marcius, cursing' (I iv 29 s.d.), and his volley of abuse begins:

> All the contagion of the South light on you,
> You shames of Rome! you herd of – Biles and plagues
> Plaster you o'er, that you may be abhorr'd
> Farther than seen and one infect another
> Against the wind a mile! You souls of geese
> That bear the shapes of men, how have you run
> From slaves that apes would beat! Pluto and hell! (I iv 30–6)

What is important here is not the catalogue of disease and
animal imagery, but the 'thunder-like percussion' (I iv 59) of

Marcius's wrath. The breaking off in 'you herd of –' is not felt as a gap, but as part of a natural rhythm in which the histrionic stress is on sound rather than sense. These images are therefore 'illustrative' because they are used as examples of Marcius's anger, and no single image nor the sequence of the group is absolutely necessary. We have the same sort of effect in Marcius's second speech in the play, an extended harangue to the plebeians:

> He that trusts to you,
> Where he should find you lions, finds you hares;
> Where foxes, geese. You are no surer, no,
> Than is the coal of fire upon the ice
> Or hailstone in the sun. . . . (I i 174–8)

These are metaphors but they could as easily have been similes, for the analogy that is drawn is very explicit and limited. The animals have traditional, proverbial associations that are fairly well fixed: the lion is valiant, the hare fearful, while the fox represents shrewdness and craft, and the goose foolish simplicity. We do not feel any breadth of meaning in these images. But we must remember that it is Marcius who is speaking, and he is neither a poet nor a politician, but only a straight-forward man of war. He tags plebeian faults with what is for him a suitable imagery, and if it seems familiar and trite, that in itself is a comment on his image-making powers.

It is significant, too, that the thirty-six lines of soliloquy in *Coriolanus* – the same number as in *As You Like It* – represent the minimal use of this device in Shakespeare. By itself, this proves nothing, but it keeps us aware of the lack of inwardness in the play and the fact that Coriolanus is the least articulate of Shakespeare's tragic heroes. At an opposite pole is the brooding, meditative Hamlet, who resorts to the soliloquy as a 'natural' form of expression.[10] The few soliloquies in *Coriolanus* have a very particular dramatic effect. In a play so full of politics it is not often that we see a lone figure on stage speaking as if to himself. We have been accustomed to seeing troops moving about and crowds of plebeians and patricians wrangling with each other. In this context the soliloquy, the stage im-

age of isolation, emphasizes Coriolanus's own inner state. The
two soliloquies in IV iv, for example, call attention to the
spiritual alienation of Coriolanus as an exile and traitor in the
country of the Volscians. In II iii his proud soliloquy in the
gown of humility sets him completely apart from his plebeian
petitioners. He speaks to himself on stage not to unburden his
conscience nor to express his inner purposes, but because he
feels himself to be a lone and humiliated figure.

The style of *Coriolanus* is not so much 'Roman', implying as
this does a Stoic self-control, as objective and public. This is
seen very vividly in the great amount of public ceremony in the
play, with its accompanying music or noise. The ominous
shouts of 'mutinous *Citizens*' open the action, and these are
reinforced by '*Shouts within*' (I i 47 s.d.) from the mob on the
other side of the city. We then have an elaborate range of
sound directions for the battle scenes: '*They sound a parley*' (I iv
12 s.d.), '*Drum afar off*' (I iv 15 s.d.), '*Alarum far off*' (I iv 19 s.d.),
'*Alarum, as in battle*' (I viii s.d.), '*Flourish. Alarum. A retreat is
sounded.*' (I ix s.d.), and '*A flourish. Cornets.* Enter *Tullus Aufidius*
bloody, with two or three *Soldiers.*' (I x s.d.). These directions
graphically convey the changing fortunes of war. We also have
a number of acclamations of Marcius's valor: '*They all shout
and wave their swords, take him up in their arms and cast up their caps*'
(I vi 75 s.d.) and '*A long flourish. They all cry,* "Marcius! Marcius!" *cast up their caps and lances*' (I ix 40 s.d.). In Coriolanus's
triumphal procession there is '*A shout and flourish*' (II i 172 s.d.),
'*A sennet. Trumpets sound.*' (II i 178 s.d.), and '*Flourish. Cornets.
Exeunt in state, as before.*' (II i 220 s.d.). In the conflict between
Coriolanus and the plebeians in Act III we have confused
shouting as '*They all bustle about Coriolanus*' (III i 185 s.d.), and
when he is banished, '*They all shout and throw up their caps*' (III iii
135 s.d.). Coriolanus's decision to spare Rome is celebrated
by musical jubilation: '*Trumpets, hautboys, drums beat, all
together*'[11] (V iv 51 s.d.), '*Sound still with the shouts*' (V ii 60 s.d.),
and '*A flourish with drums and trumpets*' (V v 7 s.d.). The final
scene of the play also puts strong insistence on public
ceremony as '*Drums and trumpets sound, with great shouts of the people*' (V vi 48 s.d.), and Coriolanus enters 'marching with *Drum
and Colours. . .*' (V vi 69 s.d.). As in *Hamlet*, the play ends with

solemn music: '*A dead march sounded*' (v vi 155 s.d.).

The public style of *Coriolanus*, so forcibly conveyed by the sound directions, is in some sense an expression of the imaginative limitations of the play; the characters use language and imagery that are natural and appropriate to them. Coriolanus himself renounces rhetoric and seems to equate a plain style with integrity, for the heroic virtues of war and the soldier do not demand an elaborate poetic imagery. Perhaps part of the difficulty in appreciating this play stems from an overemphasis on verbal imagery. If we consider the play from a dramatic point of view, it has surprising force and vitality, as the production directed by John Houseman at the Phoenix Theater in 1954 seemed to indicate. The poetic speech is remarkably tight and sinewy, from Volumnia's familiar 'Pow, waw!' (II i 157) to Marcius's formal renunciation of 'acclamations hyperbolical' (I ix 50). There·is also a brilliant use of short choric scenes which comment on the main action without making obtrusive analogies; for dramatic economy, I iii and IV ii are among the best scenes of this sort in all of Shakespeare. It is along these dramatic lines, I think, that we may understand the otherwise bewildering remark of Eliot that *Coriolanus* is, 'with *Antony and Cleopatra*, Shakespeare's most assured artistic success'.[12]

SOURCE: extract from 'Style in the Roman Plays', in *Shakespeare's Roman Plays: The Function of Imagery in the Drama* (1961) pp. 29–40.

NOTES

1. E. K. Chambers, *William Shakespeare*, I 479–80. Chambers thinks *Coriolanus* may have been produced early in 1608. The dating of *Antony and Cleopatra* before 1608 partly depends upon the assumption that Daniel made changes in his new edition of *The Tragedie of Cleopatra* in 1607 after he had seen or read Shakespeare's play (see Chambers, I 477–8). This assumption has been challenged by Ernest Schanzer, who finds evidence that Daniel influenced Shakespeare in some small verbal details. Schanzer would therefore date *Antony and Cleopatra* after the spring of 1608 ('Daniel's Revision of His *Cleopatra*', *R.E.S.*, new. ser., VIII (1957) 380 and n.1). The arguments are

summarized in Kenneth Muir, *Shakespeare's Sources* (London, 1957), and in Arthur M. Z. Norman, ' "The Tragedie of Cleopatra" and the Date of "Antony and Cleopatra" ', *M.L.R.*, LIV (1959) 1–9. Norman dates Shakespeare's *Antony and Cleopatra* in 1606–7.

2. See D. A. Traversi, *An Approach to Shakespeare* (1938) pp. 216–34.

3. A. C. Bradley, 'Coriolanus', *Proc. Brit. Acad. 1911–1912*, v 459 [reprinted in this volume].

4. D. J. Enright, '*Coriolanus*: Tragedy or Debate?' *Essays in Criticism*, IV (1954) 16–17

5. See W. Clemen, *Shakespeare's Imagery*, p. 5. This is one of Clemen's theses about Shakespeare's development.

6. Kittredge, following Tyrwhitt, emends the Folio 'Ouerture' to 'coverture'. Thiselton clarifies the Folio text by regarding 'him' as the dative instead of the objective case. Coriolanus would then be making a scornful overture to the parasite to fight in the wars. When the soldier's steel becomes as soft as the parasite's silk, it is time for the parasite to go to the wars and for the soldier to stay at home (*Variorum Coriolanus*, pp. 145–58, esp. p. 157).

7. See Paul A. Jorgensen, *Shakespeare's Military World* (Berkeley, Calif., 1956) ch. 5.

8. Ibid., ch. 6.

9. *Johnson on Shakespeare*, ed. Walter Raleigh (London, 1908) p. 179 [see Part One above].

10. Morris Le Roy Arnold, *The Soliloquies of Shakespeare* (N. Y., 1911) p. 25. Arnold counts fourteen soliloquies of 291 lines in *Hamlet*.

11. This is the punctuation of the Folio, which Kittredge changes to '*Trumpets, hautboys; drums beat; all together*'. See H. Granville-Barker, *Prefaces*, II 270.

12. See also Eliot's unfinished *Coriolan*, which is based on Shakespeare's play (*The Complete Poems and Plays 1909–1950*, N. Y., 1952, pp. 85–9).

Una Ellis-Fermor

'SECRET IMPRESSIONS: THE DRAMATIC DEFINITION OF *CORIOLANUS*' (1961)

In the plays of his maturity, Shakespeare reveals by secret impressions the underlying natures of his characters, so that, with the knowledge thus conveyed to us, we redress at unawares the balance of evidence given not only by those characters but by other parts of the play. Many of those in which this process can be clearly discerned are minor or subordinate figures, but a few are co-partners with the greatest[1] and it is found to some degree in all. Of none can we say with certainty that we know them until we have taken into account the hidden evidence thus disclosed, and it is probable that our unconscious awareness of every character is influenced by it. But in one play at least Shakespeare seems to determine by this mode our apprehension of the central figure itself; and this so modifies the total effect of the play, as to re-colour our interpretation of nearly every aspect. No detailed analysis of such a character can be attempted within the limits of this volume, but some indications may be given of the process by which unconscious knowledge finds its way into our imaginations.

The character I have in mind is Coriolanus; and the discrepancy between speech and fact, a certain conflict between the character's professions and his actions may prompt us to look further into the mind from which both, though seemingly incompatible, derive. And this in turn may lead to successive readings that reveal depth below depth in his nature, re-interpreting the surface for us and modifying our first inferences from it.[2]

With the character of Coriolanus we observe first the strife and turmoil created by his passions on the world around him, shaking the State of Rome and bringing him to destruction, then the presence of bitter conflict in his own mind. From this point onward we are guided, I think, by deeper-lying and less evident indications of motive, until we reach a point where we depend wholly upon 'secret impressions' for the final interpretation. When we have reached this, we begin to travel backwards, in reascending order, as it were, to the surface which we first observed and to reconsider these earlier and it may be mistaken conclusions in the light of that final discovery.

Our first impression of Coriolanus in the first three acts of the play is familiar to all Shakespeare's readers and on this there may be little disagreement. He is a man still young[3] and of evident military genius, as brave and brilliant in battle as Hotspur, with powers of leadership in the field and a grasp of strategy akin to that of Henry V; a man whose valour and heroic wrath inspire men to follow him and carry them to victory (I iv 30 seq.; I vi 66 seq.). As a statesman, he shows in an emergency the same grasp of the essential factors; he is a clear and pitiless judge of the plebeians and a shrewd and fearless prophet of the immediate future. His impatient scorn of the people's cowardice and treachery, of the contemptible custom of vote-begging (accepted even by his fellow patricians), though fierce and heedless, is also of a heroic mould. He is a man of equally strong attachments within his own class, to his fellow generals Cominius, Menenius, and Titus Lartius, to his wife and above all to his mother; a sincere man, hating flattery, with an irritable dislike of praise, even when he has fairly earned it. These are the elements of a noble character and he reveals them clearly in action and eloquently in speech. On immediate political issues he is as sound a judge as on the conduct of a campaign; great intelligence as well as firm definition of thought shine through the courage and vigour of his speech (III i 37–40, 104–11, 124–38, 141–60). His military genius (and, within these limits, his statesmanship) exceed the others' as his imagination surpasses theirs. In these two domains he appears to achieve full and untrammelled expression; passion and thought are in triumphant union. And the fruits of this may be seen in the liberal frankness of his manner during the first three acts to his fellow-generals and to Menenius; this is a man in at least momentary harmony with his immediate world.[4] If we accept this reading, his fall results directly from behaviour of a piece with what he has already shown us, from his intolerant, unsympathetic and heroically undiplomatic treatment of the insolent Roman mob. But after his fall the balance of his nature seems to change, and though some change might follow naturally upon the shock of his banishment, it is not altogether easy to interpret this as a direct development from his earlier behaviour. Darker moods and purposes than we or his fellows had suspected in him take possession and lead to his unnatural alliance with the Volscians, his vengeful attack on Rome and so to his death.

Thus already, in the reading these brief indications suggest, we find ourselves troubled by a seeming hiatus[5] at this point in the play. The haughty, heroic, and magnanimous patrician of the earlier acts is transformed into a vengeful soldier of fortune. The man who could not stay to hear his nothing monstered now sees himself as a lonely dragon whom his fen makes feared and talked of, and he who could not speak mildly to save his consulship flatters Aufidius's fellow-officers to win control of a war of vengeance.

And so a second impression begins to modify our first, though still drawn from the evidence of character and conduct revealed by the outward action of the play. For in seeking, as we must, to reconcile these two contradictory phases of conduct, to trace them to a common root in character, we have in fact already assumed the second to be inherent in the first. And so we begin to look for indications, for flaws that may be no more than faint inconsistencies; but that points us back or forward to the presence of something hitherto unnoticed in his nature, secretly at work, it may be, upon his experience, transforming it to something whose effects are incalculable to him, to us, and to his Roman world. One of the most evident of these flaws is the hyper-sensitive modesty of the early acts, churlish and ungrateful sometimes in its repudiation of praise that was in part at least kindly and courteous (ɪ ix 36–40, 40–53). It is, as we have already noticed, in flat contradiction to his growing preoccupation, towards the end of the play, with the effect he is producing on other people and so belongs, presumably, to a part of his nature later submerged by the crucial act of treachery. But, more important than this, it is also hard to reconcile with our first impression, that of a man in full and glorious exercise of his power as a soldier, a confident man who, though vehement and irascible, yet expresses his political vision with full and satisfying vigour, a man secure in his close, affectionate relations with his friends and the members of his household. Beneath the confidence and the security, then, we recognize disharmony. And we ask from what it derives.

This leads us to consider other passages in the play, where openly declared difference of principle and conviction breaks out in the scenes in which Volumnia and the patricians force Coriolanus to conciliate the Roman mob he has defied (ɪɪɪ ii esp. 16–20). This might be no more than a clash between two positive natures, each equally confident and secure in its own convictions, but that, as we observe, the divergence proves wider than Volumnia had supposed and its disclosure takes her by surprise. And we recall, too, an earlier moment of insistence on her part and uneasy acquiescence on his, where we are momentarily aware of something in him that she has not recognized. 'My mother, Who has a charter to extol her blood, When she does praise me grieves me' (ɪ ix 13–15). This is not idle talk; it reveals a deep division of idea, even an unrecognized division of ideals. Comparing the two passages, we recall what we have learnt of Volumnia's influence over Coriolanus, of her heroic ambition which has moulded his character and career (ɪ iii etc.). We have been seeking to reconcile two contradictory phases of conduct in Coriolanus and have been led to assume the presence of division in his own mind. Now this assumption, at first suggested by that exaggerated sensitiveness, ungracious, ill-proportioned and at odds with his customary mood, is confirmed by the passages between him and Volumnia, which reveal not only the unexpected depth and inwardness of the division between them, but a like unfor-

mulated division in the mind of Coriolanus himself. For
Coriolanus has been moulded in the ideals of his world
(epitomized in his mother's) and though much in him has
given them a willing response, we begin to question now
whether they have been entirely of his own initiating, and
whether they have in fact satisfied the whole of him. If his conduct, first in little, perplexing details of behaviour and finally
in a great and catastrophic revolution, has pointed to a civil
war within the mind of Coriolanus and if his mother's bearing
and his relation to her has suggested a sufficient cause for this,
can we go further and say that Shakespeare has revealed to us
something of the nature of this war and of the conflicting
elements involved, by further hints, in single phrases it may
be, in momentary betrayals of something invisible and unknown to the speaker himself? For this would, if true, lead us
to reconsider our earlier conclusions with the help of these impressions and so perhaps to come nearer to understanding
what lies below the contradictions that first prompted our inquiry.

What picture does Shakespeare give us of this Roman
civilization with which Coriolanus is in these passages at odds,
which has yet shaped his habits, which has been his world and
his devotion, to which his mother has dedicated him and to
which he has offered his genius in eager and triumphant service? We might set aside the part played by the mob (which,
to his fellow-patricians as to him, is hardly Rome at all and
certainly not Rome's civilization, but rather an enemy within
the gates) were it not that the values revealed by its behaviour
have a disquieting affinity with some that we find among the
patricians and that it is precisely their submission to its
demands that calls forth the opposition from Coriolanus that
prompted our inquiry. For the truth is that Shakespeare has
sometimes drawn the patrician world in harsh, blunt lines.
Bold, vigorous, and spirited, the Roman nobles are insensitive
to nobility except for the specialized virtues of warfare and are
redeemed largely by their generous respect for these qualities
in each other and by the aristocratic imperturbability, the sar-
castic detachment with which they face annihilation at the
end.[6] Cominius is a good general, brave in war but no

fire-eater, sensible and conciliatory in politics, knowing well
the importance of Coriolanus's achievements and making a
sane plea for public acknowledgment of it (I vi, I ix esp.
53–5); a just man but no idealist; a man who lets himself be guided
by custom and events instead of shaping them. He, Menenius
and Volumnia alike believe in maintaining a balance between
ideals and complaisance; convictions are one thing; to act
upon them implacably, as would Coriolanus, is another.
Volumnia betrays this as often as she speaks of the Volscian
wars (I iii, II i), but she adds much also that the other
patricians do not openly express. There is something crude
and coarse-grained in her enumeration of Coriolanus's
wounds; at least half her pleasure is in their market-value,
they are something 'to show to the people' (II i 165–72). Her
restless ambition is short-sighted and limited, carrying in it
the seeds of bitterness and ultimate defeat; her son has 'out-
done his former deeds doubly' (II i 151–2), but we question to
what positive good this cumulative record-breaking is to lead.
And so when she meets in him a resistance she cannot understand she assumes it to be a trivial folly (III ii). But the reader,
guided imperceptibly by signs invisible to her, begins to
recognize that her limited and crude ambitions owe such
dominion as they have over Coriolanus to childhood's training; his affections have made them in some sort sacred to him,
the only images in which he could clothe his innate aspirations
and ideals.

The ideals of this Rome in fact are sometimes base, and
precisely because of their limitations (II i 216–20); Volumnia
gloats over Coriolanus's wounds as a profitable investment,
and crude butchery wins the respect even of Cominius, taking
high place in his official speech to the Senate on Coriolanus's
triumph (II ii 87–127). If these are indeed the roots of Rome's
code and values we have much ground for disquiet; perhaps,
at the end of the play, as we listen to Volumnia's noble prayer
to Coriolanus for the Rome that has ruined him (V iii) we hear
also a discordant echo of her exultation over the slaughter in
Corioli (II i 175–8). Perhaps, after all, the mob are but the
crudest element in a state in which even the patricians
sometimes accept low values and condone base customs.

Cominius and Menenius admit fairly and frankly (IV vi
112–18, 137–9; v iv 35–8) that they deserve destruction for
abandoning Coriolanus to the mob's decree and this is the
belated recognition, by two of Rome's best men, that they
have hitherto identified themselves with some of the very
things he had denounced.

This, then, is the obverse of that image of Rome to whose
service Coriolanus had once dedicated himself, and after the
overturning of his world, it, or something very like it, takes the
place of that earlier image in his mind. In Corioli he sees no
other. As to those Roman friends with whom he had been in
close and happy relationship – 'He could not stay to picke
them in a pile Of noysome, musty Chaffe.' 'Rome and her
rats' are no longer now 'at point of battle', but infamous allies.

But has this reversal come, after all, without all warning?
Of the process by which Coriolanus finds his way from the
first image of Rome to its opposite we can only guess, for it is
hidden in silence – the silence of his disappearance into exile
from a stage he had hardly quitted before, the silence of his
strange new taciturnity and later the even deeper silence,
though more significant, of smooth concealing speech [see
below, page 137]. But the new picture is so sharply defined
that it seems to spring all but complete from some area of the
mind where it has long been secretly forming. Can this be so?
If this is Shakespeare's intention here, perhaps we shall find
Coriolanus already, before the crisis of his fortunes, more
nearly aware than he dare admit of the two Romes in his own
mind; perhaps we, the readers, have had intimations offered
us of that uneasy relationship.

Such intimations of the hidden depths of the mind we shall
seek most naturally at the points of fissure, those moments
when his behaviour is most nearly inexplicable to us, to his
fellows, and to himself. We go back to the passages, that is,
when his recoil from the customs of his world is most evident;
in his abnormal hatred of its praises and in his deep-seated
loathing of the election tactics of the patricians. In the second,
he only hates more deeply (though from widely differing
motives) a tradition that the patricians themselves dislike; he

and they are at one so far. But in the first, in his discourteous
rebuff to courtesy, his wanton repudiation of popularity, that
draws down Cominius's merited rebuke (I ix 41–53), he finds
unbearable something that the patricians approve, a ritual
that for them has significance and value. This is a wide breach
not to be explained away by modesty or even by vanity. 'It
does offend my heart' (II i 185). We have no reason now to
take these words at anything but their face value; something
contaminates the acclamations and praises poured upon him,
so that they touch him at heart; there is nausea in the recoil.
And thereupon, we observe, he turns to the figure that has
stood mute in the midst of the clamour, to Virgilia. 'My
gracious silence, hayle' (II i 192). Perhaps these words too
mean precisely what they say; perhaps there is there
something lacking else in his world, a source of grace and
wisdom, a silence the vehement cannot touch.

Light can be thrown back upon the question at this point by
certain habits of speech that grow upon him towards the end
of the play. The first clear signs of change appear when he
parts from Cominius, Menenius, Volumnia, and Virgilia at
the gates of Rome (IV i), when both bearing and language
begin to reflect the deep shock given to his spirit by his banishment. Already he is the 'lonely Dragon that his Fenne Makes
fear'd, and talk'd of more than seene' (IV i 29–31). Moreover,
it is he now who counsels calm and submission, quoting what
were formerly Volumnia's own stoic *sententiae*. He sets up certain barriers between them and himself by this ominous
steadiness of demeanour, this unnatural, even and measured
phrasing. He behaves like a man who has summoned up a
stoic dignity to compensate for loss, conceal a wound or deny
humiliation; a man who has lost at once his world and his integrity. From this scene onward, the familiar outbursts of rage
disappear.[7] Paradoxically, the shock appears to have integrated his character. (More probably, as we already divine,
it has cut deeply into it and left him to rescue and integrate
one part only.) From now, he practises a rigid and seemingly
unbreakable control over his emotions, a cynical shrewdness
in planning his treatment of men, an unscrupulous exercise of
flattery in subduing them (V vi 21–6, 71–84). But, there are

indications that this inflexible rigidity belongs only to the surface of his mind and that is now the surface only of a part.
This demeanour is more ominous than the former,
ungoverned outbursts of rage or irritation; the man is for the
time hardly sane, though his madness does not touch, what
nothing has ever troubled, his military genius. He appears
rather as a man playing a part or a succession of parts and
watching himself as he does so.[8] And in the end this declares
itself in a habit of speech which throws light back over the
whole play.

For again and again, especially in the crucial scene of the
last act, Coriolanus speaks of himself as an actor or as a man
determined to deny nature (v iii 24–5, 35–7, 40–2, 83–4, 184–
5). The two recur in sinister conjunction and these related
and iterative images begin to stir the reader's imagination.

The climax of this headlong career of perversity comes in
the fifth act, when the man who revolted against a conventional untruth and hated even the semblance of exaggerated
praise has now put his imagination at the service of deliberate
fantasy and built between himself and the world a gigantic
façade of megalomaniac shams. The familiar images of the actor recur here and the language and rhythms of his speech are
a clear index of the severance of his conduct from his nature.[9]
The complex syntax, the florid vocabulary, the imagery at
once banal and theatrical, the slow and weighty rhythms that
reverberate like a hollow structure are as far removed from
those of the earlier acts, from the ringing athletic movement,
the crisp hammer-blows of the syntax and the vivid, shining
imagery, as this later Coriolanus is from the gallant and impetuous aristocrat of the beginning.

We ask ourselves whether this seemingly new habit is of
purely recent growth, derived solely from his spirit's
catastrophe and sequent experience, or whether this, like that
major image, the new picture of the Roman state, has its roots
also in some earlier phase, had already, in fact, been long
preparing in secret recesses of his mind. And this question
leads us back again to the middle of the play, to the
triumphant return from the Volscian war and to the consular
elections. For it is upon these scenes that we must turn such

light as we can derive from the final phases of Coriolanus's behaviour.

'It is a part that I shall blush in acting' (II ii 149–50). The words are spoken in protest to his fellow patricians when they urge him to put on the 'vesture of humility' and beg the people's votes in the open forum. And in a later scene he recurs at intervals to this image (III ii 15–16, 105–6 (109–10, Volumnia), 112–15). To his fellow-patricians, this is something to be argued away by appeals to common sense and to custom, even if need be, by Volumnia's impatient scolding. But the disproportionate outbursts of anger as he resists and the persistent return to the images that accompany them point to something genuine in the words and deeper in the motive. Nor is the cause of it the pride of which Volumnia and the tribunes accuse him.[10] It is clear that he fears some consequences far graver than they, who think only of the practical effects, and that though his fear is instinctive and only half-articulate, he is aware of some deep inward harm that threatens if he consents. And as the pressure upon him increases, in the later scene (III ii), and his resistance becomes more desperate, we realize that he is right, though he cannot communicate his reasons to them. Their demand is dastardly and his ultimate consent disastrous, not because his failure brings ruin on him, but because the result is precisely what he foretells, and because in consenting to play a part he does indeed 'teach his Minde a most inherent Baseness' (III ii 120–3). To them the impersonation that they counsel is a sensible piece of complaisance and no man of the world would think twice of it. But to him the pretence, the attempt to be something other than himself, means the forfeit of his integrity. What follows, from the decision of III iii to the end of the play is determined by this and if Coriolanus, after the shock of his banishment, appears to hide himself in a succession of parts, culminating in that of the inhuman world-conqueror which Volumnia herself is compelled to destroy, it is because he has lost the power to 'honor mine owne truth' (III ii 121), and has no other stay against the tide of hitherto unknown passions that sweep him onward.

If, moreover, we were right in thinking that this baser

Rome, present alike in the easy-going patricians and in the violent and sentimental mob, acted unconsciously as an irritant in Coriolanus's mind, if we are persuaded that, by conceding to it the service of a lie, he has in his own eyes forfeited his honour and debased his mind, if we think that his loss of the integrity that has upheld him is the real cause of the histrionic and vindictive treachery of the last acts, can we go a step further and ask why this experience, which Volumnia would have carried so lightly, brings psychological disaster to her son? If we would do this, we must attempt to guess at what has all this while lain hidden, that part of Coriolanus's nature which was not expressed in the double career of heroic soldier and forthright but discerning statesman, that part which was outraged by the customs his closest friends took as matters of course, that part whose resistance was broken by his own consent to a lie. I think that here too Shakespeare has given us certain impressions that can guide us to a conclusion justified in the context of the play.

Some words of Volumnia's spoken at the height of her exasperation when Coriolanus, after winning their votes, has provoked the mob to fury, surprise us by their evident misunderstanding of the nature of his impulse. 'You might have beene enough the man you are With striuing lesse to be so' (III ii 19–20). Is there any truth in this or is it in fact valuable precisely as a mis-reading of his character serving to point us to an opposite truth? For, despite his confusion, Coriolanus appears to be striving rather to be the man he is, a man, it may be, that neither he nor she knows; the very fact of the strife is perhaps an index of his frustration. She accuses him of being 'too absolute' (III ii 39) and, again, this absoluteness may but indicate a man not yet on terms with himself and struggling to preserve what he cannot define. Her argument here (III ii 47–57 seq.) that the union of 'honour and policy' in war are a true parallel to the conduct she now urges upon him is specious and fallacious. For uprightness and deliberate deception in a statesman are incompatible, while valour and strategy in war are not. 'They do not go together' (A. C., IV xv 47) and this he certainly knows even if he cannot define or articulate his knowledge. The strife that is native to his mind is

not this deep, inward conflict, but a forthright, eager strife for
some glory, that cannot be measured or satisfied by success. It
is a great part of his tragedy that this glory is undefined;
nevertheless, his desire for it fires his valour as does Tamburlaine's aspiration or Hotspur's 'bright honour'. It has no
commerce with Volumnia's well-defined aims of power and
dominion (II i 188–94). The Coriolanus we see in the play, for
lack of a clearer sight or worthier image, struggles to satisfy
this passion for glory with things that breed in him disquiet
and disgust. The state he serves, the class to which his love
and loyalty are bound, are content with mundane aims baser
than his, with ideals that offer him no scope.[11] The
preoccupation with his rival Aufidius (I i 236–8), which
appears early in the play, may be but another indication of
this restless search for an ideal objective; Aufidius becomes in
some sort a focus, though but a nebulous one, for this desire
for splendour of life that the summit of achievement in Rome
could never offer. Antium, 'this Enemie Towne' (IV iv 23–4),
already in the third act calls forth a line ironic but also
prophetic, 'I wish I had a cause to seeke him there' (III i 19).
In this passionate desire to image an undefined aspiration
(and, it may be, unrecognized ideals) Antium becomes the
city of his dreams. 'A goodly City is this *Antium*' (IV iv 1; cf. III
iii 133), and the violent recoil from Rome in the fourth act
makes it certain that he will rush to embrace that world that
his imagination has already sought in secret. For what has all
along looked like pride in Coriolanus is but rebellion against
standards and concessions that repel him; the reaction has
been negative, disgust and repudiation, because he cannot
focus his aspiration, but aspiration is there in him, as strong as
ever it was in Hotspur or Tamburlaine, though stifled and
perverted.

And so we return to the words whose significance we hoped
to illuminate with the help of secret impressions made upon us
by other passages in the play. 'My gracious silence, hayle!'
The words are sometimes read as a kindly, half-teasing
greeting; affectionate and gently bantering. If we have come
near the truth in what we have suggested already, they will
now mean more than this. They may well be the only overt ex-

pression in the play of two things deeply hidden in the mind of
Coriolanus, of a longing for the balancing silences, graces, and
wisdom banished from the outer world but vital to wholeness
of life, and an acknowledgement, albeit inarticulate, that in
Virgilia these values were preserved. The clamour around him
is his everyday condition, the easily articulated code of his
community, at once heroic and insidiously base, the only
system of values he has seen defined. But the source of aspiration such as his, an instinctive longing for poetry of living,[12]
contains within it an innate love for silence and grace and even
for that Valley of Humiliation whose air Bunyan knew to be
sweeter than all others. His need is for wholeness of life and he
has harnessed the poetry of living to battle and bloodshed.
What his aspiration sought of life was that it should be
radiant, clear and significant. And for this bread of life his
world has offered him success and dominion preserved at the
price of complaisance.

> I thinke hee'l be to Rome
> As is the Aspray to the Fish, who takes it
> By Soueraignty of Nature. (IV vii 35)

This sovereignty, this greatness is probably our final impression, that and the simplicity inseparable from greatness that
has been his undoing. It is not the military greatness that his
fellow-soldiers Roman and Volscian acclaim throughout the
play, though that is a partial image of it. It is something that
they cannot define, in spite of their many attempts at definition (I iv 52–61; III i 254–9; IV v 66–8; IV vii 33–5, 48–53; V vi
126–8), yet it is something that each in turn perceives, gladly
or grudgingly, and the reiteration of the word noble[13] reveals
their momentary recognitions. But an unholy alliance
between the debased and limited ideals of his world and the
heart's affections that a meaner man would have put aside has
impressed upon his imagination an image of that ideal as in-
sufficient for him as it was too great for the thing it imaged.
This magnitude of spirit and imagination was moulded from
birth in the worship of the Roman state. But in time that imagination substituted for itself an ideal Rome, as, later, an

ideal Antium, both nobler than the actual and indeed non-existent. This was the inevitable result of the attempt to bind such potentialities within such limitations and its outcome could only be the destruction of one or both. The movement towards destruction set in when, under pressure of the Roman state and its ideals, Coriolanus renounced his own undefined but hitherto unquenched aspiration. Then the surest principle of his being was contaminated and the sovereignty of his nature perverted.

I have attempted to show here ... that it is by secret impressions that Shakespeare conveys to our imaginations the nature of such a character as Coriolanus. So great is the contradiction between his outward seeming and his hidden self, so blinded and incomplete his self-knowledge, that nothing but some such disclosure could have led us to understanding (imperfect though it is) and nothing but the supreme tact of an evocative mode could have pointed us the way. Coriolanus cannot himself reveal to us his nature and motives, for part of that nature is denied and part undeveloped. No other character in the play can direct us, for the presence of such a person, articulate and clear-sighted, would have provided him with an ally against his own confusion and the limitations of his world. Only Virgilia seems to preserve for him some source of peace, silence, and wonder from which the thirst of his spirit can be assuaged and it is in his words to her that we find one of the most potent of those secret impressions that work powerfully upon the imagination.

SOURCE: 'Coriolanus', in *Shakespeare the Dramatist* (1961) pp. 60–77; the chapter was originally read as a paper to the Conference of the International Association of University Professors of English, at Cambridge in August 1956.

NOTES

[Most of the play-reference notes in the original have been incorporated in the text, with renumbering of the notes presented here – Ed.]

1. Such is the figure of Falstaff in which Maurice Morgann first discerned this method at work.

2. The likelihood of an ultimate contradiction of his earlier judgement is sometimes suggested thus to the interpreter by the presence of conflict in and about the character, while sometimes it is conveyed rather by an uneasiness of mind recognized by the character himself but provoking no outward conflict. Sometimes, it may be, the contradiction offered to the surface and its evidence is so slight as to pass almost unobserved, as with the characters of Henry IV, Henry V, Volumnia and others.

3. Coriolanus won his first campaign at the age of sixteen, like the historical Edward III, and has thus had time for much experience of war without becoming middle-aged by the time of the play. This makes Aufidius's taunt at the end – 'boy' – something that may justly infuriate and not a piece of mere gutter-snipe rudeness.

4. Never is this modest magnanimity more clearly revealed than in the scene during the consular campaign where he puzzles in simple bewilderment over his mother's disapproval of his conduct (III ii 7–16).

5. Menenius perceives this too (IV vi 72–4).

6. Ironically, Coriolanus never sees the best of those aristocrats whom he hates for the sake of the city, the scenes in which, awaiting destruction in Rome, they mock the craven repentance of the 'clusters' (IV vi and V i).

7. To reappear once more only, at the end of the play, after his reconversion.

8. This is an almost complete reversal of his former behaviour. The modesty is gone and he courts publicity; resolved to 'exceed the common', he deliberately makes himself 'feared and talked of'. His 'love's upon this enemy town' and the measure of his reasoning delusion is to be found in his assumption that he will not find in Antium the human nature he had 'banished' in Rome. He is as short-sighted in his estimate of Volscian hero-worship as he was shrewd in his condemnation of the Roman.

9. Especially in V iii 56–67, and 183–9. On the rhythms of Coriolanus's speech here see also *Shakespeare the Dramatist*, p. 135.

10. The word 'pride' is used nearly a dozen times in the course of the play and some six or seven of the other characters agree in thus accusing him; the first citizen, Sicinius (twice), the first Senate Officer, Brutus (twice), Volumnia (III ii 126, 130 and v iii 170) and Aufidius, explicitly in I v vii 8 and by implication from that point onward. But it is to be noticed that all but one of these are prejudiced utterances; even Volumnia's are to clinch an argument or reinforce an appeal.

11. Volumnia to the end never perceives this, but two other characters, Cominius and Menenius, come near to doing so when in the fourth and fifth acts they acknowledge that his fellow patricians have in some sort betrayed Coriolanus and identified themselves with what was base and contemptible in Rome.

12. Certain of Coriolanus's images bear out this. It is at first glance surprising that he does not, like Antony, draw his images from the battle-field, but sometimes, both in the earlier and in the later part of the play, from a quite different world of fancy or imagination. There are sudden, momentary flights from the immediate and actual; in the midst of his abuse of the mob comes the picture of them throwing up their caps, not as though they would lodge them on the Capitol, but 'as they would hang them on the hornes o' th' Moone' (I i 217) and from the often hollow imagery of Act v, scene iii, there flashes out the description of Valeria 'Chaste as the Icicle That's curdied by the Frost from purest Snow, And hangs on Dians Temple' (v iii 65–6). Images from nature thus break through, 'pebbles' and stars, the 'mutinous windes' that 'Strike the proud Cedars 'gainst the fiery Sun' (v iii 60) and are at once in sharp contrast with the hyperbole and self-consciousness of the actor and suggestive of something escaping from the depths of his mind under the final strain of this scene. My attention was first drawn to the presence of these images in Coriolanus's speech by Miss Jacqueline R. Dunn.

13. Some twenty-five in all are spoken of Coriolanus, but the word has echoes in the traditional application to the patricians as description of rank and the somewhat similar use among the Volscian gentry. The following are some of the references to Coriolanus: I i 169, 253; Iiv 52; Iix 66; II ii 45, 134; II iii 9, 93, 141; III i 233, 254; III ii 40; IV ii 21; IV v 68, 112, 122 (all spoken by Aufidius); IV vi 109; IV vii 36; v iii 145, 154; v vi 126, 145, 155. (Aufidius's earlier images and 'devil', 'viper', etc.).

A. P. Rossiter

'POLITICAL TRAGEDY'
(1961)

Shakespeare may have felt some disappointment with *Coriolanus*. He would not be the last; for I think that few see or read it without feeling that they 'don't get as much out of it as they hoped to' or that it 'somehow doesn't seem to *pay*' or is 'less profitable than others I could think of'; or something like that. But whatever he thought he meant by the play is likely to be very different from what *we* make of it, unless we keep our attention fixed on what was going on inside Shakespeare's head in 1607 – and what was going on in the year 1607 too. I do not mean that unless we know the barley-markets for 1606–8 and the state of malt-investments, we cannot understand *Coriolanus*. I suggest only this: that there are many ways of interpreting this play, and the one that begins nearest to Jacobean times is one that is necessarily a long way from our own. Moreover, so far as I can judge, the interpretations that arise spontaneously in our own times are so violently opposed to one another, and lead so inevitably into passionate political side-tracks, that almost any line of thinking that gets us away from them gives the play a better chance: a chance as a tragic play.

'Political': there I said it. *Coriolanus* is about power: about State, or *the* State; about order in society and the forces of disorder which threaten 'that integrity which should become 't' (III i 159); about conflict, not in personal but political life; and – the aspect which catches our minds first – about the conflict of classes. I put that last deliberately, for two related but separable reasons. First, if we begin at that end, the play's

tragic qualities are endangered at once: it tends to be seen as
political, i.e. to be filled with imported feelings which are too
partisan for the kind of contemplation which is tragedy. It also
readily becomes polemical and seems to be giving *answers*,
solutions to human conflicts, which tragedy does *not*. Secondly, it suffices here to summarize a few conclusions, merely as
examples of 'passionate political side-tracks'.

   1. Hazlitt: 'The whole dramatic moral . . . is that those who
have little shall have less, and that those who have much shall
take all that others have left. The people are poor; therefore
they ought to be starved. They are slaves; therefore they ought
to be beaten. They work hard; therefore they ought to be
treated like beasts of burden.' [1] And so on. It is only necessary
to read the text, to say that Hazlitt's Jacobinical comments
are false and nonsensical. No question of politics arises: it is
simply one of reading.

   2. In December 1933, *Coriolanus* was played at the *Comédie
française*. Every performance turned into a demonstration by
Right-wing groups (it was the time of the Stavisky affair, and
Parliamentary government itself seemed to be quite likely to
come to an end); and the Royalists cheered every outburst
against the 'common cry of curs', the populace, and the bald
tribunes whose power should be thrown in the dust. The play
was withdrawn; M. Daladier dismissed the director, put the
chief of the Sûreté in his place; and events went forward to the
great riots of 6 February 1934. [2] While one can admire the
French enthusiasm for making Shakespeare really about
something that matters here and now, this is still something
other than Shakespeare-criticism. For the view that Caius
Marcius should be – or ever could be – the good and great dictator, the integrator of a shaking state, is one that the play
cannot support for a moment. Shakespeare's source, Plutarch,
had indeed said precisely the opposite; and Shakespeare has
put enough into the mouth of Aufidius alone (IV vii 35 f.) to
make further reference superfluous.

   3. I have been told that the Russian view is (or was) that
this is an entirely acceptable play, on the class-war; but showing how the Revolution is betrayed by self-seeking
demagogues who mislead the workers for their own private

ends. So that Brutus and Sicinius are wicked persons (with their modern counterparts in the Labour Party, I suppose), since the deviationist is worse than the despot. This is only what I have been told.

4. But Mr. Donald Douglas, in the *Daily Worker* (March 1952), saluted the Stratford production with the interpretation that *Coriolanus* is a revolutionary play, but one gone wrong, and patched up at the end to appease the censorship. The crack can be seen in IV vi, when the First Citizen leads the rest astray by saying

> For mine own part,
> When I said banish him, I said 'twas pity.
> SECOND CIT. And so did It.
> THIRD CIT. And so did I; and, to say the truth, so did very many of us;

– and it is not the Party Line at all. For the rest, let Mr. Douglas speak for himself: 'In the citizens' revolt against the Roman profiteers who are hoarding corn against a rise in prices ... we have the fact of the people's power. In the banished Coriolanus, vowing destruction on his native city ... we have the counterpart of the modern capitalist determined to ruin his country if only he can destroy the people.'

Those four views will do. I shall not argue with any of them, beyond saying that, given similar latitudes of interpretation (not to say perversion) of Shakespeare's words, I will demonstrate that Coriolanus is an allegory of more than one political idealist of our time, who followed his own inner counsels, despised common humanity, betrayed his trust, to become a lonely dragon in a fen; and then felt some new promptings of human nature, and threw away the game he had given away – to end in ruin and the mystery of the darkness of a mind that has set itself to stand

> As if a man were author of himself
> And knew no other kin.

Is that so far-fetched? In a sense, the three tragedies which

belong to this stage of Shakespeare's writing are all about
traitors and treachery. But treacheries of a particular kind. I
remember Donne in *Twicknam garden*:

> But O, selfe traytor, I do bring
> That spider love, which transubstantiates all,
> And can convert Manna to gall.

Coriolanus, Antony, Timon of Athens: all could be called
self-traitors, and their spider loves examined as Bradleyan
'tragic flaws'. But that is no line of mine; it will only lead
round to moral advice, moral answers: and though moral are
worth more than political answers, they cannot be the tragic
heart of a tragedy. The 'tragic flaw' analysis is far too simple.
It will never do to say that Coriolanus's calamity is 'caused' by
his being too proud and unyielding and just that; for one of
the play's central paradoxes is that though Caius Marcius
appears as a 'character' almost unvaryingly the same, yet, for
all his rigidity, he is pliant, unstable, trustless: traitor to
Rome, false to the Volsces, then true to Rome and to home
again, and twice traitor to himself. It is this 'self-traitor' element which makes one feel reservations over applying those
words of Charlotte Brontë's in *Shirley*. Caroline Helstone
recommends the play to Robert Moore, the factory-owner,
whom Caroline wants to see that he cannot haughtily pass
over the feelings of common men. He asks: 'Is it to operate like
a sermon?' She replies: 'It is to stir you; to give you new sen-
sations. It is to make you feel life strongly.' Taken by
themselves, those words suggest a stirring experience, the
romance of power, the stimulating contact with great
characters or great events, a glory in history. It is assumed
that to 'feel life strongly' has the opposite of a depressant
effect. Yet the conclusion of *Coriolanus* is not one bit like that. It
is flat, hurried, twisted off and depressing. One traitor steps
off the other traitor's dead body: 'My rage is gone'; and turns
sentimental traitor to his own successful treachery: 'And I am
struck with sorrow.'

Look at it one way and you can say, 'That is exactly the way
in which the unstable and trustless emotions of politics always

do switch and swivel.' And sardonically wait for Aufidius to turn on the stock-rhetoric, as he does: capitalizing the occasion as glibly as Antony over the dead Brutus. How well we look, assuring our dead foes of 'a noble memory', a grand funeral! And it is only a Gilbertian candour that adds 'and fireworks in the evening. You won't be there to see them, but they'll be there all the same.' Look at it a little more deeply, and that is how *History* goes. Is it perhaps only Shakespeare's sense of fitness that makes his end so inconclusive, so unsatisfying? Because history does not end conclusively? Look at it like that, and the play not only takes on more meaning, but ends in utter blackness. To say that that was the outcome of 'feeling life strongly' would stamp me as a pessimist. Yet is it not the outcome of feeling history strongly? of a strong feeling for *political* life, epitomized in a Roman example? That is the approach I make to the play. It is a History, and about the historic process. It is political. And, being both these things, it makes intellectual demands which cause people to find it (in T. S. Eliot's phrase) 'not as "interesting" as *Hamlet*'.[3]

By 'political' I do not mean the class-war, nor even narrowly the Tudor system of God-ordained order. I mean *Coriolanus* plays on political feeling: the capacity to be not only intellectually, but emotionally and purposively, engaged by the management of public affairs; the businesses of groups of men in (ordered) communities; the contrivance or maintenance of agreement; the establishment of a will-in-common; and all the exercises of suasion, pressure, concession and compromise which achieve that *will* (a mind to *do*) in place of a chaos of confused appetencies. I have the impression that many who believe they feel strongly about politics (in the sense of this party or that) have but little of this 'political feeling' I am trying to suggest to you. They find it easy to back a 'side' (as if at a Cup Final), but not to feel about what makes a 'side' an entity – as the result or resultant of the forces of many separate wills. In the extreme case, such people are 'partisans' with no sense of State whatever. No, more than that: they lack all sense of party as an organic thing; for they desire the 'victory' of their party, and desire it so childishly, that, if they had the power, they would destroy the very principle by which party exists: the recognition of conflict and uncertainty in human minds, confronted with the complexities and uncertainties of human events. The partisan would destroy all opposed groups. That is, he would see complex human situations and eventualities only in his own terms.[4] That is, see them only simplified to his one-eyed creed. And that is, not see them at all. His assumption is that, given the power, right action is *easy*. All history refutes that. As W. Macneile Dixon said (on tragedy), 'In this incalculable world, to act and to blunder are not two, but one.'[5]

The political feeling of *Coriolanus* is different: utterly so. It concerns you (if at all) with the workings of men's wills in the practical management of affairs; with the making (by some), the manipulation (by others) of 'scenes', emotional eruptions of individual or group will; with all that unstable, shifting, trustless, feckless, foolish-shrewd, canny, short-sighted, self-seeking, high-minded, confused, confusing *matter* which makes up a State's state of mind; with all that can be made – but only through feeling – its determined will. Lack of feeling about such things means that much of the play seems frozen. For there lies its excitement. If you cannot be excited about what happens to the Roman State (a branch or *exemplum* of what happens in *States*), then you cannot feel the play. For it is a kind of excitement very different from that generated by 'What happens to George?'

The advantage of such an approach – 'political' in the sense of the word in Aristotle's *Politics* – is that it leads you out of any academic or antiquarian restrictions, without landing you in the troubles which arise from prejudices about democracy imported from the nineteenth century or later. The terms in which the mob is described need not worry you. 'The mutable rank-scented many', 'the beast with many heads': those are Elizabethan commonplaces. The root phrase was Horace's (*belua multorum capitum*), and that was not original; a Stoic, Ariston of Chios, called the People *polycephalon therion* and versions and variants can be found in Bacon, Chapman, Dekker, Marston, Massinger, Middleton, Ford and (as we should expect) Beaumont and Fletcher. To get in-dignant with Shakespeare for such expressions is quixotic absurdity. He did not insult his audience, for the simple reasons that they knew nothing of voters' vanity, and *did* know, quite certainly, that they were *not* a mob. Yet, when I say that, do not imagine that a man does not *mean* a 'commonplace', merely because it is a commonplace. The many-headedness of those expressions is, surely, a measure of Shakespeare's fear: his fear of disorder, civil commotion, the disintegrated State. I shall return to that point.

The other advantage of responding to political feeling in the play is that we need not freeze it to a rigid Tudor-myth pattern of order. That is, we need not narrow it to what it doubtless showed to many *c.* 1607–8: an exposition of the evils which arise in the God-ordained microcosmic State when degree is neglected; when pride and Luciferian ambition make a great soldier into a 'limb diseased' of the body-politic; and when subjects attempt to judge what rulers are good for them – which is (as the 33rd Homily said, in a very convenient phrase too) 'as though the foot must judge of the head: an enterprise very heinous, and must needs breed rebellion'. That is by far the easiest way to systematize or pattern the play. Make the Fable of the Belly the key; turn all to Tudor-political moral allegory; throw in all the images of the body, disease, physic; and it all comes out pat. But you will have lodged the play back in Tudor distances, stopped all live political feeling, and set yourself the task of imaginatively thinking about the State solely in terms which can mean nothing whatever to your political self – unless you are highly eccentric and an anachronism in the twentieth century.

None the less, some imaginative attempt of that kind must be made; for the explicit political principles in the play are mainly put into the mouth of Coriolanus; and particularly in III i, where he makes what is in effect a single political utterance, though in several parts. He says that the power of the people has increased, and must be diminished; the Senators have nourished the cockle of rebellion by the corn-dole: made themselves no better than plebeians to let these Tribunes play the Senator with their 'absolute "shall" '; the people think that concessions have been made through fear; no stable or ordered policy can come from direction by ignorant numbers through 'voices' (votes); and the State is ruined and disintegrated unless this power of disordering policy and vetoing wise decisions is taken away from them. No statement of policy could be more sincere: none less well-timed. It is Marcius's 'tragic blunder' (the Aristotelian *hamartia*) to state these convictions when he does. Yet so far as Shakespeare tells us what is right for the State in the play, there we have it. We may dislike it: we can say it belongs to a past age (and that Charles Stuart lost his head because he did not see that that age was past); we can say that we dislike the man who speaks (and there is no reason that I can see to *like* Coriolanus at any stage of the play). But the personality of Caius Marcius is one thing, and the convictions of Coriolanus are quite another. The rightness of a man's ideas or convictions is not affected by his unpleasantness; *or* by his popularity, his 'popular "shall" '. Indeed, being right is rarely too conducive to popularity. What is amiss with demagogy, but that it confuses popularity (what people like hearing) with rightness (expediency)? What do Brutus and Sicinius display, but just that?

In considering what Shakespeare gave Coriolanus to think right, we cannot overlook the fact that in May 1607 there was an insurrection which began in Northamptonshire and soon spread to other counties. It was a peasant insurrection; and partly about corn – anway, about food. It was mainly against enclosures; but the engrossing of corn was a simultaneous grievance: an endemic economic evil of the day. The insurrection of the *Romans,* as told by Plutarch, was about *usurers* (they get a line at I i 79; but nobody would see it unless told to look for it). I wish no emphasis on Shakespeare's role as investor in malt. I only say: There were these risings, they kept happening in Elizabethan times; and if you ask what is his fear of the mob and disorder, it is answered at once in Marcius's mouth:

> my soul aches
> To know, when two authorities are up,
> Neither supreme, how soon confusion

> May enter 'twixt the gap of both and take
> The one by th'other (III i 108 f.)

Taking that with what we find elsewhere, in this and other plays, I cannot doubt that those lines are heart-felt. They are (for once) what William Shakespeare also thought – in 1607. It follows that we must swallow our democracy, and, if we would grasp the play, accept it that the political convictions of Marcius are *right*.

The personality of Caius Marcius, his attempts to manage men everywhere but on the battlefield, are, you may say, wrong throughout. But his convictions about the State are good and right, however impolitically he may phrase or time them. There you have a tragic clash: the basis of a political tragedy, not a Tudor morality. And to achieve that, Shakespeare had to twist his source, for he and Plutarch are entirely at odds. . . .

Menenius's significance is one thread to take hold of the tragic pattern by: he is (what Marcius is not) a political mind which moves with the dialectic of events. As he can *think* (and will) *dialectically*, he remains true to the major loyalties: Rome and himself. Marcius, the man of 'principle', does not. In this play, Bradley's generalization is entirely true: 'To meet these circumstances something is required which a smaller man might have given, but which the hero cannot give.'⁶Thus Marcius's 'greatness' is fatal to him. But *is* it great? I do not propose to answer that: only to insist that the comic ironies of the action (and phrasing) push the question at us; and that reflection offers the paradox that Menenius is 'greater' in mind that Marcius.

The valuation of Marcius is, however, offered by Shakespeare himself: in Aufidius's speech at the end of Act IV (IV vii 35 f.), a speech which perplexed Coleridge utterly.⁷ It is, as he rightly says, 'out of character'; but in it Shakespeare sums up Marcius. He was first 'a noble servant' to Rome; but whether from pride, or defect of judgement, or unadaptable rigidity of nature (which made him attempt to manage peace as he did war) – and he had 'spices' of all these – he came to be feared, hated and banished. That he epitomizes any of these

faults is explicitly denied. But two of them particularly concern what I used Menenius to focus: the qualities of a political
mind, able to remain effective in a changing world of events.
Whatever pride may be, rigidity (however high-principled)
and 'defect of judgement' are the opposites of those qualities.
But Aufidius (and Shakespeare) adds:

> So our virtues
> Lie in th' interpretation of the time.

Now that, in one and a half lines, gives the essence of the play.
Run over the whole action, act by act, and each is seen as an
'estimate' or valuation of Marcius: enemy of the people –
demi-god of war – popular hero home in triumph – Con-
sul-elect – and then (through his assertion of what he always
had asserted) public enemy and banished man, 'a lonely
dragon' (IV i 30). Throughout all this, he himself is almost an
absolute *constant*. Then, on his way to Aufidius at Antium, we
have his one soliloquy:

> O world, thy slippery turns! Friends now fast sworn,
> Whose double bosoms seems to wear one heart,
> Whose hours, whose bed, whose meal and exercise
> Are still together, who twin, as 'twere, in love
> Unseparable, shall within this hour,
> On a dissension of a doit, break out
> To bitterest enmity (IV iv 12 f.)

It is strangely reminiscent of the sad midnight reflections of
Henry IV, looking back over Richard's time; yes, and thinking
about history. But what is Marcius's speech about, if not that
same world of history, where all is change, nothing absolute;
where all 'virtues' lie in the interpretation of the time, and all
times lie about the virtues they have lost the use for?

   This is very near to what Ulysses tells Achilles about Time's
wallet and the 'one touch of nature' that 'makes the whole
world kin'. The 'touch' is an incessant writing-off of past
values, an interminable revaluation-series. This is what
happens in the historical process: history always *goes on*; goes

on, if you like, to the sad and cynical tune of *Frankie and John-
nie:*

> This story has no moral,   .
> This story has no end,
> This story only goes to show
> That there ain't no good in men ...

Or shall we say, 'There is not enough good of an effective kind,
in men as they appear in the historical process'? Be that as it
may, this is what happens in that process. History always goes
on; and in this play even Bradley could not say that
re-established order and rightness are left to console us. There
is no Albany; not even a Fortinbras or a Malcolm; the survivor
is Tullus Aufidius.

Coriolanus is the last and greatest of the Histories. It is
Shakespeare's only great political play; and it is slightly
depressing, and hard to come to terms with, because it is
political tragedy. The idea of the State runs through it:

> the Roman state; whose course will on
> The way it takes, cracking ten thousand curbs ... (I i 67)

And ten thousand men. Yet it is *not* the ideal or cosmic state of
the other plays: rather, an abstraction from an organism, or a
real state. Real states are dynamic: hence the constant irony
in the play, especially of Marcius and Aufidius saying what
they *will* do, and then not doing it or doing it in a way that
neither had foreseen.[8] Hence too the changing valuations of
the same Marcius by Aufidius, or by the comic servants in Antium, who snub him muffled and then say they knew all along
he was Somebody. This re-estimation of Marcius goes on to
the bitter end: to Aufidius's stepping off his stabbed body –
'My rage is gone' – and calling for a hero's funeral. 'O world,
thy slippery turns!'

But, in a sense, Caius Marcius *Coriolanus* was dead already.
That fine speech which Shakespeare made by transforming
North –

My name is Caius Marcius, who hath done
To thee particularly, and to all the Volsces,
Great hurt and mischief (IV v 65 f.):

what is it but the equivalent of a *dying*-speech, a summary of
expiring greatness? 'Only that name remains' is no more than
truth: he is no more *Coriolanus* – as Aufidius will tell him,
before he stabs him.

The final depressing paradox is that Marcius's un-
yieldingness and would-be self-sufficiency make him so pliant
to force of circumstance. All told, he is as unstable and
trustless as those whom he abused with:

>   you are no surer, no,
> Than is the coal of fire upon the ice
> Or hailstone in the sun . . .
> . . . and your affections are
> A sick man's appetite . . . (I i 170 f.)

Shakespeare spares him that last twist of bitter reflection: the
words were spoken to the mob. But the reflection is there, in
the play. And on my view, it ends – as J. W. N. Sullivan says
that Beethoven's *Coriolan* ends – 'in utter darkness': the
darkness of history, from which Shakespeare finally absconded – with *Cymbeline*. I cannot accept Bradley's hint to make
this the bridge-head towards the Romances: but I rejoice to
concur with Mr. Eliot: *one of* Shakespeare's most assured
aristic successes – as perfect in control as *1 Henry IV*.

SOURCE: extracts from '*Coriolanus*', in *Angel with Horns*
(1961) pp. 235–43, 249–52.

NOTES

1. *Characters of Shakespear's Plays* (1817) [see Part One – Ed.].
2. See the 'Class War by the Avon', *Manchester Guardian* (21
March 1952).
3. He says this in the context of the comment that *Coriolanus* is,

'with *Antony and Cleopatra,* Shakespeare's most assured artistic success'. [See Eliot's comment, reprinted in Part One above.]

4. Like Brutus and Sicinius with the slave who brings the bad news from Antium: they want him whipped until he shares their desire to deny the inconvenient facts.

5. *Tragedy* (1924) p. 136.

6. *Shakespearean Tragedy,* p. 21.

7. *Lectures on Shakespeare* (1818) [reprinted above].

8. Examples are Marcius's statements about what he will do to Aufidius:

> Were half to half the world by th'ears, and he
> Upon my party, I'd revolt, to make
> Only my wars with him (i i 231–3);

and

> At Antium lives he? . . .
> I wish I had a cause to seek him there,
> To oppose his hatred fully (iii i 18–20).

Others are: Aufidius's early threat to murder Marcius 'were it/At home . . . even there/Against the hospital canon' (i i 24–6); and Marcius's assurance to his mother, as he leaves Rome in exile, that he 'Will or exceed the common or be caught/With cautelous baits and practice' (iv i 32–3). Here the irony is double: both things happen, but in no foreseeable sense.

G. K. Hunter

THE LAST TRAGIC HEROES
(1966)

The modern outlook which sees *King Lear* as the central Shakespearian statement, and the modern interest in the Last Plays as repositories of symbolic wisdom – these are not entirely separate aspects of modernity. For *Lear* is treasured as the play which, more than any other, tested and proved the 'positive values' of the Last Plays; it is this view, I suppose, that causes Traversi to speak of '*Lear* and the plays which follow: *Pericles, The Winter's Tale, The Tempest*, and even *Cymbeline*' – as if the subjects of this essay. *Timon, Macbeth, Coriolanus, Antony and Cleopatra*, had sunk without trace from the Shakespearian horizon.[1] It is one of my principal purposes here to complicate the relationship of *Lear* to the Last Plays by suggesting ways in which the group of 'Last Tragedies' acts as intermediary, charting the direction of Shakespeare's mind between the 'Great Tragedies' and the Romances.

The word which most clearly leads the modern eye straight from *Lear* to the Last Plays is the word 'reconciliation'.[2] *Lear* is seen as the greatest of the tragedies because it not only strips and reduces and assaults human dignity, but because it also shows with the greatest force and detail the process of restoration by which humanity can recover from this degradation. Lear is exiled from his throne, his friends, his dependants, his family, even from his own reason and his own identity:

Doth any here know me? This is not Lear:
Doth Lear walk thus? speak thus? Where are his eyes?
. . . . .

Who is that can tell me who I am? (I iv 246) [3]

But what is lost on one side of madness and exile is seen to become unimportant when set against what is discoverable on the further shore:

> We two alone will sing like birds i' th' cage
> . . . . .
> And take upon's the mystery of things
> As if we were God's spies.

When Lear leaves the warmth, the society, the 'civilization' of Gloucester's castle he might seem to be leaving behind him all of the little that is left to make life bearable. But the retreat into the isolated darkness of his own mind is also a descent into the seed-bed of a new life; for the individual mind is seen here as the place from which a man's most important qualities and relationships draw the whole of their potential. Lear continues to assert his innermost perceptions (that justice is a word with meaning, that there is an order in nature, broken by ingratitude and immorality), and continues to do so even when it is only through madness that he can pursue the tenor of his own significance, when it is only in this context that he can set at naught the palpable success of opposite views. But by preserving these 'mad' assumptions the hero is, in fact, preserving the substance of a moral life, of which comfort, dignity and society are only the shadows. . . .

The life of Alcibiades, who fled and conspired against his country, provides a natural bridge between Timon, who forecast his career (as Plutarch tells us), and Coriolanus, who formed his Roman 'parallel'. Certainly Shakespeare's *Coriolanus* provides the obvious instance of exile and hatred to be compared with that in *Timon*. And, again, the speech spoken at the point of exile serves to focus the attitude of the hero:

> You common cry of curs, whose breath I hate
> As reek o' th' rotten fens, whose loves I prize
> As the dead carcasses of unburied men

That do corrupt my air – I banish you.
    . . . Despising
For you the city, thus I turn my back;
There is a world elsewhere. (III iii 120)

The gesture is magnificent, but the same reservation still
applies: it is inhuman, or rather anti-human. The 'world
elsewhere' of Coriolanus does not turn out to be in the least
like Lear's world of introspective anguish and revaluation; it is
only the same Roman political world, at a certain
geographical remove, and equally resistant to the
monomaniac individual. And however proud that individual,
he continues to need a populace, a city, that accepts his
dominance. *Coriolanus* makes quite clear what is only implicit
in *Timon*: the political nature of the scrutiny to which these
later heroes are subjected. The aspirations of Hamlet,
Othello, and Lear relate centrally to their families; their principal effort is to comprehend and adjust the strains and tensions arising in that context; the wider sphere of politics is present only as a background.[4] But the difficulties of the later
heroes involve organized society in a much more direct way:
Macbeth, Coriolanus, Antony all feel the pressure to pursue a
political course which runs against their natural in-
dividualities. Moreover the 'family life' of Coriolanus, as of
Macbeth or Antony, is only a particular aspect of this general
social pressure. Volumnia, the type of the Roman matron,
sees home as a parade-ground for training in leadership; the
pressure of her love is always exercised for a political end.
Indeed the play shows a paucity of relationships which are entirely private in intention. One might indeed allow Virgilia to
be unswayed by public interests; but it is notorious that
Virgilia is the most ineffectual character in the play. There is
no evidence that her love is any more listened to than that of
Flavius the steward in *Timon*, who is dismissed as statistically
meaningless, too exceptional to count; in the political or social
contexts of these plays the humble and disinterested love of
the private individual can exercise little power, for the minds
of their heroes are too little attuned to such cadences. . . .
    Lear's curses when he goes into exile ask the gods to in-

tervene or at least to observe; Timon's only ask that the *human*
observances of religion (seen as symptoms of order) should
cease to exist. Coriolanus manages to curse his banishers
without mentioning the gods at all. The gods are invoked constantly, of course, even in this markedly secular play. There is
a notable example in Coriolanus's speech after his capitula-
tion in Act v

> Behold, the heavens do ope,
> The gods look down, and this unnatural scene
> They laugh at. (v iii 183)

But the gods who appear out of Coriolanus's heaven are quite
different from those who, in *Lear,* 'keep this dreadful pudder
o'er our heads'. Coriolanus's gods only reflect back the human
scene; most often, indeed, they appear to be the mere con-
veniences of Roman political faction;[5] certainly a gulf of irony
separates them from involvement in the tragedy of any one individual.

Their withdrawal from possible involvement further isolates
the hero, leaves him alone with his own standards and the
political urge to fulfil the sense of individual greatness in terms
of distinction from and dominion over his fellows. Unfor-
tunately for Coriolanus's fulfilment, the *distinction* and *dominion*
are not entirely compatible. He desires to be a nonpareil, to
behave

> As if a man were author of himself
> And knew no other kin.

He speaks of the people

> As if you were a god, to punish; not
> A man of their infirmity. (III i 81)

Like Timon, he denies reciprocity. 'He pays himself by being
proud', his wounds 'smart to hear themselves remembered'.
His condescensions are general, hardly at all concerned with
individuals. An episode, which seems to mirror Shakespeare's

desire to make this point obvious, is that in which we see
Coriolanus pleading for the exemption of a Volsci who had
once sheltered him – but he cannot remember his name. As
the bastard Faulconbridge tells us:

> . . . new made honour doth forget men's names:
> 'Tis too respective and too sociable. (*John,* I i 187)

Coriolanus's pretension to be a god takes him rather further
into action than does Timon's, and this undoubtedly reflects
his greater involvement in politics, his interest in leadership:

> He is their god; he leads them like a thing
> Made by some other deity than Nature,
> That shapes men better. (IV vi 90)

But his involvement is also his destruction. To fulfil his distinction above other men he has to seek dominion over them;
but he is bound to fail in this because the distinction is too
great; he is too inhuman. Indeed the more godlike he seeks to
be, the more *inhuman* he becomes. The play has very usefully
been seen in relation to Aristotle's celebrated dictum: 'He that
is incapable of living in a society is a god or a beast'; or (as the
Elizabethan translation expanded it): 'He that cannot abide
to live in company, or through sufficiency hath need of
nothing, is not esteemed a part or member of a Cittie, but is
either a beast or a God.'[6] The ambiguity of Aristotle's remark
is nicely adjusted to the ambiguity that I find in these last
tragedies, the moral ambiguity of heroes who are both godlike
and *inhuman.* The inhumanity of Coriolanus is conveyed to us
in terms both of a beast and of a machine. Sometimes the two
are combined as in the following:

he no more remembers his mother now than an eight-year-old horse.
The tartness of his face sours ripe grapes; when he walks, he moves
like an engine and the ground shrinks before his treading. He is able
to pierce a corslet with his eye, talks like a knell, and his hum is a
battery. He sits in his state as a thing made for Alexander. What he
bids be done is finished with his bidding. He wants nothing of a god
but eternity, and a heaven to throne in. (v iv 16)

Coriolanus, like Timon, and like Macbeth, searches for an *absolute* mode of behaviour, and like them he finds it; but the finding it is the destruction of humanity in him, as it was in them. And as far as it concerns personality, the process is as irreversible for Coriolanus as for Timon or Macbeth; he can, however, avoid that final stage, where the absoluteness of the individual is only to be guaranteed by the destruction of his society. He is unable to sustain the absoluteness of 'Wife, mother, child, I know not'; but I do not think we should see the collapse before Volumnia as a great triumph of human love.[7] The play's judgement on the beast-machine nature of 'absolute' man stands unchanged. Only death can chillingly enough satisfy the hunger for absoluteness; and the final scene in Corioli, with its ironic repetition of the political and personal pattern already set in Rome, makes it clear that nothing in Coriolanus has altered or can alter. Greatness is seen as a doubtful and destructive blessing; love is powerless to change it . . . .

The theme of exile, which bulks so large in these later tragedies, does not wither away when Shakespeare turns to the writing of the 'Romances'. Pericles, very obviously, lives his life around his exile; Belarius and Posthumus are exiled from the British Court; Perdita and Camillo live in banishment (though she does not know it); Prospero's exile provides the whole subject of *The Tempest*. The societies which exile these characters are all corrupt ones; but, as in the later tragedies, the corruption is viewed as something basic in human nature so that it has to be dealt with by compromise and acceptance rather than by extirpation. It is as if the figure of Timon were to be removed from the play that bears his name and the attitude of Alcibiades developed as the basis of the plot. The hero, whose quest for absoluteness has been scrutinized in these last tragedies and whose mode of life has been seen as inhuman, now ceases to be the magnetic centre of interest. *The Tempest* is rather exceptional in this respect and will be dealt with separately. Certainly *Cymbeline* and *The Winter's Tale* lack dominating central figures, whose developing feelings carry us along the main channel of the play's movement. In these plays (and in *The Tempest* and even *Pericles*

as well) it is in terms of the social embodiment of virtue that
the play develops, rather than towards the achievement of virtue in the individual conscience. We are less interested in the
'redemption' of Leontes or Posthumus than in the complex of
interests and attitudes inside which their redeemed lives will
have to be accommodated. The state of exile is not here (as in
Lear) an opportunity to discover the true quality of humanity;
it is rather that the structure of society is seen as coming to
recognize its need for the elements it has rejected. This is true
of *Timon* and *Coriolanus* as well; but there our point of view
remains closely attached to the exile himself; we see society's
repeated offers of compromise from his viewpoint and we
recognize that he owes it to his absoluteness to refuse them. In
the Last Plays the individual is seen much more as an inex-
tricable part of the social group, and his actions are followed
from that standpoint. Alonso's need for Prospero's comfort,
Leontes's for the friends and family he dispersed, and (most
clearly of all) Britain's need for soldiers like Belarius and
Posthumus, finds a natural answer in a restoration of the
original social alignments. This does not occur because the individual has changed in his exile; it is not even that society has
changed in any basic way. The mixture of good and evil is
much as it was; it is only that time has brought the unchanged
elements into a new arrangement. Clearly we are meant to rejoice at this; but (the mode of vicissitude so obvious in the construction of these plays serves to insist) time will change all
things again. Time himself tells us so when he appears before
us in *The Winter's Tale*:

> I, that please some, try all, both joy and terror
> Of good and bad, that makes and unfolds error
>   . . . so shall I do
> To' th' freshest things now reigning, and make stale
> The glistering of this present. (IV i 1)

Mutability is not an important theme in *Lear*; but the heroes
of the last tragedies all live within its scope, though they try to
outface it; the Last Plays accept it as basic and inevitable, and
the natural result is a diminution in the scope of the in-

dividuals who initiate action. The exiles of *Cymbeline* and *The Winter's Tale* return, not to take any 'absolute' revenges, but rather to accept again the society in which we first saw them – the place to which they belong.

It is only thematically that the situations of these plays are similar to those of the last tragedies. But in *The Tempest* Shakespeare returns also to a plot-line which is parallel. Prospero is exiled from political office, and exiled for an absoluteness of temperament which made him too much like a god and too little like a man. And the 'god' image is now more than a metaphor; Prospero's magic gives him the power to enact what the curses of Lear, Coriolanus and Timon only imagined:

> I will do such things –
> What they are yet I know not; but they shall be
> The terrors of the earth. (*King Lear,* II iv 283)

But here again (as, most notably, in *Coriolanus*) the power to execute such threats can only be bought at the price of inhumanity; Ariel's sense of what is proper to a man reveals the quality of the danger:

> Hast thou, which art but air, a touch, a feeling
> Of their afflictions, and shall not myself,
> One of their kind, that relish all as sharply,
> Passion as they, be kindlier mov'd than thou art?
> (*The Tempest,* v i 21)

Prospero's acceptance of *kindness* – the feeling of necessary fellowship between one member of the human *kind* and the rest of the species – implies the rejection of his earlier notion that he could isolate himself:

> being transported
> And rapt in secret studies. (*The Tempest,* I ii 76)

It also implies the rejection of his later delusion that he could change mankind, or execute justice upon it. The recognition here of the isolated individual's ultimate powerlessness picks up what I take to be the central theme of the later tragedies. The splendid self-will of the last tragic heroes existed in defiance of this recognition; and, given their celerity in dying, they may even be said to *defeat* it. For in death (and only in death) they are able to fix the image of greatness they lived by, and free it from the necessary decay of still-living things. The last tragedies explore that *splendour*; the Last Plays describe the quality of the *living*; both groups of plays accept that the two concepts will appear on opposite sides of the dramatic conflict; and it is this that gives their worlds their common and unique quality.

From the views advanced in this essay it follows that the Last Plays have to be greatly simplified before we can see them just as fables of reconciliation. Their relation to the last tragedies suggests a different point of view; the capacity to accept the world-as-it-is has had to be bought by a sacrifice of heroic pretensions, by a loss of confidence in the heroic individual. In reading the Last Plays we should feel the sense of this loss even as we rejoice in the sweetness of their reconciliations.

SOURCE: extracts from 'The Last Tragic Heroes', in *The Later Shakespeare,* eds J. R. Brown and Bernard Harris (1966) pp. 11–12, 16–17, 19–21, 25–8.

NOTES

1. Derek Traversi, *An Approach to Shakespeare* (1938) p. 102. Cf. his p. 112.

2. Bradley thought that *Coriolanus* and *Antony* were too concerned with reconciliation to be real tragedies (*Shakespearean Tragedy*, p. 84). Tillyard (*Shakespeare's Last Plays*, pp. 20 f.) quotes this and denies its truth. He is fairly representative of the modern position in finding the last tragedies to be a blind alley, from which Shakespeare escaped only when he came to *Cymbeline*: 'the hints of a regeneration in the mind of Othello count for more than all the dying ecstasies of Antony and Cleopatra or Coriolanus's yielding to his mother' (p. 21). In this view the Last Plays pick up the genuine reconciliations of the Great Tragedies, and thus 'develop the final phase of the tragic

pattern' (p. 20); for 'in the last three plays [*Cymbeline, Winter's Tale and Tempest*] the old order is destroyed as thoroughly as in the main group of tragedies' [Bradley's four, I suppose].

3. All quotations in this chapter are of Peter Alexander's text, with line references to the Globe edition.

4. Brutus might seem to be an exception to the division being attempted here: he is an 'early' hero, whose dramatic life is concerned with politics and hardly at all with family. But Brutus cannot justly be assimilated into the later group of heroes: his real life remains locked inside his self-consciousness; the political scene does not ever come to seem the whole of his life. His relationship with Portia remains set apart from his political life, and closer to his heart.

5. E.g. I i 191; I viii 6; I ix 8; II iii 142; III i 290; III iii 33; IV vi 36; v ii 104.

6. F. N. Lees, 'Coriolanus, Aristotle and Bacon', *R.E.S.*, I (1950) 114–25.

7. It has been so represented by Bradley and (more ecstatically) by G. Wilson Knight.

Kenneth Burke

THE DELIGHTS OF FACTION
(1966)

This paper will involve the safest and surest kind of prophecy;
namely: prophecy after the event. Our job will be to ask how
Shakespeare's grotesque tragedy, *Coriolanus*, 'ought to be'.
And we can check on the correctness of our prophecies by con-
sulting the text.

We begin with these assumptions: Since the work is a
tragedy, it will require some kind of symbolic action in which
some notable form of victimage is imitated, for the purgation,
or edification of an audience. The character that is to be
sacrificed must be fit for his role as victim; and everything
must so fit together that the audience will find the sacrifice
plausible and acceptable (thereby furtively participating in
the judgment against the victim, and thus even willing the victimage). The expectations and desires of the audience will be
shaped by conditions within the play. But the topics exploited
for persuasive purposes *within* the play will also have strategic
relevance to kinds of 'values' and 'tensions' that prevail *outside*
the play.

There is a benign perversity operating here. In one sense,
the aesthetic and the ethical coincide, since a way of life gives
rise to a moral code, and the dramatist can exploit this moral
code for poetic effects by building up characters that variously
exemplify the system of vices and virtues to which the code explicitly or implicitly subscribes. But in another sense, the
aesthetic and the ethical are at odds, since the dramatist can
transform our moral problems into sources of poetic entertainment. Any ethical 'thou shalt not' sets up the conditions for an

author to engage an audience by depicting characters that variously violate or threaten to violate the 'thou shalt not'. And many motivational conflicts that might distress us in real life can be transformed into kinds of poetic imitation that engross us. Thus in the realm of the aesthetic we may be delighted by accounts of distress and corruption that would make the moralist quite miserable.

The moral problem, or social tension, that is here to be exploited for the production of the 'tragic pleasure' is purely simply a kind of discord intrinsic to the distinction between upper classes and lower classes. However, a certain 'distance' could be got in Shakespeare's day by treating the problem in terms not of contemporary London but of ancient Rome. A somewhat analogous situation is to be seen in Euripides's tragedy of *The Trojan Women,* which appeared some months after the Athenians had destroyed the little island of Melos, though on its face the play was concerned with the Trojan war, the theme of the *Iliad.* When *Coriolanus* appeared, there had been a long history of suffering due to the Enclosure Acts by which many tenants had been dispossessed of their traditional rights to the land; and a year or two before, there had been a riot. Both of these plays may, in their way, have gained strictly contemporary relevance from the allusive exploiting of a 'timely topic'. But in any case, each was dealing with a distress of much longer duration, in Euripides's case the horrors of war, and in Shakespeare's case the *malaise* of the conflict between the privileged and the under-privileged, as stated in terms of a struggle between the patricians and plebeians of old Rome.

If we are going to 'dramatize' such a tension, we shall want first of all a kind of character who in some way helps *intensify* the tension. Where there are any marked differences in social status, in the situation itself there is a kind of 'built-in pride', no matter how carefully one might try to mitigate such contrasts. And despite polite attempts to gloss things over, the unresolved situation is intrinsically there. By the nature of the case, it involves *exclusions*.

But for our purposes the main consideration is this: Whereas a hostess, or a diplomat, or an ingratiating politician, or a public relations counsel might go as far as possible towards *toning down* such situations, the dramatist must work his cures by a quite different method. He must find ways to *play them up*. In some respect, therefore, this play will require a kind of character who is designed to help aggravate the uneasiness of the relationship between nobles and commoners.

For this aspect of his role, our chosen victim is obviously a perfect fit. In contrast with the suave Menenius, who has been addressing the mutinous citizens with such a cautious mixture of gravity and humor, our chosen victim's first words to the people are: 'What's the matter, you dissentious rogues,/ That, rubbing the poor itch of your opinion,/ Make yourselves scabs?' Thereafter, again and again, his gruff (or, if you will, arrogant) manner of speaking is designed to point up (for the audience) the conflict intrinsic to the class distinctions with which the play is 'drastically' concerned. (It's well to recall here that, in earlier medical usage, a 'drastic' was the name for the strongest kind of 'cathartic'. Also, the word derives etymologically from the same root as 'drama'.)

The Greek word *hubris* sometimes translates best as 'pride', sometimes as 'excess'. And in Athenian law *hubris* was also used to designate a civil offence, an insulting air of superiority, deemed punishable by death. When you note how neatly all three meanings come together in the role of Coriolanus, I think you will realize at least one reason why I find the play so fascinating. The grotesque hero is *excessively* downright, forthright, outright (and even, after his fashion, upright), in his unquestioned assumption that the common people are intrinsically inferior to the nobility. Indeed, though the word 'noble' suggests to most of us *either* moral *or* social connotations, Coriolanus takes it for granted that only the *socially* noble can have nobility of any sort. (The word appears about 76 times in the play. In half of these contexts it is applied to Coriolanus himself. And, to my knowledge, it is never used ironically, as with Mark Antony's transformations of the word 'honourable'.) Coriolanus is excessive in ways that prepare the audience to relinquish him for his role as scapegoat, in accentuating a trait that the audience also shares with him, though seldom so avowedly.

More 'prophesying after the event' is still to be done. But first, perhaps we should pause to give a generalized outline of the plot, having in mind the kind of tension (or factional malaise) that the drama would transform into terms of purgative appeal:

After having gained popular acclaim through prowess in war, a courageous but arrogant patrician, who had been left fatherless when young and was raised by his mother, is persuaded by his mother to sue for high political office. In campaigning, he alienates the plebeians who, goaded by his political rivals, condemn him to exile. When in exile, making an alliance with the commander of the armies he had conquered, he leads a force against his own country. But before the decisive battle, during a visit by his closest relatives, his mother persuades him not to attack. In so doing, she unintentionally sets in motion the conditions whereby the allied commander, whom he had formerly vanquished and who envies his fame, successfully plots his assassination.[1]

It is impressive how perfectly the chosen victim's virtues and vices work together, in fitting him for his sacrificial function. The several scenes in the first act that build up his prowess as a soldier not only endow him with a sufficient measure of the heroics necessary for tragic dignification. They also serve to make it clear why, when he returns to Rome and, against his will, consents to seek the office of consul, he is bound to be a misfit. Shakespeare himself usually gives us the formula for such matters. It is stated by the Tribune, Brutus, in I I I iii: Get him angry, for

>   He hath been used
> Ever to conquer, and to have his worth
> Of contradiction. Being once chafed, he cannot
> Be reined again to temperance; then he speaks
> What's in his heart, and that is there which looks
> With us to break his neck.

He is not the 'war games' kind of military man, not the 'computer mentality'; thus we spontaneously accept it that his valiant though somewhat swashbuckling ways as a warrior will make him incompetent in the wiles of peaceful persuasion, which the wily Shakespeare so persuasively puts in a bad light, *within* the conditions of the play, by his treatment of the Tribunes. Though Shakespeare's theatre is, from start to finish, a masterful enterprise in the arts of persuasion, high among his resources is the building of characters who are weak in such devices. Indeed, considered from this point of view, Coriolanus's bluntness is in the same class with Cordelia's fatal inability to flatter Lear. Later we shall find other reasons to think of Lear in connection with Coriolanus's railings. Meanwhile, note how the Tribunes' skill at petition is portrayed as not much better than mere cunning, even though somewhat justified by our high-born goat's arrogance in his dealings with the commoners. He finds it impossible even to simulate an attitude of deference. And once we have his number, when he sets out to supplicate, armed with the slogan, 'The word is "mildly",' the resources of dramatic irony have already prepared us for the furious outbursts that will get the impetuous war-hero banished from Rome, a climax capped perfectly by his quick rejoinder, 'I banish you!' As a fearless fighter, he is trained to give commands and to risk his life, not to supplicate. And the better to build him up, in the role of the Tribunes Shakespeare makes the art of political supplication seem quite unsavory.

All told, Coriolanus's courage and outspokenness make him a sufficiently 'noble' character to dignify a play by the sacrificing of him. And excessive ways of constantly reaffirming his assumption that only the *social* nobility can be *morally* noble indicts him for sacrifice. But more than this is needed to make him effectively yieldable. . . .

Fundamentally, then, the play exploits to the ends of dramatic entertainment, with corresponding catharsis, the tension intrinsic to a kind of social division, or divisiveness, particularly characteristic of complex societies, but present to some degree in even the simplest modes of living. (I take it that the presence of a priesthood or similar functionaries dealing with things of this world in terms of a 'beyond', is on its face evidence that a society is marked by some degree of social differentiation, with corresponding conflicts of interest. And at the very least, even tribes that come closest to a homogeneous way of life are marked by differentiation between the work of men and women or between youth and age.)

This malaise, which affects us all but which in varying degrees and under varying circumstances we attempt to mitigate, is here made insultingly unforgettable. Coriolanus's *hubris* (whether you choose to translate it as 'pride' or as 'excessiveness') aggravates the situation constantly. And when he dies (after a change of heart that enables us to pity him even while we resent his exaggerated ways of representing our own less admirable susceptibilities, with their corresponding 'bad conscience'), he dies as one who has taken on the responsibility and has been appropriately punished. Thereby we are cleansed, thanks to his overstating of our case.

Along with this tension, which is of long duration in societies, I considered the likelihood that, when the play originally appeared, it also exploited a 'timely topic', the unrest caused by the Enclosure Acts, when new men of means took over for sheep-raising much land that had traditionally been available to small farmers, and these 'legally' dispossessed tenants were in a state of great frustration. Many were starving while the monopolists were being made into patricians. It was a time when many *nouveaux-riches* were being knighted – and as Aristotle points out, it is *new* fortunes that people particularly resent.

An ironic turn of history has endowed this play with a new kind of 'timely topic', owing to the vagaries of current dictatorships. But I would incline to contend that this 'new immediacy' is more apparent than real. In the first place, Coriolanus isn't a good fit for the contemporary pattern because the frankness of his dislike for the common people would make him wholly incompetent as a rabble-rouser. A modern demagogue might secretly share Coriolanus's prejudices – but he certainly would not advertise the fact as Coriolanus did. His public heart would bleed for the poor, even while he was secretly shipping state funds to a Swiss bank, against the day when his empire would collapse, and he would flee the country, hoping to spend his last years in luxurious retirement on the Riviera. Presumably our nation is always in danger of pouring considerable funds down such rat-holes. Thus, I feel that the attempt to present *Coriolanus* in the light of modern conditions can never quite succeed, since these conditions tend rather to conceal than to point up the cultural trends underlying its purgative use of the tension between upper and lower classes. Or should we call it a 'tension behind the tension'? I have in mind a situation of this sort:

The Renaissance was particularly exercised by Machiavelli because he so accurately represented the transvaluation of values involved in the rise of nationalism. A transvaluation was called for, because *religion* aimed at *universal* virtues, whereas the virtues of *nationalism* would necessarily be *factional*, in so far as they pitted nation against nation. Conduct viewed as vice from the standpoint of universal religious values might readily be viewed as admirable if it helped some interests prevail over others. This twist greatly exercised Machiavelli. But though (from the universal point of view) nations confront one another as factions, from the standpoint of any one nation factionalism is conceived in a narrower sense, with nationalism itself taking over the role of the universal.

In Shakespeare's day, as so many of his plays indicate, the kind of *family* factionalism that went with feudal relationships was being transformed into the kind of *class* factionalism that would attain its 'perfection' (if we may apply that term to so turbulent a development) in the rise of nationalism, with its drive towards the building of the British Empire. And here Shakespeare tackled this particular tangle of motives in a remarkably direct manner, except of course for the kind of 'distance' (with corresponding protection) the play got by treating the subject in terms of ancient Rome rather than his contemporary London.

All told, the motivation splits into four overlapping loci: national, class, family, individual. And in *Coriolanus* we witness a remarkably complex simplification of these issues, dramatically translated into terms of action and character.

Individualism may come and go, but there is a compelling sense in which the individual is always basic. The centrality of the nervous system is such that each of us is unique (each man's steak and his particular toothache being his own and no one else's). And even those who are killed *en masse* nonetheless die one by one. Symbolicity (by assigning proper names and attesting to the rights of private ownership) strongly punctuates this physical kind of individuality. And Shakespeare adds his momentous contribution by building so many plays on the 'star' system, with a titular role. I think it is safe to say that *Coriolanus* most thoroughly meets this description. Think of such lines as: 'O, me alone! Make you a sword of me?' (I vi); 'Alone I fought in your Corioles walls' (I vii); 'Alone I did it.' (v vi) – or his resolve to stand 'As if a man were author of himself' (v iii) – or a Tribune's grudging tribute to him: 'He has no equal' (I i) – or his own mother's formula: 'You are too absolute' (III ii). And the play backs up such statements by incessantly making him the center of our attention whether he is on the stage or off.

Yet even his name is not his own, but derives from the sacking of a city. And when he is threatening to lead an army against Rome, he does not know himself; and the sympathetic Cominius tells us (v i) that he 'forbade all names./ He was a kind of nothing, titleless,/ Till he had forged himself a name o' th' fire/ of burning Rome' – and that's precisely what, in obedience to his mother's pleadings, he did not do.[2] Incidentally, the longer one works with this text, the more ingenious Shakespeare's invention seems when, just before Coriolanus is killed, he *apologizes* because he had fallen into a rage: 'Pardon me, lords, 'tis the first time ever/ I was forced to scold.' But he is addressing the *lords* of Antium, not the commoners. Shortly thereafter the Conspirators will shout, 'Kill, kill, kill, kill, kill him!' thereby, as they slay, modifying poor impotent Lear's line, 'Then, kill, kill, kill, kill, kill, kill!' (IV vi 192).

But such considerations bring us to the next locus of motives, the *familial,* which the play brings to a focus in the 'mother, wife, child' formula, used variously by Menenius (v i 28–9), himself (v ii 78), and Volumnia (v iii 101), hers being the most effective, when she bewails the sight of him for 'Making the mother, wife, and child to see/ The son, the husband, and the father tearing/ His country's bowels out'. Yet to say as much is to move us almost as quickly into the realm of *class* and *nation,* since his family identity was so intensely that of a *patrician,* and his individualistic ways of being a patrician had brought him into conflict with all Rome.

Here you confront the true poignancy of his predicament, the formula being: individualistic prowess, made haughty towards the people by his mother's training, and naturally unfit for the ways of peaceful persuasion with regard to the citizenry as a whole. The *class* motive comes to a focus ter-ministically in the manipulations that have to do with the key word, 'noble'. But the *nation* as motive gets its forceful poignancy when the play so sets things up that Coriolanus maneuvers himself and is maneuvered into a situation whereby this individualist, mother-motivated, patrician patriot is all set to attack his own country, which at the beginning of the play he had defended with such signal valor, despite his invective against the commoners. As Granville-Barker has well said: 'Play and character become truly tragic only when Marcius, to be traitor to Rome, must turn traitor to himself.'

Yet, so far as I can see, the treatment of this motivational tangle (individual–family–class–nation) is not in itself 'cathartic', unless one uses the term in the Crocean sense rather than the Aristotelian. (That is, I have in mind the kind of relief that results purely from the well-ordered presentation of an entanglement. Such a complexity just *is*. But Shakespeare transforms this motionless knot into terms of an irreversible narrative sequence, the 'cure' here residing not in a sacrifice as such, but rather in the feeling of 'getting somewhere' by the sheer act of expression, even though the scene centered in conditions when Coriolanus was totally immobilized, a quite unusual state for so outgoing a character.) My soundest evidence for catharsis of this sort (whereby the sheer unfolding of expression can impart a kind of relief to our kind of animal, that lives by locomotion) is the nursery rhyme:

> The grand old Duke of York
> He had ten thousand men
> He marched them up to the top of the hill
> Then he marched them down again.

> And when they were up they were up
> And when they were down they were down
> And when they were only halfway up
> They were neither up nor down.

I'm among the company of those who would call *Coriolanus* a 'grotesque' tragedy. So our final problem is to make clear just wherein its grotesqueness resides, and how this quality might also contribute to its nature as medicinal.

Obviously, in contrast with the typical sacrificial victims of Greek tragedy, Coriolanus rather resembles a character in a satyr-play. He is almost like a throwback to the kind of scurrilities that Aristotle associates with the origins of the tragic iamb, in relation to the traditional metre of lampoons. (See *Poetics* IV.) So some critics have called it a 'satiric' tragedy. But 'grotesque' seems closer, since Coriolanus is *not* being satirized. The clearest evidence that he is being presented as a *bona fide* hero is the fact that *every* person of good standing in the play admires him or loves him and is loyal to him, despite his excesses. What does all this mean?

Still considering the problem from the standpoint of *tensions* and their exploitation for dramatic effects (that is to say, poetic delight), can we not find another kind of tension exploited here for medicinal purposes? It concerns the function of Coriolanus as a 'railer', a master of vituperation. Dramaturgically, such a figure is at the very least of service in the sense that, by keeping things stirred up, he enables the dramatist to fish in troubled waters. When a cantankerous character like Coriolanus is on the stage (and Shakespeare turns up many such), there is a categorical guaranty that things will keep on the move. Yet, beyond that sheerly technical convenience (whereby Coriolanus does in one way what Iago does in another, towards keeping a play in motion), there is the possibility that such a role in itself may be curative, as a symbolic remedy for one particular kind of repression typical of most societies.

I might best make my point by quoting some remarks I made elsewhere about another scurrilous tragic victim,

Shakespeare's Timon of Athens. There, however, the cut is different. Coriolanus throughout is respectful to the patricians and directs his insults only to the plebeians. But Timon, beginning as a great lover of mankind, ends as a total misanthrope. These paragraphs bear upon Timon's possible appeal as vilifier in the absolute:

Invective, I submit, is a primary 'freedom of speech', rooted extralinguistically in the helpless rage of an infant that states its attitude by utterances wholly unbridled. In this sense, no mode of expression could be more 'radical', unless it be the closely allied motive of sheer *lamentation,* undirected wailing. And perhaps the sounds of contentment which an infant makes, when nursing or when being bedded or fondled, mark the pre-articulate origins of a third basic 'freedom', *praise.*

Among these three, if rage is the infantile prototype of invective, it is a kind of 'freedom' that must soon be subjected to control, once articulacy develops. For though even praise can get one into trouble (for instance, when one happens to praise A's enemy in the presence of A, who happens also to be both powerful and rancorous); and though lamentation can on occasion be equally embarrassing (if one is heard to lament a situation among persons who favor it), invective most directly invites pugnacity, since it is itself a species of pugnacity.

Obviously, the Shakespearean theatre lends itself perfectly to the effects of invective. Coriolanus is an excellent case in point. Even a reader who might loathe his politics cannot but be engrossed by this man's mouthings. Lear also has a strong measure of such appeal, with his impotent senile maledictions that come quite close to the state of man's equally powerless infantile beginnings. . . . And that delightfully run-down aristocrat, Falstaff, delights us by making a game of such exercises.

Though one has heard much about the repression of sexual motives, in our average dealings invective is the mode of expression most thoroughly repressed. This state of affairs probably contributes considerably to such 'cultural' manifestations as the excessive violence on TV, and the popular consumption of crude political oratory. Some primitive tribes set aside a special place where an aggrieved party can go and curse the king without fear of punishment (though if our society had such an accommodation, I'm sure there'd be a

secret agent hiding behind every bush). In earlier days the
gifted railer was considered invaluable by reason of his expert
skill at cursing the forces deemed dangerous to the welfare of
the tribe (see on this point some interesting data in Robert C.
Elliott's book, *The Power of Satire: Magic, Ritual, Art,* and above
all his suggestive and entertaining Appendix on 'The Curse').
At the very least, in figures such as Coriolanus we get much of
such expressiveness, without the rationale of magic, but under
the 'controlled conditions' of a drama about political unrest.
And if he dies of being so forthright, downright, and outright
(if not exactly upright), it's what he 'deserved'. For as regards
the *categorical* appeal of invective, it resides not so much in the
particular objects inveighed against, but in the sheer process
of inveighing. And Coriolanus, like Timon, has given vent
with fatal over-thoroughness to untoward tendencies which, in
our 'second nature', we have 'naturally' learned to repress.

In conclusion, then, where are we? We have been considering
Coriolanus's qualifications as a scapegoat, whose symbolic
sacrifice is designed to afford an audience pleasure. We have
suggested: (1) His primary role as a cathartic vessel resides in
the excessiveness with which he forces us to confront the dis-
criminatory motives intrinsic to society as we know it. (2)
There is a sheerly 'expressive' kind of catharsis in his way of
giving form to the complexities of *family, class,* and *national*
motives as they come to a focus in the self-conflicts of an *individual*. (3) There is the 'curative' function of invective as
such, when thus released under controlled conditions that
transform the repressed into the expressed, yet do us no
damage. And (4) the attempt has been made to consider the
'paradox of substance' whereby the chosen scapegoat can 'be
himself' and arrive at the end 'proper to his nature' only if
many events and other persons 'conspire' to this end, the persons by being exactly the kind of persons they are, and the
events by developing in the exact order in which they do
develop. To sum it all up, then, in a final formula for tragic
catharsis: (a formula that I wrote with such a play as
Coriolanus in mind, though it could be applied *mutatis mutandis*
to other texts): [3]

Take some pervasive unresolved tension typical of a given social order (or of life in general). While maintaining the 'thought' of it in its over-all importance, reduce it to terms of personal conflict (conflict between friends, or members of the same family). Feature some prominent figure who, in keeping with his character, though possessing admirable qualities, carries this conflict to excess. Put him in a situation that points up the conflict. Surround him with a cluster of characters whose relations to him and to one another help motivate and accentuate his excesses. So arrange the plot that, after a logically motivated turn, his excesses lead necessarily to his downfall. Finally, suggest that his misfortune will be followed by a promise of general peace.

SOURCE: extracts from '*Coriolanus* – and the Delights of Faction', *The Hudson Review*, XIX (1966) 185–9, 195–202. Reprinted in *Language as Symbolic Action* (Univ. of California Press, 1966).

NOTES

1. To bring out the steps of the plot by proposing titles for the five acts:

I. 'Coriolanus Gets His Name.' Or, 'His Mother's Son.' The first three scenes establish successively: his arrogance towards the people, his rivalry with Aufidius, his relation to his mother. The rest establish his prowess as a warrior (by the sacrifice of supernumerary victims) – and at the end, Aufidius sets the arrows of our expectation by telling of his resolve to dispose of our hero, in whatever way he can.

II. 'The People's Misgivings.' Or, 'The Tribunes Start Trouble.' 'Know, good mother,/ I had rather be their servant in my way/ Than sway them in theirs.' (He, who is at home with force, can't petition. He can't capitalize on his valor by displaying his wounds.) Here petition, as a form of persuasion, is presented in a bad light. It is the trade of the Tribunes. (Quite different from Socrates's prayers to Peitho.)

III. 'Coriolanus Banished.' Or, 'Coriolanus Banishes His Banishers.' In the first scene, Menenius gives us the formula: 'He has been bred i' th' wars/ . . . and is ill schooled/ In bolted language.' ('Bolted' means 'sifted', 'refined'.) When he says, in the second scene, 'The word is "mildly",' things are set up for his fatal outburst of rage.

IV. 'Coriolanus and Aufidius Allied.' Or, 'Alliance With the Enemy.' This being, as usual, the pity act in a Shakespearean tragedy, there is the poignancy of Coriolanus's departure. As regards the pointing of the arrows, all comes to a focus in Aufidius's aside: 'When, Caius, Rome is thine,/ Thou art poor'st of all; then shortly art thou mine.'

V. 'The Fatal Petition.' Now the theme of supplication comes to fulfillment. But ironically. For Coriolanus, who has been an ineffective suppliant, yields to his mother's entreaties, and thereby helps set up the situation that leads to his death.

2. Since he got his name 'Coriolanus' from his role in the destruction of Corioli, had he persisted in his campaign against Rome he could have been called none other than 'Romanus'!

3. Originally printed in *Arts in Society*, II 3 (1963).

Derek A. Traversi

'THE WORLD OF CORIOLANUS' (1969)

It would be harder to imagine a greater gulf than that separating the world of *Coriolanus* from the one of *Antony and Cleopatra*. The poetry of the latter play takes in with effortless ease the fortunes of a world in conflict, the former achieves its effects through intense concentration upon the familiar and the material.[1] Its prevailing imagery is rigid and unadorned, more appropriate to a village or a country town than to a capital of historical significance. The aristocratic ladies of Rome sit at home upon their 'stools'[2] and the people carry 'bats and clubs' (I i) to their riots; the action abounds in references to simple pastimes, such as 'bowls' (v ii), or turns upon disputes over the immediate necessities of life, 'corn', 'coal', and 'bread' (I i and *passim*). To a great extent the difference is imposed by history; whereas the world providing the background to Antony's fall concerned an empire that spanned the known world, the one conditioning the tragedy of Coriolanus is concentrated within the limits of a city and its immediate surroundings and reflects the tension between its classes, the threat to its indispensable unity.

This tension, this threat, marks the struggle for power in a world at once restricted and pitiless. The sense of this struggle is conveyed almost immediately by the patrician Menenius when, in rebuking the citizenry for their rebellion against constituted authority, he embarks upon a fable which reveals more than he can himself realize of the true situation in Rome. The central image of the fable, derived from Plutarch, but considerably developed, is that of the functioning of the human body in its related parts:

> There was a time when all the body's members
> Rebell'd against the belly: thus accused it:
> That only like a gulf it did remain
> I' the midst of the body, idle and unactive,
> Still cupboarding the viand, never bearing
> Like labour with the rest; where the other instruments
> Did see and hear, devise, instruct, walk, feel,
> And, mutually participate, did minister
> Unto the appetite and affection common
> Of the whole body. (I i)

The wording of the parable tends to the transformation of a political commonplace, a theoretical vindication of natural 'degree', into a criticism, not of this attitude or that, but of Roman society itself. The impression of a general obstruction of all vital activity communicates itself through the unhealthy stagnation of 'idle and unactive', the coarseness of 'cupboarding'. These effects are set against the very noticeable livening of the verse when Menenius turns to the 'other instruments', the senses and active faculties of the body which represent, however, not the class he is defending but its enemies. These contrasted elements, thus concentrated, in a manner profoundly typical of the play, upon images of food and digestion, answer to the real state of the Roman polity. Stagnation and mutual distrust, mirroring the ruthlessness of contrary appetites for power, are the principal images by which we are introduced to the public issues of *Coriolanus*. . . .

This initial confrontation does not lead immediately to disaster. Rome's need of its warrior hero is stressed by news of the Volscian rising, which he welcomes as offering the authorities an opportunity to 'vent' the 'musty superfluity' of the state into a foreign adventure. But before Marcius is set in motion on the first, ascendant stage of his career, we are offered a revealing glimpse of his family circle, and more particularly of the mother whose demands upon him will determine the course of his tragedy. The First Citizen has already linked these demands to his martial prowess when he has said, in explanation of his service to Rome, that 'he did it to please his mother and to be partly proud' (I i). This pride proceeds from a strange mixture of solicitude and ruthlessness, possession and renunciation in Volumnia's own nature. Remembering 'the only son of her womb' as 'a tender-bodied child', the repository of all her affection, whom 'for a day of kings' entreaties' she would not 'sell an hour from her beholding', she can yet recall how she found herself 'considering how honour would become such a person' and how she directed his youth to a stern and fanatical conception of duty. Fearing that her son might 'picture-like hang by the wall', she willed that he should 'seek danger where he was likely to find fame'; and as she dwells on this decision, her thoughts rise to a severe exaltation of the sacrifice which she imposed upon her affection and which she is now determined to assert as freely and responsibly taken. 'To a cruel war *I sent him:* from whence he returned, his brows bound with oak' (I iii). Seen in this way, the hero's glory becomes the reflection of his mother's purpose, a compensation for the sacrifice which sent him forth, in despite of a mother's natural attachment, to affirm in dedication to 'honour' the exalted destiny she has chosen for him.

Before long, and in the course of the same scene, this concentration rises to a ruthlessly masculine participation in her son's achievements. Her ideal, to which he will amply correspond, ceases to be human, becomes the exaltation of an engine impersonally dedicated to destruction. Marcius will 'pluck Aufidius down by the hair', be shunned by his enemies as children 'fly from a bear'; as she imagines him defying the Volscians it is as if she were herself engaged in the bloody work, sharing in its ruthless fascination. The picture of her victorious son –

> his bloody brow
> With his mail'd hand then wiping, forth he goes
> Like to a harvest-man that's task'd to mow
> Or all, or lose his hire – (I iii)

balancing against a touch of spontaneous poetry the grim aspect of the warrior bathed in blood, is not allowed to deflect

her from the dedication which her nature so insistently
demands. When Virgilia, with wifely concern, pleads 'no
blood', her answer is ferociously concentrated on the idea
which entirely possesses her. 'Away, you fool': the repudiation
ends in a glorification of bloodshed more fantastic and inhuman than all that has gone before:

> the breasts of Hecuba,
> When she did suckle Hector, look'd not lovelier
> Than Hector's sword when it spit forth blood
> At Grecian sword, contemning. (I iii)

Even at this moment of supreme dedication to her martial
ideal, the thought of maternity lingers on as an obsessive
presence in the mother's mind. Sacrificed to the masculine
cult of 'honour', its survival emphasizes the moral in-
completeness which will bring her son to ruin.

These narrow and perverse intensities are not allowed to
pass without implicit comment. This is provided by Volumnia's picture of her grandson in the nursery:

O' my word, the father's son; I'll swear, 'tis a very pretty boy. O' my
troth, I looked upon him o' Wednesday half an hour together; has
such a confirm'd countenance. I saw him run after a gilded
butterfly; and when he caught it, he let it go again; and after it
again; and over and over he comes, and up again; catched it again:
or whether his fall enraged him, or how 'twas, he did so set his teeth,
and tear it; O, I warrant, how he mammocked it! (I iii)

There could be no better comment on the deadly lack of feeling which has surrounded Marcius from birth and of which
his child, in turn, partakes; the boy is, after all, 'the father's
son'. To complete the effect we need only the crushing, if unconscious, irony implied in Valeria's observation, 'Indeed, la,
'tis a noble child'. The entire episode, with its glimpse of the
father's narrow and inhuman concentration mirrored in the
precocious savagery of his child, makes a revealing introduction to the episodes of war which follow.

All this, however, acutely and finely observed as it is, is only

one side of the picture which this strangely inconsistent hero
presents. On the other, and not less real, we are made to feel
in this same exclusive family circle the reality of an affection so
intense, so concentrated, that it binds the son irrevocably to
his mother, making him indeed a hero and the savior of his city, but finally, in its onesided possessiveness, leading to his
ruin. Subject from birth to the relentness pressure of his
mother's affection, Coriolanus has grown into a man at once
capable of the deepest feeling and unable to give it free expression, even at times ashamed of what he feels: the man who at
one moment can salute his wife, on his return from the
hazards of war, with a marvelous, shy tenderness –

My gracious silence, hail!
Would'st thou have laugh'd had I come coffin'd home,
That weep'st to see me triumph? Ah, my dear,
· Such eyes the widows in Corioli wear,
And mothers that lack sons – (II i)

and who, at another, thrusts aside his own heroic deeds,
bashfully and awkwardly, as scarcely worthy of mention or
recall: in other words, at once a hero, an inexorable fighting
machine, and a childishly naïve and undeveloped human being. The play is consistent in presenting Coriolanus under
both these aspects. As a warrior, neither material rewards nor
normal pity can make him other than a superb but inhuman
engine of war placed at his country's service; as a son, his intimate resolution is helpless before his mother's successive
demands upon him, and he is brought to isolation and disaster
by following the strain of natural sensibility which lies present
in the deepest recesses of his nature, but which he has never
really been brought to consider or to understand.

This combination of nobility and weakness is fully revealed
in its true nature when Coriolanus returns to Rome to
celebrate his victory at Corioli. The victory has been won in
the name of his city's aristocracy, the ruling patrician class to
which he is so proudly conscious of belonging, and in the pur-
suit of personal rivalry with Tullus Aufidius. The common
soldiery whom he regards with contempt as the 'musty' raw

material for slaughter have had no share in his exploits: so
much so that, when he rallies them on the field of battle, they
watch him go, as they think, to meet his fate behind the closing gates of the enemy city to the accompaniment of an indifferent comment: 'To the pot, I warrant him' (I iv). Now, as
he receives the offer of supreme authority in Rome, the virtues
which have made him a hero are balanced against his lack of
flexibility and human understanding, both wonderfully present in the great eulogy with which Cominius, his peer and
colleague, proposes him for the supreme office. The speech
underlines by its weight and gravity a decisive turning point in
the action. At this dangerous moment in the hero's career,
when his triumph and his ruin stand face to face, it stresses the
energy, the splendor of superabundant power, made manifest
in his victorious campaign. This impression of life is conveyed
not only in the triumphant image which mirrored his youthful
rise to glory – 'he waxed like a sea' – but in the intensity which
records in terms of vivid sensation his inexhaustible response
to the challenge of danger:

> the din of war 'gan pierce
> His ready sense; then straight his doubled spirit
> Re-quickened what in flesh was fatigate. (II ii)

This magnificent rousing of the spirit to the sounds of conflict
carries us back to the nostalgia felt by Othello for 'the
spirit-stirring drum, the ear-piercing fife' (O., III iii); both
passages convey, in their respective evocations of what is, for
each of these heroes, life and fulfillment, a sense of the imagination reaching out to the confines of sensual intensity.
The exaltation of the warrior as he advances toward his goal,
the crowning of triumph with the 'garland' of victory, im-
presses itself through a fine keenness of sensation, this play's
parallel to that which, at certain moments, transfigures the
utterances of passion in Antony and Cleopatra.

Just, however, as Antony and Cleopatra does not finally invite
to uncritical romantic surrender, so the celebration of the
soldierly virtues in Coriolanus is balanced by a contrary impression. Side by side with its superb sense of vital energy,

Cominius's speech asserts the presence of a dead heaviness, an almost grotesque insensibility. The expansive splendor of 'he waxed like a sea' is immediately qualified by the ponderous, dead impact of

> in the brunt of seventeen battles since,
> He *lurch'd* all swords of the garland; (II ii)

even as the hero attained with manhood the complete martial assertion of his being, the power so revealed converted itself into a heavy indifference to life. From the comparison, at once splendid and sinister, of the warrior to a 'vessel under sail', bearing down upon the lives which he regards as 'weeds', we pass to the evocation of his sword as 'death's stamp', invested with the destructive weight of a battering-ram. As the eulogy draws to its close, its object is converted into a mechanical instrument of carnage, indifferent to the ruin he has caused:

> from face to foot
> He was a thing of blood, whose every motion
> Was timed with dying cries. (II ii)

The impression of inhumanity is further reinforced by the irresistible impact with which the hero 'with a sudden reinforcement' *struck* Corioli 'like a planet'; the effect is to make Coriolanus no longer a mere soldier but an instrument of 'shunless destiny' launched against 'the *mortal* gates of the city'. In the word 'mortal' is contained not only a sense of the frailty of those who sought to bar his progress, but the protest of downtrodden life against the power which began as an affirmation of vital energy and is now revealed in ruthless dedication to destruction. Then, to balance the effect yet again, the machine quickens in response to new perils in the lines about 'the din of war' and the effect of 're-quickening' to which it leads: a revival followed, however, by the renewed callousness of

> he did
> Run reeking o'er the lives of men, as if
> 'Twere a perpetual spoil; (II ii)

until we are left, as Cominius bows to the acclamation which greets his close, with a final picture of Coriolanus pausing to 'pant' like a hot-blooded bull after his orgy of carnage.

On the tide of emotion which the speech rouses, Coriolanus is lifted to the culmination of his public glory. If he fails to remain there it is because his true enemy lies finally, not in those around him, but in himself. The prospect of addressing himself to the people produces in him a deep-seated, almost physical repugnance associated with the fear of finding himself 'naked', intimately exposed in his hidden weakness. In this reaction the tribunes see an opportunity which they hasten to press home. The people '*must* have their voices'; they will never 'bate one jot' of the 'ceremony' which they know to be their due. The growing rift is healed for the moment by Menenius and the hero is left to 'blush' boyishly and to express an unwillingness to 'brag' which, however creditable in itself, answers to motives deeper than he can readily understand. The entire situation is already variously and impossibly fragile. The demagogic demands of the tribunes are balanced by an unreasoning obstinacy in the warrior, who is being compelled, against every instinct of his stubborn nature, to exhibit his most intimate feelings to further ends which others have imposed upon him.

In this situation the final triumph of the hero's enemies is assured. Before they finally achieve their end, however, Coriolanus, feeling himself lost, at sea in a world too complicated for his understanding, turns, as he has always been accustomed to turn, to his mother, seeking from her a confirmation of what he regards as his sacred integrity, his belief in himself: only to find himself *there*, in the very place where all his confidence has rested, inexplicably betrayed. For it is indeed Volumnia who now strikes the decisive blow at his consistency by calling him 'too absolute' – as if he could be so in his own esteem – and by wrapping her counsel in what must strike him, being what he is, as a deep moral ambiguity. In war, she urges, it is in accordance with 'honour' to seem 'the same you are not' and to shape 'policy' accordingly; why then should it be 'less or worse' to do precisely this in an emergency of peace? From this opening, which he can only receive in

bewilderment ('Why force you this?'), she goes on to urge him
to dissimulation:

>   now it lies on you to speak
> To the people; not by your own instruction,
> Nor by the matter which your heart prompts you,
> But with such words that are but rooted in
> Your tongue, though but bastards and syllables
> Of no allowance to your bosom's truth. (III ii)

The wording of this advice is calculated to bring home to
Coriolanus the moral monstrosity, as it must seem to him,
which it implies. To tell such a man that he must speak, not
from the 'heart', according to the dictates of that 'honour'
which is life to him, but according to the promptings of expediency is to run counter to the self-respect, the narrow but
absorbing sense of fitness, for which he has been taught to live.
Most shocking of all is the assumption that dissembling is an
acceptable and even a necessary part of the warrior's oc-
cupation:

>   Now, this no more dishonours you at all
> Than to take in a town with gentle words,
> Which else would put you to your fortune and
> The hazard of much blood. (III ii)

The one-sidedness, the artificial simplicity, of the hero's attitude to his martial profession could hardly be more
devastatingly exposed. When his mother tells him,

>   I would dissemble with my nature, where
> My fortunes and my friends at stake required
> I should do so in honour, (III ii)

the notions of 'honour' and 'dissembling', hitherto so clearly
separated in his mind, are presented to him as intolerably
mingled, have become pointers to disorientation and inner
doubt.

The manner in which Volumnia goes on to depict the piece

of play acting she is urging upon her son can only add to his shame. His 'bonnet' is to be stretched out in supplication, his knee to be seen 'bussing the stones'; the 'waving' of his head must correct the impulse of the 'stout heart', which is to become

> humble as the ripest mulberry
> That will not hold the handling. (III ii)

Worst of all, the hero is to prostitute his soldiership, declaring himself the servant of the people and exhibiting himself as tongue-tied and unapt of speech:

> being bred in broils,
> Hast not the soft way which, thou dost confess,
> Were fit for thee to use, as they to claim,
> In asking their good loves. (III ii)

By the end of this harangue, Coriolanus is a hero shattered in his inner integrity, exposed to the play of forces which can have for him no intimate reality. It is supremely ironic that Volumnia, having achieved her purpose by tying up her son in doubt and self-mistrust, should claim at the last to have left him free: 'Do thy will.' In fact, his will is now for his friends and, above all, for her to dispose of. As he goes to meet the populace, with the words 'honour' and 'mildly' ringing inarticulate and clashing changes in his stunned thought, we know that they have prevailed. The consequences of their victory for Rome and for himself will emerge in the remaining course of the tragedy. . . .

The final confrontation between the hero and his family (v iii) is beyond doubt one of Shakespeare's most moving and eloquent creations. Coriolanus, bracing himself instinctively to meet the challenge which it implies, calls on his Volscian allies to witness what he intends to be a demonstration of his firmness; but when Volumnia actually stands before him, with his wife and child, a notable admission of natural feeling escapes his lips —

> I melt, and am not
> Of stronger earth than others – (v iii)

before he takes refuge in further emphatic denials of instinct
and family alike. The expression of these is, indeed, revealing.
Coriolanus seeks, by sheer emphasis of assertion, to return to
the simplicity of purpose which his being craves. Let the
Volscians, whom he has so often defeated in his country's service, 'plough Rome' and 'harrow Italy'. To 'obey instinct' by
accepting the validity of the intimate emotion he has just
allowed himself to reveal is – so he seeks to persuade himself –
to confess himself a 'gosling', incapable of asserting integrity
of will in his new situation. Self-depreciation here is a cover for
doubt and inner contradiction. To smother the powerful voice
of 'instinct' Coriolanus needs to postulate the impossible, to
assert that a man may be 'author of himself' and 'know no
other kin'. The effect is to make him a renegade, not only to
his city and to the family which has bred him, but – in a sense
deeper than he can fully understand – to his own being.

When he ceases to speak, enough has been said to show
where the hero's resolution will be vulnerable. The first indication of what is to come is a recognition of the clumsiness
with which, like a 'dull actor' who has forgotten his lines, he
moves toward the exposure of his 'full disgrace'. The admission leads naturally to a more personal expression of the
emotions which, do what he will to smother them, remain so
close to his heart. 'Best of my flesh', he salutes his wife, and
goes on to beg forgiveness for the 'tyranny' which his attitude
toward her implies; but, once feeling has thus forced its way to
the surface, he makes yet again to cover it, pleads to be
allowed to maintain the fiction he has chosen to present to the
world:

> do not say,
> For that, 'Forgive our Romans.' (v iii)

The plea, however, is already advanced in the name of a lost
cause, and the emotion he seeks to repudiate finds issue in a
further lyrical outburst which gains enormously by contrast

with Virgilia's reticence and his own assertions of iron sufficiency:

> O, a kiss
> Long as my exile, sweet as my revenge!
> Now, by the jealous queen of heaven, that kiss
> I carried from thee, dear, and my true lip
> Hath virgin'd it e'er since. (v iii)

Beneath the depth of feeling, the sense of a return, through emotions so long and so perversely excluded, to the natural foundations of the speaker's being, there lies a further revelation of character. The emphasis on virgin purity answers to an essential simplicity of nature: the simplicity which underlies, on its more positive side, the code of martial 'honour' for which he has lived and which he cannot, without involving himself in ruin, sever from its intimate inspiration. Because the simplicity is true, Coriolanus's downfall must affect us as truly tragic; because his own perverse choices have led him to deny it, a pitiless element of irony shadows his end.

Once so much has been admitted, the gesture of natural submission at once imposes itself:

> sink, my knee, i' the earth;
> Of thy deep duty more impression show
> Than that of common sons. (v iii)

There could be no better comment on the determination, so recently asserted, to show himself 'author' of his own decisions, autonomous, released from the ties of nature. As the hero's knee bends, a frame of tense and self-imposed rigidity bows to the reality it has sought to evade, even while it seeks, in a vestige of obstinate pride, to assert its devotion in terms more absolute than those afforded to the rest of men. The emphasis cannot conceal the reality of the transformation which is taking place under our eyes. Nature, so long and so vainly denied, has begun to reassert herself. The way is open for Volumnia to press her plea and to compass, through her

very success, the downfall which her son's choices have from
the first implied.

It is highly significant that Coriolanus should have gone so
far in admission before his mother has really had occasion to
marshal the full force of her arguments. In her marvelously
eloquent reply she pleads, in fact, for all the pieties that she
has instilled into him, which have made him what he is, and
which he has so unnaturally been brought to deny. Her plea
gains its end because, as we have already been shown, there is
nothing true, nothing but inner emptiness, beneath the resolution that the exile has sought to oppose to it. As she ceases, he
is left 'silent', holding her by the hand and contemplating the
sorry spectacle of his shattered integrity. When at last he
speaks, the effect is overwhelming in its recognition of personal disaster. 'O mother, mother,' he exclaims, "What have
you done?" (v iii) The question comes from one bewildered,
conscious not of a true resolution to his conflicting loyalties,
but of obscurely threatening deities who look down upon an
'unnatural scene' and 'laugh' at what they see. The sardonic
note which has throughout lent the scene a distinctive quality
finds issue at this point in a vision of life, as it presents itself to
the hero, finally desolate and meaningless:

> O my mother, mother! O!
> You have won a happy victory to Rome;
> But, for your son, believe it, O, believe it,
> Most dangerously you have with him prevail'd,
> If not most mortal to him. (v iii)

At this moment, if anywhere, we are face to face with the
tragic contradiction on which the entire action has rested.
Coriolanus's submission, made under the eyes of a withdrawn
and notably non-committal Aufidius, represents an affirmation of natural feeling, but one made in vacancy, which
answers to the pathetic crumbling of an impossible purpose
with nothing real or consistent to take its place. He has spared
Rome, but cannot in the nature of things return to it. The
patriot is left without a country to serve, the son, having
chosen a course which is now seen as in turn enslaving him, is

debarred from accompanying his mother. Uprooted, with a
strange, almost adolescent gesture of clumsiness, he turns
away for the last time from the women and the child before
him: turns away to what he knows already to be his ruin.
The ruin, indeed, is not long in coming. In the city he has
left forever, a new mood of 'merriment', of relief from tension,
makes itself felt in a poetic transformation which bursts the
iron bonds that have habitually restrained imagination in the
public scenes of the play. The messenger is as certain of the
truth of his tidings of peace as he is that 'the sun is fire', and he
follows up his assertion with a most graphic picture of the
returning tide –

Ne'er through an arch so hurried the blown tide – (v iv)

as the 'recomforted' swarm in jubiliation through the city
gates. 'All together', as the stage direction has it,

The trumpets, sackbuts, psalteries and fifes,
Tabors and cymbals and the shouting Romans
Make the sun dance. (v iv)

The restoration of peace, however, though it restores Roman
society to sane unity and produces these manifestations of life
and joy, is powerless to ward off the hero's own fate. Aufidius,
who no longer has any use for his former enemy, finds it easy
to accuse him of betraying his new masters. Returning to
Corioli, which he had once conquered in the name of Rome,
Coriolanus is taken unawares, surrounded and stabbed ig-
nominiously to death. His reaction, somewhat like that of
Othello before him, is a last pathetic glance back to the days of
his glory: the days when he had been a triumphant warrior in
the service of Rome, and before division had become the substance of his soul:

If you have writ your annals true, 'tis there,
That, like an eagle in a dove-cote, I
Flutter'd your Volscians in Corioli;
Alone I did it. (v vi)

'Alone': perhaps here, in the turning into a heroic virtue of
what is in fact a weakness, the isolation from his fellow men
which birth and prejudice have combined to impose upon
him, lies in great part the key to Coriolanus's tragedy. Both
the angry scolding and the attempt to reaffirm a lost dignity
represent some aspects of the truth about this strangely
divided, inopportune hero; and since these aspects do not har-
monize, since he cannot now hope to recover the shattered
simplicity which he abjured when he turned his back on his
city and his family, the tide of vengeance flows over him with
the repeated clamor of 'Kill' and Aufidius, in a last gesture of
gratuitous brutality, 'stands on his body' in triumph.

SOURCE: extracts from 'Coriolanus', in An Approach to
Shakespeare, 3rd ed. (1969) pp. 536–7, 542–9, 553–7.

NOTES

[Play-references in the notes of the original have been incorporated
in the text, with renumbering of the notes presented here – Ed.]

  1. This aspect of the poetry of Coriolanus has been well brought
out by G. Wilson Knight in The Imperial Theme (Oxford, 1930).
  2. Stage direction to I iii.

Reuben A. Brower

THE DEEDS OF
CORIOLANUS (1971)

> It is held
> That valor is the chiefest virtue and
> Most dignifies the haver

The modern reader feels less confident than the editors of the Folio in referring to *Coriolanus* as a 'tragedy', particularly just after reading *King Lear* or *Antony and Cleopatra,* plays many will regard as prime examples of that ever debatable term. George Bernard Shaw has called *Coriolanus* Shakespeare's 'finest comedy'; one critic has described it as a satire,[1] another as a debate[2] rather than a tragedy. Although we may consider none of these descriptions adequate, we can agree that when we call Coriolanus a 'tragedy', we mean something rather peculiar, something that was almost certainly not in the minds of Shakespeare's first editors. The aim of this chapter is to offer some clues toward defining that admirable 'peculiarity'.

I ARMS AND THE MAN

One fairly obvious clue is the closing processional speech, which . . . marks the death of a hero in the great tradition:

> Take him up.
> Help, three o' th' chiefest soldiers; I'll be one.
> Beat thou the drum, that it speak mournfully;
> Trail your steel pikes. Though in this city he
> Hath widowed and unchilded many a one,

Which to this hour bewail the injury,
Yet he shall have a noble memory.
Assist.   *Exeunt bearing the body of Marcius.*
           A dead march sounded.

An audience used to this type of conventional ending would be
better prepared than we to appreciate the special force of
'deeds' in the great encomium[3] spoken by Cominius in Act II
[quotes II ii 83–123, 125–31].

Let us consider the growth of the picture of Coriolanus in
this speech and, in particular, certain words and phrases important for defining the special character of his tragedy.
Menenius's comment at the end, 'right noble', is the key to the
encomium, and as in *Antony and Cleopatra,* one of the more important thematic expressions for interpreting the hero's
career. The meaning of 'noble'[4] – as often in Shakespeare
equivalent to 'heroic' – is summed up in this tremendous survey of the 'deeds of Coriolanus'. The theme is anticipated at
the start by direct statement: 'It is held/ That *valor* is the
chiefest virtue...' (84–5), 'valor' being used here as in
Elizabethan translations for ancient Roman 'virtue'.

In the earlier part of Cominius's story, the stress falls first
on Coriolanus as wonder boy, as the beardless youth with
'Amazonian chin' (92) – a description that reminds us oddly
of his potent mother, Volumnia. We next see him crowned,
'brow-bound with the oak' (99); then we get an impression of
boyhood swiftly thrust into manhood: 'His pupil age/
Man-ent'red thus' (99–100). The brusque compound renews
the physical energy of 'ent'red' ('initiated into'), especially as
it is linked with 'waxed like a sea' (100), an image that turns
the 'man' into a vast natural force. Again Coriolanus is
crowned: 'He lurched all swords of the garland' (102); but
how oddly this is put, as if men were swords and swords wore
garlands, as if the man himself now wore the ornament of
'swords'. He stands a 'rare example' (105) against the 'fliers',
who appear as mere 'weeds before/ A vessel' (106–7). With
'below his stem' (108), the man becomes the 'stem', the bow of
a ship. From pointed bow, the image glides in true
Shakespearian fashion to 'sword', to 'stamp' (108), a die for

stamping a coin or a medal. Where the 'stamp' made its 'mark', its cutting edge 'took' (109): it killed.[5] The sword is seen now as a great sword-machine coming down on its victims, quite literally 'impressing' them. Then Coriolanus himself is dehumanized, turned into a mere blood-thing (110), with 'every motion . . . timed' (110–11), working with mechanical regularity, yet incongruously dripping with blood.[6]

'Alone' – once more the 'rare example' – he entered the 'mortal', the fatal, gate by which death comes (111–12). He 'painted it / With shunless destiny' (112–13): the bloody instrument smeared it with the gore of dying men, made it one with the deaths of men who could not escape their fate. The abstractness of idiom fits in with the whole style of Shakespeare's vision in the speech and in the play, imparting to the hero the added impersonality of a divine power. We may recall Volumnia's awesome image:

> Death, that dark spirit, in's nervy arm doth lie,
> Which, being advanced, declines, and then men die.
>
> (II i 166–7)

She too sees Coriolanus as the great sword-sweeping arm of Death.

He 'struck / Corioles like a planet' (114–15). Now Coriolanus is a more terrifying force of nature, 'striking' with fatal disease as the planets were believed to do, by the death-ray of the Elizabethan cosmos. There is a final impression of swift action and 'reeking' gore before Cominius's summing up (125–30). Coriolanus's reward for his 'deeds' lies in the pure doing, in 'living it up in action'. Heroic violence, it is suggested, is self-destructive: in killing time, the hero is killing himself.

We recognize – as the more literate and the more theatrically experienced members of Shakespeare's audience would have done more quickly and more certainly – that the core of this speech is an heroic narrative in the Graeco-Roman manner. The more 'judicious', of whom Hamlet speaks, would have

caught in 'noble' and the 'deeds of Coriolanus' an echo of
phrases like Homer's *klea andron* – 'the glorious deeds of great
heroës dead', as Chapman translated it. In 'the man I speak
of' they might have heard Virgil's *arma virumque cano*, and felt
the special force that 'man' and 'virtue' had acquired through
repeated use in heroic contexts of Elizabethan plays and
translations.

Shakespeare's knowledge of the traditional heroic style and
character in their ancient and Renaissance forms had been
refreshed, as when he was writing *Julius Caesar* and *Antony and
Cleopatra*, by his reading of Plutarch. The concept of the true
hero assumed in the *Life* of Coriolanus (and in other
Plutarchan *Lives*) is close to the Renaissance ideal implicit in
Chapman's [*Iliad*] translation, as can be seen from some of the
more general comments on the character of Coriolanus:

... this Martius naturall wit and great harte dyd marvelously sturre
up his corage, to doe and attempt notable actes. But on the other
side for lacke of education, he was so chollericke and impacient, that
he would yeld to no living creature: which made him churlishe, un-
civill, and altogether unfit for any mans conversation. Yet men
marveling much at his constancy, that he was never overcome with
pleasure, nor money, and howe he would endure easely all manner
of paynes and travailles: thereupon they well liked and commended
his stowtnes and temperancie. But for all that, they could not be
acquainted with him, as one citizen useth to be with another in the
cittie. His behaviour was so unpleasaunt to them, by reason of a cer-
taine insolent and sterne manner he had, which bicause it was to
lordly, was disliked. And to say truely, the greatest benefit that learning bringeth men unto, is this: that it teacheth men that be rude
and rough of nature, by compasse and rule of reason, to be civill and
curteous, and to like better the meane state, then the higher. Now in
those dayes, valliantnes was honoured in Rome above all other vertues, which they call *Virtus*, by the name of vertue selfe, as including
in that generall name, all other speciall vertues besides. So that *Virtus* in the Latin, was asmuche as valliantnes.

                                         (North's *Plutarch*, II 144)

To begin with, there is the high praise of Martius's 'great
harte' and 'notable actes', '*But on the other side*'– in what follows
North sounds exactly like Chapman: 'for lacke of education,

he was so chollericke and impacient, that he would yeld to no
living creature . . .'. North re-enforces this with a remark showing clearly that 'education' is very nearly 'learning' in Chapman's sense of the word: 'And to say truely, the greatest
benefit that learning bringeth men unto, is this: that it
teacheth men that be rude and rough of nature, by compasse
and rule of reason, to be civil and curteous . . .' But in the next
sentence we are reminded (in North's rather back-handed
way) that Coriolanus was the pattern of Roman *Virtus*. According to North's view – and it would be Chapman's too –
Coriolanus was not fit to be 'a prince' or 'governour', because
he 'lacked the gravity, and affabilitie that is gotten with judgment of learning and reason . . .' (p. 160). He has another
characteristic that is connected with his 'choller' and his 'over
selfe will and opinion' (we should say, 'pride'): 'he remem-
bred not how wilfulness is the thing of the world, which a
governour of a common wealth for pleasing should shonne, being that which Plato called solitariness.' It is worth noting that
Coriolanus's obstinacy and pride are described as
'solitarines', the uncivil 'aloneness' of men 'who will never
yeld to others reason . . .'.

Bearing in mind North's picture of heroic Coriolanus, and
the tradition behind it, we can now account better for certain
features of Cominius's narrative; the august and at times coldly Latin style, the *nobility* of this display of *virtue,* the terrifying
and repellent energy of a man who is a lone instrument of
death and destiny. Coriolanus emerges as a hero like Achilles[7]
in his most vengeful phase, choleric and impatient, hurrying
for slaughter, who 'did/ Run reeking o'er the lives of men'. We
recall how in earlier scenes Shakespeare has stressed by imagery and stage business the 'bloodiness', 'aloneness', and
other non-human qualities underlined in Cominius's portrait.
Coriolanus has been 'mantled', 'painted', 'smeared', and
'masqued' in blood; heard with the 'thunder-like percussion'
of a cannon; seen swordlike 'outdaring his senseless sword'
and fighting alone, apart from his plebeian followers – both
impressions being vividly merged in the scene when his men
'*wave their swords*' and '*take him up in their arms*':

O me alone! Make you a sword of me? (I vi 76)

Whether these cries are to be read as questions or as ex-
clamations – and there is no certainty[8] – in uttering them
Coriolanus sees himself in splendid isolation, like a sword
swung aloft in battle.

The extreme emphasis on a non-human aloneness is a sign
that Shakespeare was not writing an ancient heroic tragedy,[9]
not even of the Renaissance type of *Antony and Cleopatra,* and
that he had seen in Plutarch's 'solitarines' another subject and
another possible treatment.[10] 'Suppose we set our Achilles
down in the Roman forum – what then?' There are subtle
hints in Cominius's speech of this other subject and attitude:
'It is *held* / That valor is the chiefest virtue ... *If it be ...*'.
Menenius's comment at the end, 'He's right noble. / Let him
be called for', is just, but off-hand and curt in Coriolanus's
own manner. 'Enough of that', Menenius seems to say – and
irony breaks in. 'Say more, and you may remind people of this
hero's immense pride', 'his haughty obstinate mind', as North
puts it, a quality that Shakespeare stresses much more than
Plutarch. But Shakespeare does not limit himself to por-
traying a flawed proud and angry man. He had grasped in the
Lives and in the Roman historians the importance of the
forum, of the Roman state, which he viewed with his contemporaries as an example both of 'the mischiefes of discord and
civill discention'[11] and of the well-ordered society, a model of
a true commonwealth.

Shakespeare sets the 'deeds of Coriolanus' against the great
parable of Menenius, 'the body's members' and their revolt
'against the Belly' (I i 97–164). There are many contemporary
documents that show a familiarity with this figure and with
the related metaphor of the 'disease' and 'health' of the body
politic. We are reminded, as in *Troilus and Cressida,* that the
state in more than a modern figurative sense embodies
another order: the parts receive from the governing centre
'that natural competency / Whereby they live ...'. The
dramatic point of the brilliantly comic scene in which this
fable is presented does not lie in the fable, but in the way it is
acted out by Menenius in co-operation with the citizens. The

good-natured insolence and sturdy candour, the tough
repartee of the exchanges, belong to a kind of game played
between patrician and people. Both the 'Belly smile' of the
patrician, and the 'great toe' of the plebeian, help impart the
feeling of healthy relatedness in a civil society. To that, *Enter
Caius Marcius* – followed by Menenius's greeting,

> Hail, noble Marcius!

with the answer:

> Thanks. What's the matter, you dissentious rogues
> That, rubbing the poor itch of your opinion,
> Make yourselves scabs? (ɪ i 164–7)

The 'nature' of the state is henceforth counterpoised by the
'nature' of Coriolanus: 'What he cannot help in his nature',
one citizen says to another in the beginning of this same scene,
'you account a vice in him.' From here to the end of the play
Shakespeare keeps dramatizing this clash of natures until
Coriolanus, still protesting, hears 'Great Nature' cry ' "Deny
not" . . .' and

> He bowed his nature, never known before
> But to be rough, unswayable, and free. (v vi 25–6)

In North's version of the scene where Coriolanus gives in to his
mother's pleas (v iii), there is considerable emphasis on the
claims of 'nature' and the 'natural' in various senses.[12] But
there is nothing in the *Life* as a whole like Shakespeare's in-
terweaving throughout his drama of variations on this central
theme. The opposition of 'natures' in Coriolanus produces a
continuous play of irony, as every protestation of the hero, or
of his friends and enemies, is heard against a suppressed nega-
tion.

Again taking a hint from Plutarch – which he develops fully
and explicitly – Shakespeare introduces one further strand of
ironic ambiguity into his picture of Coriolanus, the link
between his heroic energy and his love of his mother. 'There's

no man in the world', she explains near the end of the play,
'More bound to's mother'. (Such is the stuff of heroes:
Achilles must have his guardian Thetis.) 'What he hath done
famously . . .' a citizen says, 'though soft-conscienced men can
be content to say it was for his country, he did it to please his
mother and to be partly proud, which he is, even to the
altitude of his virtue' (I i 36–41). More curious still,
war-making, love, and marriage are closely related and almost
identified in the minds of Volumnia and her son. 'I tell thee,
daughter,' his mother says to his wife, 'I sprang not more in
joy at first hearing he was a man-child than now in first seeing
he had proved himself a man' (I iii 16–18). Coriolanus has a
way of embracing generals as if they were brides of war:

> MARCIUS [To Cominius] O, let me clip ye
> In arms as sound as when I wooed; in heart
> As merry as when our nuptial day was done,
> And tapers burned to bedward! (I vi 29–32)

Much later – with the inevitable ironic echo – Aufidius
answers him in kind:

> that I see thee here,
> Thou noble thing, more dances my rapt heart
> Than when I first my wedded mistress saw
> Bestride my threshold. (IV v 119–22)

II ACHILLES IN THE FORUM

If we remember the many contradictions in Coriolanus's
nature and the heroic image his role evokes by similarity and
by contrast, and the vision of society symbolized by
Menenius's fable, we shall appreciate better the
Shakespearian complexity of the climactic scenes of the play
and reach a truer measure of its peculiar flavour as tragedy. In
the first of these scenes Coriolanus, about to be made consul,
makes his magnificent attack on the tribunes and their
officers. In his view, the advice to abolish the tribuneship is a
call to a godlike 'noble life':

> Therefore, beseech you –
> You that will be less fearful than discreet;
> That love the fundamental part of state
> More than you doubt the change on't; that prefer
> A noble life before a long, and wish
> To jump a body with a dangerous physic
> That's sure of death without it – at once pluck out
> The multitudinous tongue; let them not lick
> The sweet which is their poison. Your dishonor
> Mangles true judgment, and bereaves the state
> Of that integrity which should become't;
> Not having the power to do the good it would,
> For th' ill which doth control't (III i 149–61)

By this point in the play the noble life is not only being equated with the 'deeds of Coriolanus', but with the ironic qualifications of his pride. 'A *noble* life' – these words coming from Coriolanus can be taken by the tribunes and people more plainly, as 'the life of the nobles, the senate'. Coriolanus's plea for the 'fundamental part of state', his concern for the 'integrity' of the body-politic seemingly echoes Menenius's fable; but to 'pluck out / The multitudinous tongue', to eliminate the tribunes, is effectively to deny the people any part whatever in the government. Coriolanus does not want a 'blended' voice, but one; and he alone, it seems, is the proper voice of the state. He is making this plea, he says, in the interest of avoiding 'confusion' (110). But the hero who pleads for order and who fears revolution, speaks revolutionary doctrines. He of course intends a counter-revolution; but he very nearly sets a true popular revolution under way.

The metaphor that runs through Coriolanus's speech is the familiar medical one of the play (used once, but only once, by Plutarch): he offers 'a dangerous physic', and in his view he is the health of the state. But to the tribune Sicinius 'He's a disease that must be cut away' (III i 293). Menenius accepts the implication, but proposes a 'cure' rather than surgery. He would proceed by 'the humane way' of compromise; that is, by Chapman's (and Plutarch's) way of 'humane government'. But the fatality of Coriolanus's nature – his pride and 'choler',

his lack of temperance – carries him on to destroy what he
thinks he is saving. 'His nature is too noble for the world', says
Menenius,

> He would not flatter Neptune for his trident,
> Or Jove for's power to thunder. His heart's his mouth:
> What his breast forges, that his tongue must vent;
> And, being angry, does forget that ever
> He heard the name of death. (III i 254–9)

This is another image of a man who will equal the gods, a
forge-like machine of war and death, deafened by wrath.

Coriolanus's insistence on being true to his heroic nature is
constantly to the fore from this point to the end of the play. In
the next scene, where the Nobles and Volumnia urge him to
ask the people's pardon, a scene that has no parallel in
Plutarch, he asks his mother with boyish puzzlement,

> Why did you wish me milder – Would you have me
> False to my nature? Rather say I play
> The man I am. (III ii 14–16)

Volumnia's sensible advice fits Chapman's and North's concept of 'education':

> I have a heart as little apt as yours,
> But yet a brain that leads my use of anger
> To better vantage. (29–31)

Menenius comments, 'Well said, noble woman!' But this is
not Coriolanus's nobility; his is of the pure Homeric type, absolute and without compromise. 'You are too absolute',
Volumnia well says,

> Though therein you can never be too noble
> But when extremities speak. (39–41)

But Volumnia does not altogether understand her son: it is exactly in 'extremities' that the hero must be 'too noble', that his

nature cries out. Coriolanus faces a dilemma similar to Antony's – how to be both noble and politic. Volumnia attempts
to make him feel that the politic can be identified at one and
the same time with nobility, with loyalty to the better part of
the state and to the family, and most significantly, with loyalty
to herself:

> I am in this
> Your wife, your son, these senators, the nobles . . . (64–5)

Her despairing

> Do as thou list.
> Thy valiantness was mine, thou suck'st it from me,
> But owe thy pride thyself . . . (128–30)

only increases the sense of their likeness, of the bond between
them: they are one flesh and one blood.[13]

The physical intensity of the appeal is persuasive for the
moment, and for the first time in the scene, Coriolanus calls
her 'mother':

> Mother, I am going to the marketplace . . . (131)

What this curbing of his nature costs him has been suggested
earlier in the same scene, when like Othello he says farewell to
arms,

> Away, my disposition, and possess me
> Some harlot's spirit! My throat of war be turned,
> Which quired with my drum, into a pipe
> Small as an eunuch . . . (111–14)

and when he suddenly reverses himself,

> I will not do't;
> Lest I surcease to honor mine own truth,
> And by my body's action teach my mind
> A most inherent baseness. (120–3)

Though the words Coriolanus uses are very like those of Chapman, his actions have really turned the ideal upside down. While everyone is urging him to conquer his body's 'angry part' by 'framing his spirit' to 'fair speech', he sees only a betrayal of spirit by flesh.

He will seek 'a world elsewhere', outside state and family, out of the ordered nature he had known in Rome, and fight, now truly 'alone, / Like to a lonely dragon,[14] that his fen / Makes feared and talked of more than seen . . .' (IV i 29–31). With splendid irony he asserts that though outside society he will still be the same noble hero: 'You shall / Hear . . . never of me aught / But what is *like me*[15] formerly' (51–3). In the flattering talk of the Volscians he seems to recover his old nobility, 'as if he were son and heir to Mars', but this new-found independence is an illusion, as Aufidius's ominous hints make clear. Aufidius's explanation of why Coriolanus was 'hated' and 'banished' – though it neglects some reasons, and though it is not Shakespeare's 'last word' on his hero – does offer one important hypothesis borne out by much of the play:

> whether ['twas] nature,
> Not to be other than one thing, not moving
> From th' casque to th' cushion, but commanding peace
> Even with the same austerity and garb
> As he controlled the war . . . (IV vii 41–5)

In this last phase of Coriolanus's career there is, as in Achilles's last battles, something much more frightening about his pride and his wrath. 'He was', says Cominius,

> a kind of nothing, titleless,
> Till he had forged himself a name o' th' fire[16]
> Of burning Rome. (v i 13–15)

He harshly rejects his 'old father', Menenius,

> Away! . . .

> Wife, mother, child, I know not. (v ii 81, 83)

The Second Watch gives one final impression of Coriolanus's dehumanization just before the women come to beg him to save the city: 'He's the rock, the oak not to be wind-shaken' (v ii 111). What then will happen to the man who supposes he is 'author of himself', the absolute hero detached from humanity?

As when he rejected Menenius's appeal, he will attempt to separate personal allegiance from allegiance to country. When the women approach, his eye moves quickly from his wife to his mother, who claims and receives his attention during most of the scene. He speaks to her at first in the strange impersonal style that others have used of him: 'the honored mold / Wherein this trunk was framed . . .' (v iii 22–3); but at once he is stressing the close physical bond of mother and son: 'and in her hand / The grandchild to her blood'. With another typical turn,[17] he denies this and all similar bonds: 'All bond and privilege of nature, break!' He will be deliberately unnatural; but when he sees those 'doves' eyes', he 'melts' – and how wonderfully the imagery recalls the hard godlike self he has tried to be: 'I melt, and am not / Of stronger earth . . .' – he is not the metallic machine man of earlier scenes. When his 'mother bows' to him, it is indeed a 'perturbation' in Nature, and 'Great Nature' cries out against it (33).[18] Though the Renaissance hero should obey the voice of Nature, Coriolanus with an imprecation worthy of Achilles – 'Let the Volsces / Plough Rome, and harrow Italy!' – denies 'instinct', innate impulse, and, with consummate irony, declares that he is 'author of himself', as it were, self-born!

But soon he is yielding to Nature in the sense of family affection, as he gives his wife 'a kiss / Long as my exile', while still insisting that he is not yielding to Nature in the sense of allegiance to his country. When he sees his mother kneeling, he comes out with more hyperbolic oaths in the best heroic vein:

Then let the pebbles on the hungry beach
Fillip the stars! Then let the mutinous winds
Strike the proud cedars 'gainst the fiery sun . . . (v iii 58–60)

Like Othello and Lear, Coriolanus invokes the disorder he
fears, and of which he is the unconscious instrument. Like
Hector he sees his son as the reincarnation of his own heroism,
his words recalling his own nobility and his lonely strength
and inhumanity. He prays that the boy may prove

> To shame unvulnerable, and stick i' th' wars
> Like a great sea-mark, standing every flaw . . . (73–4)

But he is still trying to hold off the claims of wife and mother.
'Tell me not', he shouts, 'wherein I seem unnatural.'
Then come Volumnia's two great appeals in answer to his
poignantly absurd assertion. The keynote of the first is struck
in

>   thy sight, which should
> Make our eyes flow with joy, hearts dance with comforts,
> Constrains them weep and shake with fear and sorrow,
> Making the mother, wife, and child, to see
> The son, the husband, and the father tearing
> His country's bowels out. (98–103)

The body of the state, realized in Volumnia's words with such
physical vividness, is equated with mother, wife, and child, as
if to say, 'tearing that body is tearing us'. During the rest of
the speech, Volumnia's language intensifies this identification
until the climax,

>   thou shalt no sooner
> March to assault thy country than to tread
> (Trust to't, thou shalt not) on thy mother's womb
> That brought thee to this world. (122–5)

The violent image is Plutarch's, and the identification of the
mother with the state is suggested by one of his explanatory
comments; but the explanation shows also the relative
simplicity of his analysis and his unawareness of the emotional
confusion that Shakespeare's Volumnia exploits so
successfully:

yet he had no reason for the love of his mother to pardone his contrie, but rather he should in pardoning his contrie, have spared his
mother, bicause his mother and wife were members of the bodie of
his contrie and city, which he did besiege.

(North's *Plutarch*, II 194)

Volumnia's second appeal falls into three distinct phases.
First she urges him to reconcile the Romans and the Volsces,
offering the same kind of sensible advice she had given earlier
when begging him to be 'mild' to the tribunes. Next she makes
a masterly attack on the very nobility that stands in the way of
compromise, pointing out that the only practical· 'benefit' of
being so absolutely noble is to destroy his country and gain a
' "name . . . / To th' ensuing age abhorred" '. She enforces
her argument with a satirical picture of the godlike role
Coriolanus has aimed at, seeking 'To imitate the graces of the
gods . . .' as if he were to 'thunder' like Jove, and yet to
'charge'[19] his lightning with a 'bolt' that would only split 'an
oak (v iii 150–3). Something, yes, but hardly a cosmic
catastrophe. She keeps reminding him that she speaks for
wife, son, and mother; and in her final stroke she reinforces all
three claims:

> This fellow had a Volscian to his mother;
> His wife is in Corioles, and his child
> Like him by chance. (178–80)

Again she identifies personal and social bonds, as she reads
him out of family, Rome, and humanity. His reply is one of
the great speaking silences in Shakespeare:

> *Holds her by the hand, silent.*
> O mother, mother!
> What have you done? Behold, the heavens do ope,
> The gods look down, and this unnatural scene
> They laugh at. (182–5)

'Unnatural' – just when he is responding to all these most
natural claims! For a moment he seems to see his dilemma

more clearly, and to understand that in giving in to his mother
he is responding to the demands of his native country and
state. But he soon is talking as if all can be well: he can give in
to his mother, be false to the Volscians, and 'frame convenient
peace'.

The last scene of the play begins as an ironic repetition of
the scene in which he had 'mildly' given in to his mother's advice. At that time he had not been able to sustain the part; but
now he 'bows his nature' and comes 'marching' in, '*the commoners being with him*'. In contrast to the usual isolation of his
figure from the plebeians, Coriolanus is seen *with* the people,
and we catch another ironic reflection from the past:
Menenius's easy companionship with the lower orders.
Coriolanus seems for once to 'belong', and he cries happily, 'I
am returned your soldier; / No more infected with my country's love . . .' (v vi 71–2). What was once his health is now
disease, and loyalty to the enemies of Rome is his 'cure'. He is
so terribly unaware of what he has been doing that he
responds with dreamlike deafness to Aufidius's cry of 'traitor'
– the exact echo of the Tribunes' earlier ' 'Has spoken like a
traitor . . .' (III i 162).

When he finally takes in Aufidius's cruel caricature of how
he had been moved by his mother to betray the Volscians, he
can hardly speak: 'Hear'st thou, Mars?' His incoherent cry,
reminding us of the godlike soldier he had been, is inadequate
but dramatically concentrated in the highest degree.
Shakespeare was never more successful than in this brief
dialogue in focusing the manifold meanings of a play in the
slightest of verbal gestures. To Aufidius's slanderous 'boy of
tears' he cries:

> Cut me to pieces, Volsces, men and lads,
> Stain all your edges on me. "Boy"! False hound!
> If you have writ your annals true, 'tis there,
> That, like an eagle in a dovecote, I
> Fluttered your Volscians in Corioles.
> Alone I did it. 'Boy'? (v vi 112–17)

'Alone' and ' "Boy"?' carry the weight of Coriolanus's whole dramatic career. In 'Alone' we recognize his cult of independence, his integrity, his insistence on being 'Coriolanus'. But we hear also the opposite theme, in a play in which wholeness of the state is the public ideal, in which metaphors of the body politic keep reminding us that the great natural order is realized in a whole of which the single man is only a part. This is his final denial of nature's bond, only making clearer his real dependence on Rome, his mother, Menenius, and now on the Volscians. ' "Boy"?' in its scornful tone is Coriolanus's way of saying '*man*-hero'. But the hero cannot act in this setting; he can only utter frustrated cries. He *is* in part behaving like a boy, and he *had* responded to his mother. The single word recalls a long history of boyish irresponsibility and lack of control.

But there is another view, as always in *Coriolanus*: 'The man is noble', one of the Volscians says, 'and his fame folds in / This orb o' th' earth' (v vi 125–6). The 'deeds of Coriolanus' cannot be forgotten any more than 'the impatience' that North finds so dangerous in the 'governour' of a state. The closing processional speech, with which we began, marks the death of a hero: 'Yet he shall have a noble memory.' [20]

III CORIOLANUS AND THE HEROIC TRADITION

If we now compare Coriolanus with the model of all Greek and Roman literary heroes, Achilles, and with the Renaissance counterpart in Chapman and North, and finally with the chief characters of other Shakespearian tragedies, we can define more clearly the character of the play – surely the most original of Shakespeare's heroic dramas, whatever we choose to call it. Throughout *Coriolanus* Shakespeare is continually recalling the ancient model in imagery associating his hero with divinities and 'shunless destiny'. Like Menenius, Shakespeare has 'Godded him indeed'. Perhaps Coriolanus is most like Achilles in his passionate pride, in his 'choler', in his shifting from 'rage to sorrow', emotions that lie very close together, as Plutarch had noted. But he comes nearest to the essence of Homer's hero in his absoluteness, in his determination to imitate 'the graces of the gods', in his will to push the heroic to the limit until he destroys his own society along with his enemy's. In reducing all virtues to *virtus,* he is the Greek hero Romanized, while in appealing to 'Great Nature' and at the same time asserting the greatness of his own nature, he betrays the Stoic ancestry of the Elizabethan tragic hero.

But there is no moment when, like Achilles, he sees his anger and curses it, nothing to correspond to the scene with Priam, no vision of himself and a higher order within which his action and suffering are placed and made more comprehensible. His last gesture is like his first, to 'use his lawful sword'. He knows little of what Chapman calls the soul's 'sovereignty in fit reflection', not to mention 'subduing his earthly, part for heaven'. He is the most Roman, the least 'gentle' and the least Christian,[21] of Shakespeare's major heroes.

This Roman-ness is felt in the austerity of a style that lends itself so well to irony and that is the best index to the quality of the play. In *Coriolanus* Shakespeare seems to turn his back on the richness of language in *Antony and Cleopatra,* with the deliberate intention of creating a protagonist who will deny much that is common to his own and the Renaissance heroic ideal. And yet there are in Coriolanus the makings of a tragedy in Shakespeare's more typical manner: he is a man nobly conscious of his role, a 'governour' like Lear or Macbeth on whom the health of society depends, a person like Lear and Othello of immense impatience in a situation calling for utmost patience, a man like Antony whose action is godlike and connected with dimly perceived supernatural forces. Like Antony, too, he is an instrument of the mighty Roman state, for Romans a prime symbol of the directing power of fate.

But there is of course in this most Roman hero an obvious defect that makes even Macbeth tragic in a sense of the word that does not fit Coriolanus – the want of the troubled conscience that separates Macbeth from the tyrant he is in relation to his enemies. In the final scene with his mother, Coriolanus is barely conscious that he is betraying the Volscians, just as in his last entrance he does not realize that he has been 'infected with his country's love'. His whole career is based on an illusion of *aloneness,* the belief that a man, a general, a statesman can act alone. Hence the bafflement and humiliation when he must bow to others – feelings he can express only in rotelike speeches. It is the spectator, not Coriolanus, who feels the poignancy of this betrayal of others and himself. Like a 'dull actor', as he says, he performs dully, and when out of his part, he is completely 'out'.

For Coriolanus has only one way of meeting the world – assertion of simple soldierly nobility. In this he has much in common with Othello, who also lives by absolutes, whose world collapses at any suggestion that he is *not* a soldier. But in *Coriolanus* there is no terrible recognition by the hero, as there is in the final scenes of *Othello,* that simple soldiery and simple justice have not been enough, that they have indeed brought chaos again. Damnation, which Othello calls on himself, and which presupposes a sense of sin, is incomprehensible to this noble Roman. He is equally incapable of 'noble' Antony's 'I am so lated in the world that I / Have lost my way forever.'

One last comparison with Achilles is to the point. In comparison with Shakespeare's 'men', these two are great boys. Both are strangely allied with their mothers, both produce 'confusion' by their over-developed sense of self and their disregard of the claims of society. The difference in the end result depends on the difference noted earlier: Shakespeare sets his hero in a much more complex social world. The noble voice that calls to battle may no longer sound noble in the Capitol. Though it calls for order, it becomes indistinguishable from the voice of tyrant and traitor. The man who fears innovation, who has no gift for making compromises and dealing 'mildly', may prove the most violent of innovators, worse than a mere mob. Shakespeare's picture of the people is not flattering, but not unintelligent: one cannot build an orderly society by following the whims of the many-headed monster. But fixity of principle in a prince can be as dangerous to the state as the fickleness of a mob.

Shakespeare's state is necessarily not that of the Roman republic, since both society and cosmos have been translated in Elizabethan–Jacobean terms. His subject – apart from the peculiar character of Coriolanus – is implicit in the 'degree'

speech of *Troilus and Cressida*. It should be remembered that
Ulysses's speech was occasioned by Achilles's revolt and that
Ulysses later tried to show Achilles the evils resulting from his
loss of heroic nobility. Shakespeare returns in *Coriolanus* to the
subject implied in these scenes of *Troilus and Cressida,* but with
a new Achilles and a new certainty of aim, and with a resultant concentration lacking in the earlier play. In *Troilus,*
Achilles was an ambiguous creature, a lover and a gangster,
and the drama of disunity in the state was crossed by a drama
of disunity in love. The end appropriately is sound and fury
signifying nothing, though 'the nothing that is' (in Wallace
Stevens's phrase) is so powerfully expressed. But in *Coriolanus*
Shakespeare limits the social subject more severely, and
though his picture of the social order is highly particularized,
it does not lose a large clarity. As in *Antony and Cleopatra,* the
'wide arch / Of the ranged' Roman state is never lost from
view.

Against that ordered complexity the simple extremism of
Coriolanus stands out in all its nobility and absurdity. The
noble simplicity of the hero and the certainty with which
issues are expressed and arguments are presented by
Coriolanus and by his enemies, the high decorum of the rather
chill oratorical style take us in the direction of French classical
drama. This is, like *Julius Caesar,* a most *Latin* play.

IV BEYOND PLUTARCH

It was 'all in Plutarch', we may be tempted to say. But when
we read Plutarch we discover what Shakespeare was capable
of learning – how wonderfully he selected and how skilfully he
concentrated on his chosen themes, embodying them in particular dramatic expressions. Comparison of the play with the
Life proves again that 'source' is a very misleading term if we
are trying to describe what happens when a writer of the first
rank makes a new work out of an old one. In writing *Coriolanus,*
Shakespeare was not borrowing discrete items from Plutarch;
he was engaged in a total imaginative act, seeking to satisfy his
inner measure of what was right for his own sensibility, for his

sense of the hero's character, and for his complex 'feel' of the dramatic world coming into being as he wrote. Agreement with Eliot's judgement that the play is 'with *Antony and Cleopatra,* Shakespeare's most assured artistic success', becomes easier when we discover what Shakespeare accepted and what he rejected, and particularly when we see how he adapted his borrowings to his vision of Coriolanus and of the tragedy as a whole.

Shakespeare's vision – though for all time – was not timeless in origin, but shaped in part by the social and literary culture in which he lived and by the audience for which he produced his plays. We have noted at a number of points how the Graeco-Roman heroic ideal in its Renaissance form affected *Coriolanus* and its meaning for contemporary and succeeding audiences. The treatment of civil disorders in Republican Rome was almost certainly also affected by popular protests and uprisings in England during the late sixteenth and early seventeenth centuries, brought on by the enclosure of farm lands and by the lack of grain and the consequent 'dearth'. That Shakespeare takes the famine as the principal cause for the plebeians' complaints, rather than as in Plutarch 'the sore oppression of usurers', is almost certainly traceable to the unrest in England, more especially to the Midlands revolt of 1607.[22] The extensive emphasis in the play – as compared with the *Life* – on the body–state metaphor is probably to be explained in part by the contemporary concern with the dangers of insurrection. Shakespeare also elaborated on Plutarch's brief tale of the body and its members by drawing on Sidney's *Apologie for Poetrie,* Livy's *Roman History* (both in the original and in the translation of Philemon Holland (1600)), and William Camden's *Remaines of a greater worke concerning Britaine* (1605).[23]

The main events of the play, including the important scenes of Coriolanus's attack on the tribuneship (III i), his banishment and his joining Aufidius (IV i, v), and the climactic scene with his mother (V iii), are 'based' on Plutarch. The principal features that Shakespeare stresses in his portrayal of Coriolanus have their origin, at least in an elementary form, in the pages of the *Life.* But Shakespeare has given even greater

importance than Plutarch to Coriolanus's pride and uncontrollable temper and especially to the close emotional bond
with his mother. MacCallum[24] sees in the prominent role
given to Menenius, of which there is only the slightest hint in
the *Life*, Shakespeare's intention of diminishing the isolation
Plutarch ascribes to his hero, his unfitness for association with
other men. But it is Menenius who spends much of his time
warning Coriolanus of these deficiencies, and of the likely consequences of his heroically simple and inept behaviour. It
should also be noted that in spite of his temperamental
aloneness, Plutarch's hero, like Shakespeare's, has strong
political supporters among the patricians. Where Shakespeare
departs, and significantly, is in eliminating all references to
political manoeuvring by Coriolanus, of which there are fairly
many instances in the *Life*. Other critics have noted that
Plutarch attributes a reputation for eloquence to Coriolanus,
whereas Shakespeare seems to stress his lack of ability as a
speaker and debater. The point surely is that Shakespeare, as
Menenius explains, endows Coriolanus with the eloquence of
a soldier – violent and powerful, though often tactless
utterance. He has but one style, and hence his calls for the
defence of the state sound strangely like his calls to battle
(compare III i 149–57 and I vi 67–75).

A survey of the principal scenes wholly or largely invented
by Shakespeare will give some idea of how thoroughly he
adapted Plutarch's moral history to fit his peculiar dramatic
subject, of the Achillean hero exposed to the complexities and
necessary compromises of the Roman–Jacobean political
world. First, there are all the episodes in which Menenius
figures prominently, with the exception of that part of the first
scene in which he tells his fable. The occasion for this moral
lesson, the retreat to the Sacred Mount, is passed over by
Shakespeare, though Plutarch's narrative of it contains his
sole mention of Menneius (II 149). (In Livy's *History*
Menenius dies soon after[25] this event takes place.) All the
other scenes in which Menenius does so much to defend
Coriolanus against his enemies, or to enhance his noble exploits, or to temper his wrath, are entirely of Shakespeare's
making. In Act I I i there is the bitterly comic telling off of the

tribunes, followed by the joyous welcome of the returning hero; in II iii, the dialogue with Coriolanus and with the tribunes during the election scene; and the further exchanges with the tribunes in III i, after Coriolanus has been accused of being a traitor. Although in some of these earlier scenes Shakespeare is using Menenius to voice arguments advanced by the more politic patricians of the *Life,* he had little basis in Plutarch for the prominent part taken by Menenius in a number of the scenes that follow Coriolanus's banishment. In these scenes, as often in this play, Shakespeare telescopes two or three Plutarchan episodes into one, centring the action on one of the more important characters. The scene in which Menenius begs Coriolanus to spare Rome is – like Cominius's report of his own attempt – a substitution for one of several embassies from Rome described in Plutarch's narrative.

Shakespeare has invented all of the scenes in which Volumnia figures, with the exception of the women's embassy of v iii. The scene that introduces Volumnia, Virgilia, and Valeria (I iii), where Volumnia shows that she had indeed made Coriolanus after her own image of 'valiantness', grows from a remark in the *Life* about the 'joye he sawe his mother dyd take of him', and the telling comment that after his marriage Coriolanus 'never left his mothers house therefore'. The later scene in which she and Menenius urge Coriolanus to act 'mildly' in answering the tribunes (III ii) is an original and brilliant piece of dramatic foreshadowing, preparing for the final submission of son to mother in Act v. (One characteristic of the play is the number of scenes that have close parallels, in which Coriolanus goes through the same routines, but under changed circumstances which he alone seems not to notice. Hence the odd *déjà-vu,* almost nightmarish quality of much of the action in the latter part of the play.) Shakespeare also introduces a number of other scenes or episodes in which Volumnia has an important part, such as her rejoicing over her son's return from war (II i), her farewell at the gate and her railing afterward (iv i, ii), and her triumphant return from the final embassy (v v). The speeches and scenes in which Shakespeare builds up the ambiguous hate–love relationship between Aufidius and Coriolanus in anticipation of their meeting in IV v grow from a single reference to their rivalry in the *Life*.

But no listing of inventions, or of parallels between *Coriolanus* and Plutarch's narrative can give a true impression of how wonderfully Shakespeare has transformed the Plutarchan original even when seeming to follow it closely. The obvious example. Volumnia's great appeal (v iii 19–209), offers telling proof of the art with which Shakespeare adapted North's language to suit the immediate context while keeping in view the larger dramatic and poetic design of the play. A few instances may suggest what can be learned by comparing the scene with the original in North's translation (II 183–6). Where Plutarch's Coriolanus is 'overcomen . . . with naturall affection' even before his mother speaks, Shakespeare's hero is caught up in a violently shifting debate between the claims of nature, great and small, a conflict expressed in direct speech wholly invented by Shakespeare (lines 22–37). As we have seen, the debate is not limited to this speech, but runs deeply through the whole of *Coriolanus*. In the play, where the bond with the mother is so central to the hero's character, the son is the first to kneel, and in the wholly new passages between Coriolanus and his son, the parallel to Hector suggests that in a domestic and 'natural' moment Coriolanus becomes less Achillean; while the boy's cockiness echoes the early scene in which the boy-killer of butterflies was Coriolanus in miniature. The image Coriolanus invokes of his grown son as 'a great sea-mark' is rooted in the imagery of natural forces and 'things' so characteristic of this awesome and non-human hero. An example of where the verbal parallels between the *Life* and the play are closest will indicate the remarkable depth and consistency of Shakespeare's dramatic-and-poetic art:

VOLUMNIA   thou shalt no sooner
March to assault thy country than to tread
(Trust to't, thou shalt not) on thy mother's womb
That brought thee to this world. (v iii 122–5)

. . . thou shalt see, my sonne, and trust unto it, thou shalt no soner marche forward to assault thy countrie, but thy foote shall treade

upon thy mothers wombe, that brought thee first into this world.
(North's *Plutarch*, II 184)

Shakespeare has closely imitated in his verse the climactic
form of North's sentence, with its skilful suspension through
well-placed pauses and the repeated 'thou shalt'; but by
building the whole speech to end at this point he has exploited
the emotional climax much more fully than North, who has
Volumnia go straight on with 'And I maye not deferre to see
the daye . . .'. More important, Shakespeare anticipates the
image earlier in the speech in a way to make inescapable the
identification of the mother's physical self with 'mother
Rome'. North had Volumnia say earlier, 'making my selfe to
see my sonne, and my daughter here, her husband, besieging
the walles of his native countrie . . .'. Shakespeare brings this
triple allegiance home and focuses it in a metaphor of such
violence that even Coriolanus must feel the unnaturalness of
his behaviour and recognize in advance the implication of the
final image:

> Making the mother, wife, and child, to see
> The son, the husband, and the father, tearing
> His country's bowels out. (v iii 101–3)

The identity of 'mothers', human and national, is quietly underlined a moment later in Volumnia's passing reference to
'The country, our dear nurse . . .'. Compare with this North's
relatively aloof and cold 'the nurse of their native country'.
But the full impact of the appeal would be lost if we did not
feel back of these physical mother-and-country images the
recurring metaphors of the body politic and the dramatic and
philosophic premise they express. The personal and the
patriotic appeals, which have their origin in Plutarch, have
been fused with a local intensity of feeling and with a far-
reaching reference to Shakespeare's view both of his individual
characters and of the society in which they act. Dryden once
spoke of Shakespeare as having 'all the images of nature present to him as he wrote'. In comparing Volumnia's speech
with its 'source', we see Shakespeare writing *Coriolanus* with

one eye on North, to be sure, but with all the images of the play and all their dramatic values present to his plastic imagination.

From observing how Shakespeare remade a single speech, we can begin to recover something of his imaginative excitement as he read the *Life of Coriolanus*: his recognition that here was a subject that he had wanted to handle as early as when he was writing *Julius Caesar* and *Troilus*. What a discovery – after reading late medieval versions of the ancient heroic in which the hero is reduced to a sighing lover or worse, to find that the hero is a man who has never ceased loving his mother, a man for whom marriage is second to war, whose true love is his own heroic image. Hints of these and other traits of Shakespeare's hero – his nobility and heroic virtue, his obstinate pride and lack of self-control – can be found, it is true, in North's *Life*. Other basic features of Shakespeare's drama – the picture of the Roman state and society, the debate over the claims of nature, great and small – can also be traced to North's text. But though many separate elements of Shakespeare's total design are Plutarchan, it is Shakespeare who has 'put them together', and the 'putting together' is a major dramatic and poetic feat. For example, in reporting Coriolanus's death, Plutarch merely says that the conspirators 'all fell upon him, and killed him in the marketplace, none of the people once offering to rescue him'. There is no speech from Aufidius, and more notable, none from Coriolanus, nothing to correspond to 'Alone I did it. "Boy"?' Those few words show that Shakespeare had combined perfectly an intense and rich understanding of the hero-boy, mother's son, and noble Roman with a sharply outlined picture of the social and political world, in a total vision that makes the cry so large in reference, so poignantly absurd, so tragic in a curiously ironic sense.

SOURCE: 'The Deeds of Coriolanus', in *Hero and Saint* (1971) pp. 354–81.

NOTES

1. O. J. Campbell, *Shakespeare's Satire* (New York, 1943) pp. 198–217.
2. D. J. Enright, '*Coriolanus*: Tragedy or Debate?', *The Apothecary's Shop* (London, 1957) pp. 32–53.
3. My reading of the speech is indebted in some details to the admirable analysis by D. A. Traversi, *An Approach to Shakespeare*, 2nd rev. ed. (New York, 1956) pp. 223–6 [see preceding essay herein].
4. Menenius's '*worthy* man' has much the same force.
5. Perhaps also, 'infected fatally', like 'struck', 1. 114.
6. Concerning the association of Coriolanus with images of metal and blood, see G. Wilson Knight, *The Imperial Theme*, pp. 155–60. 'He is . . . a slaying machine of mechanic excellence', p. 168.
7. Plutarch may have suggested to Shakespeare the parallel between Achilles and Coriolanus. In defending Homer's allowance for 'our owne free wil and reason', he quotes the lines on Achilles's anger (*Iliad*, I 188–9). North, II 181.
8. The Folio reads: 'Oh me alone, make you a sword of me:' – which suggests an even more assured and boastful tone. The punctuation in my text is that of Capell. The line is assigned to *soldiers* by C. Tucker Brooke (ed.), Yale Shakespeare (1917); also by Style, Cambridge, 2nd ed., according to the Variorum.
9. Though there are parallels between Achilles and Coriolanus as heroes, Coriolanus shows little of Achilles's capacity for friendship and love. (Menenius is hardly the equivalent of Patroclus or Briseis.) On the greater place given to Menenius in the play, see herein, pp. 218–19. E. Waith, *Herculean Hero*, pp. 129–30, observes that 'In contrast to this jolly patrician, always ready to compromise, the austerity and fixity of Coriolanus stand out.'
10. The contrast is between *hero* (not professional soldier) and political man. Coriolanus is not, as Wyndham Lewis says, 'a play about a conventional military hero, existing as the characteristic ornament of a strong aristocratic system'. *The Lion and the Fox* (1927; London, 1966) p. 245. Compare with my treatment Paul A. Jorgensen, *Shakespeare's Military World* (Berkeley, 1956) pp. 292–314.
11. This point (and the quotation from William Fulbeck) is taken from T. J. B. Spencer, 'Shakespeare and the Elizabethan Romans', *Shakespeare Survey*, X (1957) 29–30.
12. Hermann Heuer, 'From Plutarch to Shakespeare: a Study of *Coriolanus*', *Shakespeare Survey*, x (1957) 52–3.
13. C. I. Barber first led me to appreciate the importance of the identification of the physical bond between mother and son with

loyalty to the state and with other political and social loyalties.

14. See J. C. Maxwell, 'Animal Imagery in *Coriolanus*', *Modern Language Review*, XLII (1947) 417–21, who puts this image in 'the more heraldic, strikingly symbolic class . . .', p. 420. It is true that the imagery of the play is in general limited in suggestiveness but it is also undeniable that certain images (e.g. of the 'body' and of Coriolanus's 'thing-like' nature) are dramatically very effective. Compare the relative absence of imagery in *Julius Caesar*.

15. Another instance of the familiar type of heroic expression: *par sibi*, 'like himself', 'like a soldier'.

16. On the frequency of fire images in the later scenes of the play, see A. C. Bradley, '*Coriolanus*', British Academy Shakespeare Lecture, 1912 [reprinted above].

17. Equally typical of Othello.

18. For a curious parallel, see *King Leir* [Anonymous, *c*. 1594]:

    CORDELLA   God, world and nature say I do you wrong,
        That can indure to see you [Leir] kneele so long.

Quoted by K. Muir, *Shakespeare's Sources*, I 164.

19. 'Charge' for the Folio reading, 'change'.

20. '. . . men came out of all partes to *honour* his bodie, and dyd *honorably* burie him, setting out his tombe with great store of armour and spoyles, as the tombe of a *warlike* persone and *great captaine*', North, II 189 (italics added). Note italicized examples of heroic diction, and compare with the processional speeches of this and other tragedies.

21. In his courtesy and generosity, pagan Antony shows the effect of North's and Amyot's 'medievalizing' of the Plutarchan ideal.

22. E. C. Pettet, '*Coriolanus* and the Midlands Insurrection of 1607', *Shakespeare Survey*, III (1950) 34–42. See also 'Accounts of Historical Sources', G. Bullough, *Narrative and Dramatic Sources of Shakespeare* (London, 1964) v 553–63.

23. Muir, *Shakespeare's Sources*, I 223–4.

24. M. W. MacCallum, *Shakespeare's Roman Plays and Their Backgrounds* (London, 1910) p. 580.

25. In 'the same yeare' that Coriolanus took Corioli. *The Romane Historie of T. Livy*, tr. Philemon Holland (1600), Bullough, v 499.

SELECT BIBLIOGRAPHY

EDITIONS

(including introductory essays on the play, and in some cases stage history)

J. P. Brockbank (ed.), new Arden edition (London, 1976).

Reuben Brower (ed.), Signet Shakespeare (New York, 1966).

Francis Fergusson (ed.), Laurel Shakespeare (New York, 1962).

H. H. Furness, Jr (ed.), New Variorum edition (Philadelphia, 1928).

G. R. Hibbard (ed.), New Penguin Shakespeare (Harmondsworth, 1967).

Harry Levin (ed.), Pelican Shakespeare (Baltimore, 1956).

John Dover Wilson (ed.), New Cambridge Shakespeare (Cambridge, 1960).

BOOKS

Harley Granville-Barker, *Prefaces to Shakespeare,* Fifth Series (London, 1947).

Clifford Chalmers Huffman, *'Coriolanus' in Context* (Lewisburg, Pa., 1971).

G. Wilson Knight, *The Imperial Theme* (London, 1931).

L. C. Knights, *Further Explorations* (London, 1965).

Jan Kott, *Shakespeare our Contemporary* (London, 1964).

Matthew N. Proser, *The Heroic Image in Five Shakespearean Tragedies* (Princeton, 1965).

William Rosen, *Shakespeare and the Craft of Tragedy* (Cambridge, Mass., 1960).

J. L. Simmons, *Shakespeare's Pagan World. The Roman Tragedies* (Charlottesville, Va., 1973).

T. J. B. Spencer (ed.), *Shakespeare's Plutarch* (Harmondsworth, 1964).

ARTICLES

Ralph Berry, 'The Metamorphoses of *Coriolanus*', *Shakespeare Q.,* XXVI (1975) 172–83..

James Calderwood, '*Coriolanus*: Wordless Meanings and Meaningless Words', *Studies in English Literature,* VI (1966) 211–24.

D. J. Enright, '*Coriolanus*: Tragedy or Debate?', *Essays in Criticism,* IV (1954) 1–19.

F. N. Lees, 'Coriolanus, Aristotle, and Bacon', *R.E.S.,* new ser., I (1950) 114–125.

Richard Marienstras, 'La Dégradation des vertus héroïques dans *Othello* et dans *Coriolan*', *Etudes Anglaises,* XVII (1964) 372–89.

Kenneth Muir, 'The Background of *Coriolanus*', *Shakespeare Q.,* X (1959) 137–45.

H. J. Oliver, 'Coriolanus as Tragic Hero', *Shakespeare Q.,* X (1959) 53–60; repr. in *The Apothecary's Shop* (London, 1957).

Catherine Stockholder, 'The Other Coriolanus', *P.M.L.A.,* LXXXV (1970) 228–36.

Glynne Wickham, '*Coriolanus*: Shakespeare's Tragedy in Rehearsal and Performance', in J. R. Brown and Bernard Harris (eds) *The Later Shakespeare, Stratford-upon-Avon Studies*, VIII (1966); repr. in *Shakespeare's Dramatic Heritage* (London, 1969).

W. Gordon Zeeveld, ' "Coriolanus" and Jacobean Politics', *Mod. Lang. Rev.*, LVII (1962) 321–34.

NOTES ON CONTRIBUTORS TO
PART TWO

A. C. BRADLEY(1851–1935): Professor of Literature at Liverpool and Glasgow Universities, and Professor of Poetry at Oxford; author of *Shakespearean Tragedy* (1904), one of the classics of literary criticism, and *Oxford Lectures on Poetry* (1909).

REUBEN A. BROWER at the time of his death in 1975 he was Cabot Professor of English Literature at Harvard University, where he had taught English and Classics since 1932. His publications include *Fields of Light: An Experiment in Critical Reading* (1962), *Hero and Saint: Shakespeare and the Graeco-Roman Tradition* (1971), other studies of Shakespeare, and works on Homer, Pope, Frost, the art of translation, and the lyric.

KENNETH BURKE Poet, essayist, short-story writer and critic, he has held distinguished professorships at several American universities, most recently at the Wesleyan University Center for the Humanities. His publications include *Philosophy of Literary Form, Language as Symbolic Action, A Grammar of Motives, A Rhetoric of Motives* and *Attitudes Towards History*.

MAURICE CHARNEY Professor of English at Rutgers University; his Shakespearean studies include *Shakespeare's Roman Plays, Style in 'Hamlet'* and *How to Read Shakespeare*.

O. J. CAMPBELL from 1936 to his death in 1970 he was Professor, and subsequently Emeritus Professor, at Columbia University; in addition to *Shakespeare's Satire* and other literary studies, he edited *The Reader's Encyclopaedia of Shakespeare*.

Una EllisFermor at the time of her death in 1958 she was Hildred Carlile Professor of English at Bedford College in the University of London. Author of studies of Shakespearean and other drama, her works include *The Jacobean Drama* and the posthumously edited *Shakespeare the Dramatist and Other Papers*.

Willard Farnham since 1959 he has been Emeritus Professor of English in the University of California at Berkeley, where he taught from 1923. His studies of Shakespeare and the drama include *Shakespeare's Tragic Frontier*, *The Medieval Heritage of Elizabethan Tragedy* and *The Shakespearean Grotesque*.

G. K. Hunter currently Professor of English at Yale University and Honorary Professor of the University of Warwick. His publications include studies of Lyly, Webster, Peele, together with works on Shakespeare's late comedies and *Othello*. He is the editor of the Casebook on *Henry IV*, and 'English' Editor of the *Modern Language Review*.

L. C. Knights formerly Professor at Sheffield and Bristol Universities, he was from 1965 to 1973 King Edward VII Professor of English Literature in the University of Cambridge. His publications include *Drama and Society in the Age of Jonson*, *Explorations*, *Some Shakespearean Themes* and *An Approach to 'Hamlet'*.

A. P. Rossiter from 1945 to his death in 1957 he was Fellow of Jesus College, Cambridge; his published work includes *English Drama from early Times to the Elizabethans* and *Angel with Horns* (edited posthumously from his lecture notes).

T. J. B. Spencer Professor of English Language and Literature, and Director of the Shakespeare Institute, in the University of Birmingham. He is General Editor of the New Penguin Shakespeare and of the Penguin Shakespeare Library, and between 1960 and 1975 was Editor of the *Modern Language Review*.

Derek A. Traversi formerly Fellow of Merton College, Oxford. His publications include *An Approach to Shakespeare*, *The Roman Plays*, *Shakespeare from Richard II to Henry V*, and *Shakespeare: The Last Phase*.

INDEX